The Making of Green Knowledge

Environmental politics and cultural transformation

Andrew Jamison

CAMBRIDGE
UNIVERSITY PRESS

PUBLISHED BY THE PRESS SYNDICATE OF THE UNIVERSITY OF CAMBRIDGE
The Pitt Building, Trumpington Street, Cambridge, United Kingdom

CAMBRIDGE UNIVERSITY PRESS
The Edinburgh Building, Cambridge CB2 2RU, UK
40 West 20th Street, New York, NY 10011-4211, USA
477 Williamstown Road, Port Melbourne, VIC 3207, Australia
Ruiz de Alarcón 13, 28014 Madrid, Spain
Dock House, The Waterfront, Cape Town 8001, South Africa

http://www.cambridge.org

First published 2001

Printed in the United Kingdom at the University Press, Cambridge

Typeface Plantin 10/12 pt.   *System* LaTeX 2_ε [TB]

A catalogue record for this book is available from the British Library

Library of Congress Cataloguing in Publication Data
Jamison, Andrew.
The making of green knowledge : environmental politics and cultural
transformation / by Andrew Jamison.
      p.   cm.
Includes bibliographical references and index.
ISBN 0 521 79252 5 – ISBN 0 521 79687 3 (pc)
1. Environmentalism.   2. Environmantal policy.   3. Sustainable development.
I. Title.
GE195 .J36   2001   363.7′05 – dc21   2001035300

ISBN 0 521 79252 5 hardback
ISBN 0 521 79687 3 paperback

For Margareta

She showed me where the berries grow,
A green and lovely thing to know.

Contents

Tables

Acknowledgments

This book has been such a long time in the making that there are many contributions to acknowledge. Let me start by thanking Aant Elzinga, who has served as mentor, friend and colleague for all these years, and who read through the almost final manuscript, giving me lots to mull over. Others who have read and commented on portions of the manuscript are Yrjö Haila, Maria Kousis, Trine Pipi Kræmer, Jesper Lassen, Rolf Lidskog, Jeppe Læssøe, David Sonnenfeld, Joe Strahl, and Bron Szerszynski, and an anonymous referee for Cambridge University Press. Thank you all; I think it has become a much better book for your efforts. Sarah Caro at Cambridge has played a crucial nurturing role which has been highly professional and highly appreciated, as has the copyediting of Christine Lyall Grant.

In developing the ideas that I present, a number of contributions have been absolutely essential. Jacqueline Cramer and Jeppe Læssøe worked with Ron Eyerman and me in the 1980s when we compared the environmental movements in Sweden, Denmark, and the Netherlands. Much of the theoretical and conceptual framework that I use in the book was developed at that time, and later, together with Ron Eyerman, in our subsequent books on social movements. Other contributions have come from Gan Lin, Bach Tan Sinh and Joe Strahl, and, in particular, Erik Baark, as we have explored the cultural dimensions of science and technology policy in a number of different guises through the years. Let me especially thank Ron and Erik for providing a very special kind of intellectual collaboration that is reflected on so many of the pages that follow.

In 1996, I had the dubious honor of being given responsibility for coordinating a project in the European Union's program on targeted socio-economic research, which provided the immediate incentive to write this book. My partners – Mario Diani, Leonardas Rinkevicius, Johan Schot, Brian Wynne, and Per Østby – are all to be thanked, as are all of our research assistants, for making the project a true learning experience in more ways than one. More recently, my students and colleagues at Aalborg University and in the Danish Center for Environmental

Social Science have been subjected to countless versions of these chapters at courses and seminars, as well as at more informal gatherings. Arne Remmen and Eskild Holm Nielsen, my collaborators in the project The Industrial Appropriation of Pollution Prevention, have been especially important in helping me to understand the Danish varieties of green knowledge-making, as well as the Aalborg style of education. The book has been written while I have participated in another European project, The Transformation of Environmental Activism, and I would like to thank my partners, and especially the project coordinator Chris Rootes, for helping me to bring my understanding up to date.

A number of people have invited me to make presentations at conferences and seminars, and have offered comments and suggestions that I have tried my best to take into account in the process of writing. Let me thank, in particular, Ida Andersen, Marianne Bender, Maurie Cohen, Hans Glimell, Mogens Godballe, Robin Grove-White, Yrjö Haila, Maarten Hajer, Mikael Hård, Per Hillbur, Richard Norgaard, Richard Rogers, Harald Rohracher, Knut Sørensen, Per Sørup, and Jane Summerton for giving me the opportunity to air my evolving ideas in public.

Research costs money, and so it is the Danish, Nordic and European tax-payers and their representatives, who, in the final analysis, have made it possible for me to write this book. In particular, I acknowledge the support of the European Union and the Nordic Environmental Research Program for the project on Public Engagement and Science and Technology Policy Options, and the support of the Danish Strategic Environmental Research Program for the project on Industrial Appropriation of Pollution Prevention. I hope that at least some of you who have paid for the projects feel that the money was well spent. On the home front, finally, Margareta and Klara have probably suffered the most as I have let this book take over far too much of my attention, and keep me from doing my share in the garden (among other places) during the last couple of years. Thank you all!

As part of my belief in recycling, portions of this book have appeared in preliminary versions in the following copyrighted publications, which I hereby acknowledge:

Seeds of the Sixties (co-author Ron Eyerman), University of California Press, 1994; The Shaping of the Global Environmental Agenda: The Role of Non-governmental Organizations, in Scott Lash, Bronislaw Szerszynski and Brian Wynne, eds., *Risk Environment Modernity: Towards a New Ecology*, Sage Publications, 1996; American Anxieties: Technology and the Reshaping of American Values, in Mikael Hård and Andrew Jamison, eds., *The Intellectual Appropriation of Technology. Discourses on*

Modernity, 1900–1939, The MIT Press, 1998; National Shades of Green: Comparing the Swedish and Danish Styles in Ecological Modernisation (co-author Erik Baark) in *Environmental Values,* no. 2, 1999: 119–218; On the Ambiguities of Greening, in *Innovation. The European Journal of Social Sciences,* no. 3, 2000: 249–264; Science, Technology and the Quest for Sustainable Development, in *Technology Analysis and Strategic Management,* no. 1, 2001: 9–22; and Environmentalism in an Entrepreneurial Age: Reflections on the Greening of Industry Network, in *Journal of Environmental Policy and Planning,* no. 1, 2001: 1–13.

Introduction

Using ideas as my maps...

Bob Dylan, "My Back Pages" (1964)

Changes in culture and personality go hand in hand with our efforts to achieve a society that is ecological – a society based on usufruct, complementarity, and the irreducible minimum – but that also recognizes the existence of a universal humanity and the claims of individuality.

Murray Bookchin, The Ecology of Freedom (1982: 340)

From recollections...

I left the United States for Sweden in August 1970 in search of an ecological society. I have not yet found it, but through the years I have caught glimpses, or premonitions, of what an ecological society might be like. This book is, among other things, an attempt to put those experiences into a broader historical and cultural perspective.

When I left for Sweden I had just graduated from a battle-scarred Harvard, having studied history of science and taken part in the antiwar movement and in the more all-encompassing "dialectics of liberation" that filled the air at the time (see Cooper 1968). I had stumbled into environmentalism a couple of years before, attracted by its combination of practicality and vision, its mixing of science and spirituality, and, perhaps especially, by its uncanny ability to make bedfellows of people with the most seemingly incompatible interests.

In those disheartening days, when the shrill, aggressive, voices of extremism were taking over the antiwar movement, and the war itself was intensifying beyond belief, environmentalism served for me to reawaken the spirit of camaraderie and collective creativity that had all but disappeared from radical politics, and were fast disappearing from public life in general. Environmentalism seemed to transcend the ideological disputes and other sources of division, like class, race, gender, and national identity, that were tearing apart the movement I had known, and had felt a part of, through much of the 1960s. It was not that the ideologies or social distinctions were not important; it was, rather, that the ways they were being discussed seemed to stem from another era. There was something fundamental about the new kinds of environmental problems that we were beginning to learn about – in our earth, in our skies, in our waters, in our homes, in our food, in Vietnam – that meant that we had to rethink most of the assumptions and beliefs that we had previously taken for granted. In particular, we had to learn to expand our ideas of solidarity and community and our notions of politics and social action so that we might be better able to take into account the diverse array of non-human beings that we shared the planet with.

The environmental movement, which some of us were starting to consider ourselves a part of, was certainly critical of the way things were, but at the same time, it/we were specific, constructive, even hopeful, in many of our emerging visions and practices. Before going off to Sweden, I had made a small contribution by writing a book about steam-powered automobiles as an "answer to air pollution" in which I presented the coterie of people who were trying to revive steam cars. They were an intriguing collection: air-pollution-control officials in California, innovative automobile mechanics, idealistic engineering professors, and even an entrepreneur of renown, William Lear of Lear jet fame, who had set up shop in Reno, Nevada, and was planning to enter a steam car in the Indianapolis 500 (Jamison 1970). I had heard that Sweden, whose government was supporting the Vietnamese, was also developing some interesting approaches to environmental protection, and I wanted to take a look, never imagining that I would stay this long. The book you are about to read is a kind of progress report on the journey thus far.

In the early 1970s much of my time was spent talking with scientists and government officials, who were justifiably proud of how effective they had been in reacting to the environmental crisis, as it was often referred to in those days. Sweden was the first country in the world to establish a state agency for environmental protection, and its parliament was the first to pass a comprehensive environmental-protection law. With some ecologists from Lund, where I was living, I visited a lake near Växjö, where advanced methods of restoration were being applied to a place where the fish had largely disappeared. Later, I ventured further north to what remained of Lake Hornborga, where millions of kronor were to be spent in the following years dredging up what had become an overgrown swamp, so that the cranes that had traditionally stopped there on their way south would one day return (they have). And I spent some days on an island in the Baltic Sea, where scientists were developing an ecological systems model of the nature – society interactions in the sea, as an input into the environmental policy process (Jamison 1971a, b, c; Jamison 1973).

Eventually I made my way to a suburban house outside of Uppsala where a young geneticist lived with his family. Björn Gillberg was creating a different kind of environmentalism, writing newspaper articles about food additives and genetic risks, standing outside of supermarkets with leaflets to warn consumers about the dangers lurking inside, and, most dramatically, washing his shirt in coffee creamer on a television program to show what a common household product could (really) do. I remember being struck by the fact that there was no toothpaste in Björn Gillberg's house – he said you didn't need it to get your teeth clean – and I was also struck by how different he was from the scientists and officials with whom I had been spending so much of my time. He was taking science to the streets (Jamison 1972).

Gillberg represented the Swedish version of the international environmental movement of which I had started to feel a part. Indeed, in the early 1970s, Gillberg *was* the movement, at least according to both his own and much of the Swedish mass media's perception of things. In 1975, when other activists wanted to broaden the fledgling movement and one of them, a left-wing journalist, wanted to alter the orientation of the newspaper that Gillberg edited, taking up environmental issues at the workplace, Gillberg let the journalist go; and at the annual meeting of the national organization that Gillberg headed, a group of activists demonstrably walked out and started their own organization instead.

I too felt that there was something missing in Gillberg's approach to environmental politics. More was required than a natural scientific education and a strong will; there was also a need for a social and economic analysis, and, even more crucially perhaps, there was a need for an alternative vision and an alternative "practice" if environmentalism were ever to appeal to, and alter the consciousness of, the majority of the world's population.

Over the next few years, after moving to an old farmhouse with a big garden outside of Lund, where I have lived ever since, I found myself increasingly drawn to developments in Denmark, where I got my first academic job in 1974, teaching a course in science and society at the University of Copenhagen. Reading Danish newspapers and getting to know some Danish activists, it soon became apparent that the environmental movement was developing quite differently in Denmark. For one thing it was more of an academic affair, strongly based on students and young teachers, especially at the new universities in Aalborg and Roskilde, where environmental issues had come to be linked, according to the fashion of the day, to the Marxian "critique of political economy." For another, it drew on a populist tradition of rural resistance that had been mobilized in the nineteenth century, when, among other things, a network of "people's high schools" had been created in the countryside to provide the farmers with a more practical, but also more spiritual, form of education. Perhaps most intriguingly it was more experimental, practicing, more ambitiously than elsewhere in Europe, an alternative, or ecological, way of life, both in the renewable energy "wing" of the movement, as well as at the rural and urban collectives that were becoming such a visible feature of the Danish landscape (Jamison 1977).

In those years I met many Danish activists, people like Oluf Danielsen, a physics teacher at Roskilde and one of the more vocal energy debaters of the 1970s, and also a founding member of the Danish journal, *Naturkampen* (Nature Struggle); Preben Maegaard, a "grass-roots engineer," who established the Northern Jutland Center for Alternative Technology and helped to start the Organization for Renewable Energy (Organisation for vedvarende energi, OVE); and Peder Agger, another Roskilde teacher, of biology, and one of the founders of NOAH, in those days the leading Danish environmental organization, and now the Danish affiliate of Friends of the Earth. Peder also helped to establish the production collective, Svanholm, which is now a center for "ecological agriculture."

As the energy debate heated up in the late 1970s I became more involved in environmental politics, and I experienced the differences between Sweden and Denmark firsthand. In Sweden, we organized our opposition to nuclear energy as a popular front, which came to be dominated by the two anti-nuclear parliamentary parties – the left Communist and the formerly agrarian Center party. I helped to edit a journal that tried to offer a socialist voice, as well as some science and technology perspectives, to the opposition to nuclear energy. I even took part in writing, with some other local activists, a contribution to the Environmental Movement's Alternative Energy Plan, which was supported by the government and which was directed from an office at a government ministry by a young activist, who found our radical alternativism a bit hard to take.

In Denmark anti-nuclear activism, as it developed into a social movement, was more open-ended and experimental. With a group of students I visited some of the sites of alternative energy technology, such as Tvind, in western Denmark, where the world's largest windmill was being built by amateurs at a newly started people's high school. It was, in many respects, the same movement everywhere – "no nukes," or, as we put it in Scandinavia, "atomic energy: no thanks" (*atomkraft nej tack*) – but it was striking how the same struggle expressed itself so differently in different countries.

In our journal we tried to develop a theory of socialist ecology that drew especially on developments in Germany – where anti-nuclear opposition was more left-wing and militant than in either Sweden or Denmark – and in Norway, where environmentalism was a part of a broader movement against European integration. In the process, Norway had also spawned a home-grown form of ecological philosophy, by Arne Næss and Sigmund Kvaloy, that was starting to be called "deep ecology." From the United States there seemed to be not one but many different kinds of movements developing: revitalized conservation organizations, locally based campaigns against nuclear plants and toxic-waste sites, the media activism of Greenpeace, as well as a number of ideologies that already then seemed to be in competition with one another: the social ecology of Murray Bookchin, the new-age politics of Mark Satin, the appropriate technology of Amory Lovins, the ecofeminism of Carolyn Merchant, to name some of those that I became acquainted with.

Meanwhile, environmentalism in other parts of the world was taking on still other shades of green, which I was able to follow rather closely, in 1978–79, as editor of the *Lund Letter on Science, Technology and Basic Human Needs*. The *Lund Letter* tried to provide a forum for discussion about the preparations for the United Nations Conference on Science and Technology for Development and, through it, I met not only a wide range of activists and academic "experts" throughout the world, but also came more closely into contact with the world of utopian practice. I went to meetings at the "free town" of Christiania, in Copenhagen, often staying overnight in a converted streetcar, and at the Frostrup camp in northern Jutland, and I soon met communards in Sweden and Norway and Finland who were living the alternative life rather than (merely) talking about it.

A stint as a journalist on the newspaper at the UNCSTD in Vienna in the summer of 1979 served to reinforce the impression that environmentalism was a broad, diverse, and extremely many-headed movement. It was in Vienna that I met Anil Agarwal, for example, who was on his way back home to India to start his Centre for Science and Environment after working in Britain for Earthscan. I also met David Dickson, a journalist for *Nature*, and one of the founders of the radical science movement in Britain, and author of the book that perhaps best captures the spirit of the 1970s: *Alternative Technology and the Politics of Technical Change* (Dickson 1974). In Vienna, I interviewed Robert Jungk, author of *The Nuclear Tyranny*, and listened to Ivan Illich, author of *Tools for Conviviality*, and, at the NGO (non-governmental organizations) meeting, which was my "beat" for the conference paper, I saw many examples of the alternative technology movement that, for me, was such a central part of the environmental activism of the 1970s.

From Vienna, I especially remember visiting the "people's forum" one evening with a fellow-journalist Ziauddin Sardar. It was a kind of gathering of the tribes, with representatives from communes and other counter-cultural organizations mixing, not too easily, with the more politically minded activists from anti-nuclear and development organizations. I recall that Zia, who was soon to go off to revolutionary Iran and discover another kind of politics altogether, had a rather similar reaction to the people's forum to mine; many of the projects that were on display were exciting and stimulating, but it seemed that the alternative, or utopian, activists had grown far too distant from the political activists. Could the gap between thinking and practicing, between theorizing about and living in the alternative ecological society, ever be successfully bridged?

... to reconnections

The 1980s were not kind to environmentalism. Rather than moving forward and gaining new members and enthusiasts, the environmental movement tended to decompose and split apart, for reasons that were not so much internal as external. There were, to be sure, plenty of disputes and debates over how to proceed most effectively. How should the opportunities that had emerged in the anti-nuclear movement – to influence policy-making, to affect industrial development, to empower local communities – best be utilized? Should environmentalists in other countries follow the example of the Germans and build a political party? Did the movement need to become more professional and hard-nosed in its modes of operation, that is, was Greenpeace the model of the future?

Lurking behind all the internal debates, however, was the recognition that a counter-revolution was under way. In Britain, Margaret Thatcher had come to power, and in the United States Ronald Reagan was elected president. Both were not merely anti-environmental but vehemently, aggressively, so. The ministers they appointed defended the rights of the exploiters, and their policies favored de-regulation, privatization, commercialization. The ideology of neo-liberalism, as it has come to be called, subsequently took on many manifestations as it spread around the world. There were both "greener" versions and "browner" versions, as corporate leaders and the public servants they supported developed their responses to the environmental challenge. The strategies that emerged to combine environmentalism and economics have grown into one of the influential "discourses" of our time – sustainable development or ecological modernization: what I will be calling here, green business; while the browner versions have supported many a "backlash," from scientists denying the existence of climate change and global warming, to consumers of ever bigger and ever more unnecessary automobiles, to companies moving their operations in the name of globalization to places where environmental controls are less stringent.

Even more insidiously, however, neo-liberalism helped to mobilize what was already afoot in some parts of Europe, and in some parts of the environmental movement: a populist reaction. By now, populist parties of the far right have taken power in many municipalities in France, Austria, and Norway, and they have become significant parliamentary actors in most European countries, as well as in many other parts of the world. Mixing patriotism with racism, and defending national sovereignty against the European Union and other transnational bodies, the populist reaction has become a force to be reckoned with – both in Europe and the United States. Populism has served to infect many environmentalists with what might be called a traditionalist, or neo-nationalist, bias, and as its political influence has increased, the public concern with the environment has tended to decline. Indeed, populism has helped to inspire in Europe an anti-ecological mobilization against "green" taxes on energy use and motor fuel, for example, among those who feel that their livelihoods are threatened by certain kinds of environmental policies emanating from the European Union bureaucrats in Brussels. In the United States, populism has fed into the revival of evangelical religion that has been extremely important politically for the past twenty years.

It has not been easy for environmentalists to navigate among globalists and populists, innovators and traditionalists, but somehow we and they have managed to keep going. Most of the people I met in the early days, for instance, are still active. Björn Gillberg has developed a form of counter-expertise through the years, by which he has contributed his particular skills and talents to the resolution of many environmental controversies in Sweden. He has helped to bring polluting companies to court, and he has advised citizens' groups about their rights. Most recently, he has become a discussion partner with corporations, encouraging them to clean their production processes and develop "environmentally-friendly" products (Gillberg 1999).

Across the water, Peder Agger and Oluf Danielsen are still at Roskilde. They have been active in a range of rather unique public arenas in which environmental issues have been discussed in Danish society: the Technology Board, now Technology Council, where citizen involvement in technology assessment, especially through the so-called consensus conferences, has attracted international attention; the Ecological Council, which provides policy pronouncements and advice to government as well as publishing the journal *Global økologi* (Global Ecology); and the Green Fund, which gives support to a wide array of grassroots projects. All three institutions are conspicuous for their absence in Sweden (and, for that matter, in the United States and Britain, as well as most other countries).

Anil Agarwal has long been one of the most respected voices of Southern environmentalism, with his active involvement in international networks and organizations, while the Centre for Science and Environment serves as a model of critical environmental knowledge production and dissemination. David Dickson produced another influential book – on the politics of American science – and served a spell as editor of *New Scientist*, and is now back writing for *Nature*. Ziauddin Sardar, who has done so much over the past twenty years to teach us about the relations between science and Islam, is editor of *Futures*. Vandana Shiva, who spent a semester with us in Lund in the early 1980s, has been at the forefront of a Third World environmental activism that has intensified over the past decade, while Amory Lovins, from his Rocky Mountain Institute, now professes a belief in "natural capitalism," a form of green business that has become an ever more significant part of the ecological culture.

This book is, in many ways, their story, or, to be a bit presumptuous, our story. For I, too, have tried to keep the banner flying through the years, primarily by writing about the environmental movement, and what I have come to call its *cognitive praxis* (Jamison *et al.* 1990; Eyerman and Jamison 1991). In the 1980s, I wrote about the "knowledge interests" that had developed within environmental movements, and in the 1990s I have tried to follow those interests as they have increasingly left the movement space behind (Jamison 1996; 1998). Most recently, I have explored the politics of participation in relation to sustainable development, as well as the transformation of environmental activism, in a number of different European countries, which has given me the immediate incentive to write this book and try to work out what it all means. I have also had occasion to see what happened to the visions of those "steam people" I wrote about in the late 1960s (Hård and Jamison 1997).

For while a great deal has been written about environmental problems and environmental politics, the actual historical trajectory of environmentalism, the dynamics of what I have come to think of as an emerging ecological culture, has tended to be neglected. Different authors have focused on different aspects of the social and cultural transformations that have been taking place over the past thirty years in the name of ecology and, as a result, all too often the forest has tended to be reduced to the trees. Instead of thinking like a mountain, and recognizing that "land is community" as Aldo Leopold put it so many years ago, all too many tend to defend their own private pieces of land (Leopold 1949). Among those who have analyzed the situation, too many authors have all too often tried to fit their stories into their own professional "discourse" or personal life-world.

There is also, as in so many other topic areas, a huge difference between American writings, with their patriotic enthusiasms and their sticking to the "facts," and European writings, with their cosmopolitan sophistication and speculative theories. Americans tend to see the rest of the world as peripheral, while many Europeans, as a kind of reaction to the American media barrage, retreat into a rather ineffectual provincialism. As an American who has lived in Europe for thirty years, I have continually been struck by the discursive dissonances, the interpretative imbalances, between the hemispheres. While Americans, for example, tend to neglect the importance of history, the past weighs heavily on many a European. All that seems to be new comes from North America, while Europeans take on the task of defending all that is old. What makes it across from both sides is thus often neither the best nor the brightest but more like the loudest and the most extreme. So while there is by now a voluminous literature on environmental politics, there still is room, even a need perhaps, for a book that explicitly tries to make connections: across disciplines and social roles, across countries and continents, across the generations, and, perhaps most importantly, across the divisions that have continued to grow between activists and academics, practitioners and theorists, the doers and the thinkers of the emerging ecological culture. There is a need, in short, for a collective memory, a usable past, an attempt to fashion a narrative of our own that might just bring us a bit closer together.

Among other things, this book tries to put into a broader historical and comparative perspective the making of what I call green knowledge in Sweden, Denmark, and the United States. In all three countries, as well as in all the other places that I will, on occasion, try to bring into the narrative, there has been an ongoing political battle for many years now, a battle for recognition, for acceptance, for influence. But there has also been a battle at the level of ideas – a cognitive battle – and, at both levels, it is not so clear who or what has won. Have the Björn Gillbergs, Amory Lovinses, and Peder Aggers of the world been forced to change their message and their mission so that they could be taken seriously in high places? Or have their activities helped to change our contemporary political cultures, making them "greener," more aware and conscious of environmental problems?

Put in this way, the answer must be a firm yes – to both questions. Yes, the activism has changed; many of those who were involved in the environmental movement in the 1960s and 1970s have become less radical (but also perhaps more realistic) in the things they say and the things they do. But yes, environmental activism has also helped to change fundamentally the ambience of our late modern, or postmodern, or not-yet-modern, industrial societies. In bringing environmentalism out of the cold and into the establishment, activists and former activists have played important roles in processes of institutional and policy reform, scientific and technological innovation and, on a more personal level, in changing values, beliefs, feelings, and behavior.

It is this circuitous process of social change, this long march through the institutions, this dialectical tension between incorporation and resistance, that forms the subject-matter of this book. I want to emphasize the diversity of processes involved, the contradictions and ambiguities, the differences among the participants that are all too often neglected, and which need to be explicitly recognized and discussed if they are ever to be overcome. There are strong forces of fragmentation and separation at work, and the greater the differentiation the more difficult it seems to retain a sense of unified purpose or to articulate an underlying meaning or coherence in environmental politics. If diversity makes some of us strong, it also seems to make many of us confused and disillusioned.

. . . and conceptual tools

This book builds on a number of earlier efforts to comprehend the relations among science, technology, and the politics of the environment. It was in a research program on Technology and Culture in the early 1980s that I first encountered what I have come to see as a fundamental, and highly debilitating, bifurcation in the ways in which these matters are understood, both in the academy as well as in the world outside. In the industrialized countries of the North, our perspectives have been dominated by the hegemony of a technocratic world-view, which posits a global *technological imperative*, propelling the world forward in a never-ending pursuit of newness and innovation and progress. In the early 1980s, the technocrats were beginning to reassert themselves after being on the defensive through much of the previous decade. Economists, for example, were rediscovering the writings of Joseph Schumpeter and engineers were envisioning cleaner technologies and the dawning of an information society. At the Research Policy Institute at the University of Lund, where I was working, several economists were joining together to develop what has since become a substantial sub-field of business economics: innovation studies and technology management.

In Asia, and particularly in India, where Erik Baark and I traveled together in 1983 as part of the research program, there was, on the other hand, an equally noticeable skepticism toward the wonders of science and technology, which we came to think of as a multifaceted *cultural critique of technology*. In India, and other developing countries, science and technology were not so much seen as providing solutions to environmental and social ills as being themselves a major part of the problem. The "paradigm," or interpretive lens through which the world was seen tended to be cultural and critical, and the frameworks of understanding were drawn from such academic subjects as history and anthropology, philosophy and psychology, as well as from the ideas of those intellectuals who were articulating the messages of critical movements. In India, for instance, the teachings and broader "experiments with life" of Mahatma Gandhi had become cultural resources that were drawn upon by just about everyone who concerned themselves with science, technology, and environmental issues (Elzinga and Jamison 1986). In a very active and noticeable way, history was being mobilized in the ongoing struggles to develop more "appropriate" technologies and strategies for socio-economic development that tried to meet what at the time were referred to as basic human needs.

This bifurcation of the disparate field of science, technology, and society studies has continued in the years since, and, in most parts of the world, the economists and the rest of us have more or less parted company. We now tend to be housed in different academic departments, usually in different faculties, adopting different terminologies and concepts to characterize the relations between science, technology, and society. And we usually speak to different audiences and relate to different segments of the public when we try to apply the fruits of our understandings to policy-making and political discussions.

In the 1980s, as the naïve young researchers we were, Erik Baark and I tried to link the two sides together in one comprehensive framework of understanding. Rather than exclusively adopt only one of the available terminologies or discourses we tried to combine them, to bring them together. The economists and the cultural critics, we suggested, were interested in different aspects of the same all-encompassing process, or problematic, and it could be valuable if at least some of us tried to "grasp the whole" and take account of perspectives from both the economic and the cultural point of view. The general idea that we came up with was that scientific and technological developments are best seen in cyclical terms, whereby periods of growth and expansion are followed by periods of stagnation and crisis, the two sides informing and influencing each other in complicated ways (Baark and Jamison 1986).

If we look into the past we see that periods of decline, in technological and economic terms, have also been periods of radical reconstruction in cultural terms. Cultural critique and critical movements have often inspired a broad reexamination, or assessment, process that has, in turn, contributed to the formulation of new criteria for knowledge-making and new forms of scientific and technological practice. The "long waves" of development that the economists were studying seemed to be followed by waves of critique and "counterculture" – something like what we had experienced in the 1960s and 1970s.

It was to help understand these cyclical relations that Ron Eyerman and I developed our cognitive approach to social movements, which was inspired by the writings of the French social theorist Alain Touraine and the Italian sociologist Alberto Melucci. Touraine has continually stressed the importance of the redefinitions of reality that take place in social movements. For him, it is the struggle to define "historicity" and the articulation of new scenarios for the future, new historical projects, that is central to social movements (Touraine 1981, 1985). Fundamental to the "new social movement" theory that Touraine developed is the recognition that, aside from the actual political struggles, there is also a cultural struggle, the making, or construction, of a collective identity, taking place in the new movements. As he once put it in reply to a critic, "a social movement, in my definition, is a collective action aiming at the implementation of central cultural values against the interest and influence of an enemy which is defined in terms of power relations. A social movement is a combination of social conflict and cultural participation" (Touraine 1991: 389).

Touraine also developed a particular approach to studying these new movements, or new social actors, which he called "sociological intervention." In order to understand the importance of the new social movements, Touraine contended, it was necessary to take part in them, to identify with their activity, and his research program involved a number of "participatory" elements, such as group interviews, dialog workshops, and collective presentation of findings. Somewhat like the so-called "action research" that has been conducted with labor organizations and other activist groups in different contexts throughout the twentieth century in both Europe and North America, Touraine argued that the sociologist had to be engaged in the activities he or she was studying. Insight had to grow out of involvement, or what he called intervention (Touraine 1988).

Touraine's perspective, in both theory and methodology, has come to be developed further by Alberto Melucci, especially in his *Nomads of the Present* (1989) and *Challenging Codes* (1996). With a dual training as both a sociologist and a psychoanalyst, Melucci has tried to uncover the underlying "codes," or rituals of protest, that take place in social movements. This focus on what movements and their members actually do has led Melucci to distinguish between latent and active periods of movement activity, and he has pointed to the fact that movements change their character and, in particular, their level of public visibility over time. In the contemporary world, social movements are perhaps best seen not as organizations but as networks, which are not as firmly or coherently coordinated as social movement organizations tend to be (Castells 1996; Della Porta and Diani 1999). What is important for Melucci is the *symbolic action* that takes place in these networks, the meanings or concepts that are articulated, as well as the bonds of solidarity and community that are established and reproduced. By calling this code-challenging symbolic action, Melucci emphasizes that there is much more than instrumental behavior going on in social movements and, indeed, in social life more generally. The concept of cognitive praxis, and the newer notion of exemplary action, which Ron Eyerman and I have used to help understand the importance of songs in social movements, can be thought of as particular categories of symbolic action (Eyerman and Jamison 1998: 20ff).

Melucci also stresses the psychological elements of collective identity formation. People take part in a social movement, or in a code-challenging network, not merely for rational or instrumental reasons, but also for more emotional reasons, such as satisfaction and fulfillment. The struggle for cultural change, Melucci emphasizes, has an internal dimension to it that we can understand only by means of empathy or personal engagement. The understanding of social movements thus requires an identification or psychological involvement in the issues, or particular projects, of the activists on the part of the analyst. The sociologist, in Melucci's approach, has to take on some of the attributes of the psychoanalyst in order to disclose the hidden, or tacit, dimensions of collective action.

Touraine's and Melucci's ideas about social movements are the product of a particular kind of European social theorizing, in which the concepts that are developed can sometimes take on a life of their own. In that respect, they resemble Ulrich Beck's notions of risk society and "sub-politics" that he has been presenting in various forms over the past fifteen years (Beck 1999: 89ff). In Beck's account it is not social movements that are seen to be the carriers of an alternative political activity, or identity, in what he terms the risk society; it is rather a much looser, much less organized conglomeration of social life or interaction that it is important to identify and support. The term "subpolitics" implies that what is most characteristic of the environmental politics of our time is the significance of what is carried out below the surface of formal politics and policy-making. Subpolitics is political in a less visible or explicit way than social-movement activities tend to be. But it is the form of politics that seems to emerge in a relatively nonpolitical, or commercial, age. This book is an attempt to explore and understand what the new kind of politics is all about.

Here, I build on these perspectives in order to explore the processes of social, cultural, and cognitive transformation that have accompanied the efforts to bring about more "sustainable" forms of socio-economic development. The analysis is based on the assumption that participants in the quest for sustainable development are, to a large extent, shaped or influenced by the contexts in which they operate. Many of the concepts that I use were originally developed with Erik Baark. In studying processes of science and technology policy reform in China and Vietnam, Erik and I came to think of the policy realm as embodied by ideal-typical *policy cultures*, each of which consists of a particular constituency, a particular cluster of actors and networks (Jamison and Baark 1995). Policy-making thus becomes a process of interaction, sometimes conflictual, sometimes cooperative, among the representatives of the policy cultures. The interactions can be thought of both as negotiations among people from different societal spheres, as well as co-constructions of projects and programs, forms of mediation and hybridization that are formed in the social spaces, or virtual interfaces, among the different cultures.

In the quest for sustainable development, I have come to think of these interactions as cultural tensions. While representatives of the bureaucratic culture – the domain of the state – tend to pursue the quest for sustainable development primarily in ways that can ensure social order, the economic and civic cultures represent broader private and public interests, respectively. The representatives of the economic culture are interested in programs and policies that are directly related to their own commercial interests, while those who represent the civic culture generally seek an integration of sustainable development with broader social and cultural concerns.

These are not easy processes to pin down and analyze, and they are especially difficult to write about at a "meta" level, as I try to do here. There is bound to be some academic jargon and hyperbole, although I have done my best to keep the book readable. Here and there, I provide a personal touch to remind us that social science is not just about abstractions, but about real live human beings.

The book is organized in the following way. In chapter 1 I sketch the overall argument and present some of the main elements of my approach. The second chapter tries to provide a broader perspective, by showing how social movements have historically influenced processes of knowledge-making. Its aim is to place contemporary environmental politics within a longer-term time perspective. Chapters 3 and 4 bring the story up to date by recounting the developmental trajectories of the environmental movement itself, first in broad strokes and then in terms of more specific national experiences, primarily those I know best – from Sweden, Denmark, and my native United States. In chapters 5 and 6 I explore the contemporary "dialectics" of environmentalism by means of illustrative examples, discussing in turn the worlds of what I term green business (chapter 5) and critical ecology, or environmental activism (chapter 6). I conclude with a few reflections on my findings and observations.

1   On the ambiguities of greening

Look at Mother Nature on the run in the 1970s...
Neil Young, "After the Gold Rush" (1970)

I am struck again and again by the difficulty of designing an adequate language, an adequate conceptual apparatus to grasp the nature of the problems we seem to be faced with. I worry that last year's conceptual tools and goals will be used to fight next year's issues in a dynamic situation that more and more requires proactive rather than remedial action.
David Harvey, *Justice, Nature and the Geography of Difference* (1996: 416)

From environmental protection to cultural transformations

Like women's liberation, rock music, and the internet, an environmental consciousness can be seen to be a product of the 1960s.[1] It was then, inspired by the spirit of the times a-changin', and exemplified by a number of highly publicized cases of waste and pollution, that humankind's diverse natural surroundings were seen to be in danger, and protecting the environment became a matter of public concern. As part of the counter-cultural critique of the "technocratic society" and the widespread questioning of the dominant values of the consumer culture, environmentalism emerged as a new political cause, a new historical project (Roszak 1973; Morgan 1991). The science of ecology, a hitherto neglected branch of biology, which seemed to provide crucially important knowledge for this newfound mission of environmental protection, became a household word, and it soon became a label, as well, for the generally polite "activists" who set out to spread an environmental consciousness among their fellow citizens.

Around the world, many universities established environmental departments, governments set up environmental protection agencies, parliaments passed new laws and created new courts to enforce them, and, here and there, groups of people banded together to form what eventually came to be called an environmental movement. By the early 1970s, protecting the environment had become an expanding public-policy sector, and some even referred to the emergence of a "pollution industrial complex" that was trying to make money out of the cleaning up (Gellen 1970). By the time the United Nations held its Conference on the Human Environment in Stockholm in the summer of 1972, environmental protection was firmly placed on the international political agenda (McCormick 1991).

Thirty years later, the politics of the environment – both the talk and the action, the rhetoric and the reality, the theory and the practice – has changed in fundamental ways (Connelly and Smith 1999). Throughout the world, the general emphasis among politicians and policy-makers – as well as for most of the experts who advise them and the activists who goad them on – has tended to shift from the protection of an external realm of non-human nature to the *greening* of our own human societies (Dobson 2000). An ecological consciousness, we might say, is in the process of being internalized in our cultures and our personalities. And while we are all invited to take part in the greening of the world, the diverse processes of greening, and of green knowledge-making, are filled with ambiguities.

The new environmental agenda is both extremely ambitious and decidedly amorphous. While nature protection and pollution control remain important, and in need of further development in many countries and in relation to many specific economic activities, the broader program of greening has come to occupy the attention of increasing numbers of people. The general idea is to integrate an environmental concern into all aspects of social and economic life. The new agenda has been given many names, but, most frequently, it is referred to as sustainable development.

The apocalyptic tones, the bad news that characterized so much of the environmental debate in the 1960s and 1970s, have tended to give way in the course of the 1990s to the encouraging, good-news rhetoric of sustainable development. The emblematic depiction of doom, identifying "limits to growth" and "population bombs," has come to be replaced by more upbeat messages and conciliatory slogans: "changing course," "greening of industry," "ecological modernization," "partnership ethics" (Fischer and Hajer 1999). Former activists regularly advise private business firms on how best to improve their environmental performance, while former plunderers of the environment, such as Shell and Exxon, do their utmost to convince us of their corporate change of heart. Even the World Bank, we are told, is building an environmental ethic into their programs these days.

As a result of these and countless other developments, environmentalism has come to be decomposed and all but reinvented in recent years as elements in constructive programs of technological, economic, and social innovation. There has also been a reorientation in much environmentally related knowledge production toward approaches that are based on so-called precautionary, or preventive principles, and which seek to eliminate waste and pollution at the source, before they have been generated. Rather than delimiting environmental protection to a separate policy sector or a specialized area of scientific–technical competence, there is a growing awareness that changes need to take place throughout the entire society if there is to be an adequate alleviation of environmental problems. No longer is environmentalism viewed by those in powerful positions primarily as a threat to the further expansion of industrial society. Instead, environmental concern has come to be seen, by many influential actors in both business and government, as an important contributor to economic recovery and rejuvenation, and, for some, even as an interesting source of profit (Frankel 1998; DeSimone and Popoff 2000).

Meanwhile, new forms of domination and exploitation have come to be identified as transnational corporations seek to transform the quest for sustainable development into business (Sachs 1999; Shiva 2000). There has emerged around the world an increasingly visible, but extremely mixed, variety of critical responses to the machinations of a green-talking but not always so green-doing global capitalist order – from activists in the Southern hemisphere, small farmers in Europe, militant animal-lovers in Scandinavia, health-minded consumers everywhere, and, even in the United States, from some of those who once mined ore and tended the machinery in the industrial heartland. Many of the resisters draw on environmental arguments, but increasingly they seem to be deflecting the ecological culture into older and more traditional forms of resistance.

As such, an environmental consciousness has largely ceased to serve as a living source of identity for a relatively small number of activists and experts, and has become instead a broader, but also much more diffuse, source of inspiration for society as a whole. What had previously been fairly limited and well-defined movements of protest against the destruction of the physical environment have come to be supplanted over the past two decades by a highly variegated and contested set of ideas and practices (Macnaghten and Urry 1998). Throughout the world, a disparate range of activity is taking place in the name of ecology and sustainable development, and yet there is a gnawing sense that there is little, if any, overall direction to the process. Even more seriously, there are increasing indications that, for all the green talk, the actual health of the planet and its inhabitants is continuing to deteriorate (French 2000).

In this volume I attempt to connect the quest for sustainable development to broader processes of cultural and cognitive transformation.

As I see it, at different sites in our societies the harbingers of an emerging ecological culture are seeking to reconstitute discursive, institutional, and scientific–technical practices. They are disseminating, among other things, a wide range of ideas and concepts, organizational procedures and policy proposals, as well as "environmentally friendly" artifacts and consumer products. And sometimes directly and sometimes indirectly, they are serving to change the way we do things, both at work and at home, in the various social worlds or contexts in which we live.

As we shall see here, the emerging ecological culture is waging a struggle on two fronts – against the rich and the powerful, who are doing their utmost to commercialize the new ideas and values and turn them into business opportunities, and against the dispersed forces of resistance, who are trying to utilize the new ideas for their own often incommensurable purposes. The transformations that we will be exploring involve a wide range of activities in different social locations, and it is important to recognize that those activities are, for the most part, governed by different kinds of rationalities, motivations, and interests.

The actual manifestations of the new environmental politics are often in contrast to more established forms of political activity. Public participation has become a catch-all phrase that is used to describe the variety of ways in which various types and groups of people are involved in these processes. But it has become a phrase, like sustainable development, that refers to many different kinds of social action. Ulrich Beck has coined the term "subpolitics" to indicate that indirect forms of pressure and informal types of action have taken on a greater significance, while Maarten Hajer has used the notion of "cultural politics" in order to emphasize the symbolic, or cultural, nature of many aspects of contemporary environmental conflicts (Beck 1995; Hajer 1996). These include debates about naming programs and defining ambitions; disputes over the construction and design of policy reforms and organizational initiatives; and disagreements, both in everyday life, as well as in the wide range of "expert worlds", over how best to develop and implement practical–technical measures.

If we are to understand these processes it is not sufficient, as many policy analysts and political scientists continue to do, to focus attention primarily on the relatively formalized domain of the state and its systems of regulation and control, for what is proposed by policy-makers and politicians is often far different from what is actually carried out in practice. Nor can the environmental strategies of companies be sufficiently understood within the terminology and conceptual frameworks of business economics, when their impact and consequences are now felt far outside of the business world. It has also become problematic to discuss the broader social aspects of environmental change within the received language of sociology and social theory, since the contradictory relations of real-life ecological transformations are often at variance with the "modernist" or cosmopolitan world-view assumptions of most sociologists. In all three of the main societal domains – state, industry, and civil society – the various doctrines, or ideologies, of environmental politics cannot be adequately understood without considering the actual practices of the actors involved and the knowledge they are making.

For while there appears to be widespread agreement, in principle, about the need to infuse an ecological consciousness as broadly as possible into our increasingly "globalized" societies, there is an enormous and highly diverse range of activity that has emerged in the quest for more sustainable paths to socio-economic development. There are differences between countries – due to various national political conditions and resource bases, as well as different national policy styles and cultural traditions – and there are also conflicts within countries, as different actor groups or social constituencies seek to redefine environmental issues in their own terms (for a recent survey, see Low *et al.* 2000).

We need to understand, in particular, the ways in which the quest for sustainable development has been affected by the overriding emphasis on economic efficiency and rationalization that has come to dominate our "neo-liberal" world. The dominant strategy has been to assign the main responsibility to the private sector, and this has meant a number of new managerial and administrative procedures that attempt to incorporate environmental concern into business and government (Hillary 1997). In many countries, however, particularly in the so-called developing world, these organizational innovations have run into major financial and institutional barriers, while many "Northern" companies have devised ways to move, or transfer, some of their more visible environmental problems – and profitable "solutions" – to the South (Agarwal *et al.* 1999). Greening in the North has thus paradoxically led to an intensification of environmental destruction in the South. As so often in the past, we see how scientific and technical ingenuity are being integrated into patterns of global inequality (Guha 2000). And, throughout the world, the processes of institutionalization have also faced what has been termed a "green backlash" from those in powerful positions who have had enough of environmental protection and are unconvinced that ecology will ever be particularly profitable (Rowell 1996; Beder 1997). Especially around issues such as global warming, where scientific assertions are extremely difficult to prove, the anti-ecological forces have been given particularly attractive opportunities to oppose an emerging ecological culture. The aggressive resistance to increased taxes on diesel fuel that spread across Europe in the summer of 2000 is only the most visible sign of this tendency.

As such, a disparate range of activity characterizes the quest for sustainable development as different actors, with very different interests, seek to entice different segments of the "public" to participate in their own favored organizational and institutional initiatives.

Reinventing nature

Underlying the recent shifts in the environmental political agenda is the recognition that the ecological problems confronting humanity have taken on ever more awesome proportions. For some, this implies that a more ambitious, or comprehensive, response is necessary, while for others, it has inspired even more refined methods of human intervention in the affairs of the non-human world. Not only has human ingenuity continued to modify the landscape and turn it into something fundamentally "man-made." In recent years, particularly with the coming of the new techniques of genetic manipulation, and the continued human encroachment into previously preserved wilderness areas, it has become increasingly apparent that an autonomous world of nature has largely ceased to exist in any meaningful sense (Turner 1996; Haila 1997). And it can be suggested that this perceived disappearance of a separate, non-human sphere of existence has helped to spawn a new definition, or conception, of the environmental problematic – from protecting nature to transforming society. In the words of Bill McKibben:

How can there be a mystique of the rain now that every drop – even the drops that fall as snow on the Arctic, even the drops that fall deep in the remaining forest primeval – bears the permanent stamp of man? Having lost its separateness, it [nature] loses its special power. Instead of being a category like God – something beyond our control – it is now a category like the defense budget or the minimum wage, a problem we must work out. This in itself changes its meaning completely, and changes our reaction to it. (McKibben 1989: 210)

It has been a series of dramatic events, or disasters, over the past fifty years, that has helped make us aware of the disappearance of a separate realm of non-human nature.[2]

Early on in the 1950s there was the mercury poisoning in Minimata Bay in Japan which, more than any other single event, announced the coming of the environmental crisis in the form of a deadly and previously unknown disease. In the 1960s there was the ecological devastation of Vietnam, and the countless discoveries of waste and pollution in fields and factories around the world – the inevitable "side effects" or social costs of postwar prosperity (Mishan 1969). But, for the most part, the tragedies of the 1960s were still far off in the so-called periphery, while the "center" of the capitalist world system had not been seriously affected.

In the 1970s, the crisis started to hit closer to home. There was the disaster in Seveso in Italy in 1976, when a factory exploded and the fumes laid waste a town in the outskirts of Milan. Soon after came the nuclear accident at Three-Mile Island in Pennsylvania, outside of Harrisburg in 1979 which, although not catastrophic, did bring on a new phase of anti-nuclear mobilization around the world. It led, for example, directly to the Swedish government's decision to hold a referendum on the future of nuclear energy, and gave serious impetus to the development of alternative, renewable forms of energy – the "softer" energy paths that Amory Lovins and many others had come to envision in the heat of the energy debate (Lovins 1977).

In 1984, there was an explosion at a Union Carbide chemical plant in Bhopal in India, killing and blinding tens of thousands of people in poisonous fumes. Perhaps the first example of a "glocal" environmental catastrophe (i.e., it took place locally but had global causes and repercussions), the Bhopal disaster led to a drawn-out legal dispute between American and Indian officials, the formation of an international support alliance for the victims, and offered a telling example of the ways in which environmental problems were being exported from the Northern industrial countries to the southern developing countries, where regulations were slacker, enforcement weaker and the apparent need for foreign investment greater than in the over-developed North.

In 1986, there was an accident at a nuclear energy facility at Chernobyl in the Ukraine, spreading radioactivity across northern and central Europe. Again, the international character of the environmental crisis was painfully brought home, but, this time, the overwhelming danger intrinsic to the continued use of poorly designed technological facilities, with insufficient mechanisms for oversight and control, was also implanted in the public consciousness (Beck 1995).

In 1989, an oil tanker, the Exxon Valdez, went aground off the coast of Alaska, spilling more oil than had been the case in any previous accident and affecting fishing and fishing-dominated communities for hundreds of miles. Besides wreaking havoc on a sensitive natural landscape, the Exxon Valdez disaster was one of the key factors that encouraged many large energy- and resource-exploiting corporations to begin to clean up their act. Soon thereafter, the Business Council for Sustainable Development was established by Exxon and other transnational corporations to present a business perspective at the upcoming UN Conference on Environment and Development, the Rio "Summit" of 1992, as well as to sponsor a transition to what has since been labeled eco-efficiency (Schmidheiny 1992).

In the 1990s, the catastrophes have continued, however, and, in many respects, they have grown even more ominous:

- vast uncontrolled fires in tropical rainforests, with the precise causes unknown but attributable, to a large extent, to inappropriate forestry practices and an ever more brutal exploitation of fragile ecosystems;
- unusually intense storms, particularly in the past few years, due, quite probably, to changing global climatic conditions;
- recurrent accidents with trains, passenger ferries, and automobiles, because of faults in operation systems, maintenance, driving capability, and inadequate regulatory regimes, but primarily due to increasing amounts of traffic, and
- the emergence of new threats, especially the so-called "mad cow disease," or BSE, due to a combination of ignorance, sloppiness, and lack of controls in such crucial matters as food production.

In contrast to earlier, more localized environmental calamities, the new problems tend to be more international, or global, in scope, reflecting the growing interconnectedness of the world's economic activity, and the attendant difficulties in keeping that activity under any kind of meaningful social control at a national, or sub-national, level. And unlike many of the environmental controversies of the 1970s, when concerned citizens organized themselves into action groups so that they might move the risks away from their own neighborhoods, these new environmental challenges cannot so easily be moved away: they are in everyone's "backyard."

As such, the so-called NIMBY ("not in my backyard") response, which was characteristic of much of the environmentalism of the 1970s, in both Europe and the United States, has become an insufficient and inadequate form of response, although it still continues to proliferate and take on new manifestations.[3] While the environmental protests of the 1960s and 1970s, in most of the industrialized countries anyway, led to the enactment of more comprehensive legislation and to the creation of substantial administrative-control bureaucracies – as well as to major efforts in scientific research and technical development in the name of environmental protection – the newer, more global dangers associated with science and technology-based production tend to resist effective management and control. Paradoxically, the more expert knowledge we have, and the more "use" we make of it, the more calamitous the ensuing problems seem to be.

At the same time as the problems have been changing character, new risks have also been identified. Or, rather, dangers that had previously been considered hypothetical have been shown to be real. There has been increasing evidence from scientists investigating the atmosphere that a hole is growing bigger in the layer of ozone that protects the planet from dangerous radiation; what was generally ignored in the 1970s as a "doomsday" prophecy is now a major topic for policy deliberations. There are also ever more frightening indications that the earth's temperature is getting warmer, not due to any one particular pollutant, but, it seems, because of the very growth of productive activity itself, and the ensuing emissions of carbon dioxide that are the unintended but inevitable result. Again, this was predicted earlier, but the idea of global warming seemed too outlandish to require any consideration of measures that might be taken.

Most ominous of all perhaps is the creation of a new set of genetic technologies that are based on the manipulation and transfer of genetic material from one organism to another. The first experiments with genetic engineering in the 1970s led to major public debates, particularly in the United States, as a result of which many of the scientists involved in the new genetic "technoscience" took their knowledge-making out of the public domain and into the private sector of commercial activity (Baark and Jamison 1990). Now, when genetically manipulated products have begun to be marketed, the public response has been intense in many countries (Durant *et al.* 1998). New forms of production are being promulgated for which there is little apparent need, and which represent a significant economic threat to those involved in food production in many parts of the world (Shiva 2000). The risks and dangers associated with these new products are extremely difficult to assess. It is impossible to know exactly what this "revolution" will entail for the natural environment and for human health, but there are many who have expressed their concern, as genetically manipulated products have begun to emerge from the research laboratories. But even in this area, with almost thirty years of warning and preparation, the possibilities for effective social control seem almost to have slipped out of reach.

An environmental social science?

One of the difficulties in coming to terms with these new challenges is that ecological issues have fallen prey to many of the same types of "tribal" conflicts and territorial disputes among the so-called experts that have affected our understandings of other areas of nature and society (Becher 1989). Already in the 1970s it was apparent that the new environmental problems required for their comprehension something more than a traditional natural-science expertise, but it has proved difficult, in the years since, to develop approaches to knowledge-making that could transcend disciplinary divisions and entrenched ways of thinking (Leroy and Nelissen 1999). What we have gotten instead is a highly fragmented array of environmental sciences – and, more recently, environmental social sciences – which typically seek to bring the new problems into the separate frameworks and theoretical programs of the specialized scientific disciplines. Ulrich Beck, in his influential book of 1986, aptly termed this process the "feudalization of cognitive practice" as he called for more "reflective" modes of sciencing in order to manage the problems of what he labeled the *risk society* (Beck 1986/1992). And while his call has definitely been heard, one can question whether the resulting forms of expertise have sufficiently escaped the dilemmas of fragmentation and specialization that he warned against.

Over the past fifteen years increasing numbers of environmental economists, political scientists, geographers, and sociologists have come to compete for academic attention, along with the natural scientists, who had earlier more or less cornered the expert market.[4] The well-known patterns of disciplinary differentiation have led to a rather unhelpful division of the subject area, and, within the disciplines, there has often been more competition than cooperation among representatives of opposing schools of thought. The economists have tended to divide themselves into "mainstream" approaches, on the one hand, applying the well-worn concepts of neo-classical economics to environmental issues, while diverse groups of ecological economists, on the other hand, have sought to adapt some of the terminology of ecology to economic relations and production processes (Costanza *et al.* 1997; Daly 1999). The ecological terminology, however, has tended to become commercialized and to develop in isolation from other disciplinary perspectives. As such, ecological economists and green business managers have all but reduced the quest for sustainable development to the sustainable growth of the individual firm or economic branch. We thus have new consulting companies setting themselves up to propose "natural steps" for businesses to take on the road to an environmentally conscious capitalism that obeys the laws of nature, offering a kind of ecological phrase book in the form of organizational learning procedures (Nattrass and Altomare 1999).

Among political scientists a different kind of disciplining has taken place, with experts in environmental policy, environmental organizations, and international relations dividing the realm of environmental politics into separate and increasingly specialized spheres of scholarship. The particular activity areas of parliamentary debates, political protest, intergovernmental negotiations, local projects, Green Party machinations, and so forth all have their experts, but the knowledge that is accumulated tends to enter into public policy deliberations in a highly fragmented and sectorial manner. Policy analysis and advice has largely come to focus on the evaluation of policy "instruments" and institutional capacity-building in particular sectors – for example, transportation, agriculture, energy, industry – while the broader, and increasingly cultural, politics of the environment have tended to be filtered out of policy-making, as if they were simply too tough to handle.

In the 1980s, environmental issues also began to be taken seriously by sociologists and anthropologists after being more or less ignored through the 1960s and 1970s. But the ways in which the issues have since come to be investigated have been subjected to the peculiar logic of sociological differentiation. What C. Wright Mills once termed "abstracted empiricism" has tended to divide environmental sociology into a number of disparate bits and pieces, narrowly defined sub-areas and subsectors (Mills 1963). There are specialists in environmental movements, environmental catastrophes, participation in environmental decision-making, environmental risks and risk assessment, and environmental values and ethics, to name some of the more popular sub-fields of environmental sociology. But the empirical or factual bias that dominates the social science disciplines (especially in the United States, where most of the practitioners are to be found) has meant that broader, more all-encompassing modes of analysis have had difficulty winning acceptance. Understanding has tended to be partial and contextually specific and all too often a reflection of the particular investigator's interests and methodological preferences.

In Europe, what Mills referred to as "grand theory" has been influential among sociologists and those in the related fields of geography and anthropology. Since Ulrich Beck in 1986 first christened our age the risk society, many are the theorists who have sought to incorporate his insights into the received frameworks of social theory, and, in particular, into the language of modernization and modernity. Beck, Anthony Giddens, Scott Lash, and others have championed something they have labeled "reflexive modernization" (Beck, Giddens, and Lash 1994; Giddens 1998), without paying too much attention to the real-life contradictions that have confronted the greening of society. At a slightly lower level of abstraction, other sociologists and political scientists have developed a theory of "ecological modernization," in which they emphasize the new kinds of innovation and new forms of dialog and cooperation that are taking place among business firms, governmental authorities, and environmental organizations in countries like Germany and the Netherlands

(Mol and Sonnenfeld 2000). Still others, in both Europe, Australia, and the United States, have imposed the language and theoretical apparatus of postmodernism (Jagtenberg and McKie 1997), social constructivism (Hannigan 1995) and neo-institutionalism, or systems theory (Luhmann 1993) on to environmental politics, and have thereby identified some of the innumerable barriers that confront the visions and programs of the emerging culture.

And so, as has been the case in many other social-problem areas, environmental social science has become a debating, or, even worse, a mutual-indifference society, filled with divergent and fragmented (mis)understandings. The problem is not so much that the analyses are unconvincing; it is rather that they are, for the most part, incommensurable and competitive, and are therefore difficult to combine in any meaningful way. The analyst is all too often forced to choose a particular terminology and theoretical approach that tends to exclude the others, at the same time as research attention, according to the methodological precepts of academic life, is customarily confined to one particular aspect of reality, or one particular sector. The differences in understanding are thus in need of synthesis and integration, and a much more active process of dialog and communication than is encouraged by the increasingly competitive and entrepreneurial value system of the academic culture as it has developed in most parts of the world. Perhaps most crucially, differences in academic understanding of the issues need to be confronted with, or tested by, the ongoing processes of social and cultural change themselves. Neither the different social science disciplines nor, for that matter, the separate natural science disciplines can retain their splendid isolation in the face of the "co-evolution" of social and ecological practices (Norgaard 1994; Haila 1998).

In this, as in so many areas of social life, we need theories that are somewhat less grandiose and exclusive in their ambitions, and more open to the flow and dynamic of (eco)social development. Reality is simply too complicated and the processes of greening are too all-encompassing – they represent too much of a moving target, we might say – to be able to be explained by any one form of academic research.

Between incorporation and resistance

A fundamental feature of the new environmental politics is that there is no one true, or trusted, form of expertise, no single path to the truth. It is increasingly recognized that all experts have interests of their own which, in complicated ways, exert an influence on the knowledge they produce. As could be expected, there have emerged a number of competing academic, or analytical, responses to the new environmental challenges, but what is more difficult to realize is that many of these responses are contradictory, or, to put it another way, many of these responses are equally true. They are, however, true in different ways in that they are based on different ideals of scientific knowledge, different "epistemic" criteria, as well as different varieties of scientific practice. What is at work, we might say, are competing social epistemologies (Fuller 1988). And this leads, in this area as in so many others, to what Aant Elzinga has termed "epistemic drift," a situation in which knowledge production is carried out without any overall accepted framework of validation or shared set of beliefs (Elzinga 1985).

Many of the experts in greening come from the first wave of interdisciplinary environmental studies or human ecology programs that were established in the 1970s, but many others, as already pointed out, are trying to deal with environmental issues from a more traditional, or specialized, disciplinary perspective. We thus have both a variety of competing schools of human, or social, or political ecology, as well as new sub-disciplines of environmental chemistry, biology, sociology, history, political science, economics, management, engineering, etc. all vying for attention, all striving to be taken seriously. And we have a range of commercial experts, who are operating in a rapidly expanding marketplace of consultation that functions, for the most part, outside of the academic world with its established procedures of quality control and peer review.

While there is a growing literature of competing, even conflicting, interpretations of the new environmental agenda, it can be suggested that they may all be placed on a continuum between two opposing poles. The one pole is optimistic, progressive, and business-oriented, and, in some of its variants, has been characterized as signaling a new stage of modernity (e.g. Giddens 1998). The other is critical, often pessimistic, and tends to put in question the very idea of modernity and the myth of progress that is so central to modernist thinking (e.g. Torgerson 1999). As has been suggested:

the germ of a culturally attuned environmental sensibility in Europe is pincered between on the one side a dominant instrumentalist managerial standardising paradigm, emptied of human meanings, and on the other a set of populist, all too humanly meaningful, parochialist, sentimentalist and antimodern defence movements. (Szerszynski *et al.* 1996: 5)

The dominant interpretation has drawn on a number of new management and organizational concepts, and reflects the fact that a growing market of environmentally friendly products and technological innovations has emerged in recent years. The general idea has been to try to build environmental concern directly into established economic practices so that undesirable "side effects" can be eliminated, or prevented, at their source. Many are the former environmental activists who have become professional experts and consultants, advising companies and politicians on how best to deal with the environmental challenges and contribute to what has been termed a more sustainable socio-economic development. At the same time, new-fangled experts in environmental management, pollution prevention, ecological communication, risk and life-cycle assessment, industrial ecology, renewable energy, and many other specialty areas have begun to be trained at our universities and are institutionalizing new forms of expertise in companies, governmental agencies, intergovernmental and non-governmental organizations.

For some of these new experts what is propounded is a change in production "paradigm," while for others it is primarily a shift in emphasis in the normal practices of research and development, innovation, accounting, management, marketing and public relations. For others still, what is involved are specific, incremental changes in particular sectors or branches. Increasingly, however, environmental concern is being integrated into corporate planning and innovation strategies, while many management and engineering schools have begun to provide courses in environmental economics, as well as in the new methods of cleaner production and eco-efficiency.

As these processes have begun working their way into established routines and practices, a very different kind of environmental politics has developed around the world. From the direct action of animal-liberation groups, motorway occupants and forest protesters to the efforts of so-called indigenous peoples to save their ways of life and their resource bases from being further exploited or colonized by corporate expansion, a new wave of environmental activism has emerged in the 1990s (see Rootes 1999). Here also, new forms of expertise have developed, both in the action repertoires of protest groups, as well as in the forms of communication with the media and in the mobilization of support. An interest has developed in understanding the connections between environmental problems and traditional ideas, belief systems, local knowledges and ways of life (Fischer and Hajer 1999). New sub-fields of anthropology and philosophy have sprung up, with at least some academic researchers attempting to apply their insights to the needs of ecological resistance. A kind of intellectual partisanship, a *citizen science* of counter-expertise, has also developed, both within environmental organizations and at the "interfaces" among environmental groups, green parties, local government and universities (Irwin 1995).

Even more significant, perhaps, are the new environmental think-tanks that have developed around the world to provide an alternative form of expert knowledge in relation to environmental politics. The Centre for Science and Environment (CSE), based in New Delhi, has been at the forefront of this new form of knowledge production with a long stream of books, reports, magazine articles, and, more recently, a journal, *Down to Earth*. Since the early 1980s, CSE has served as a model for similar efforts in public interest sciencing elsewhere, and has also been one of the important critics of new forms of ecological "colonialism" (e.g. Agarwal and Narain 1991; Agarwal *et al.* eds. 1999). Also from India, Vandana Shiva has applied her own particular eloquence to the cause of ecological resistance in a number of books and articles, and has also performed her expertise at meetings, for example, of the World Bank and the International Monetary Fund, whose policies are seen by many critics as among the main contributing factors behind the new environmental challenges (e.g. Shiva 1988; Shiva 1997).

In the United States, the Worldwatch Institute has been producing a "State of the World" Yearbook and an influential journal and report series since the late 1970s. Located at some distance from the academic world, the Worldwatch Institute produces an expertise that is meant to be put into practice (e.g. French 2000). It is an expertise of mediation or popularization that translates the findings of scientists into a more directly political language (Jamison 1996). Like the publications of the large environmental organizations, Worldwatch does not claim to be producing objective knowledge, but rather a kind of partisan or action science that takes sides and attempts to affect reality. In Europe, similar green think-tanks have developed, such as the Wuppertal Institute in Germany, the Stockholm Environment Institute in Sweden, and the Programme for Research and Documentation for a Sustainable Society (ProSus) in Norway, but, in comparison to the research efforts of the business world, they remain fairly weak. In the new "dialectics" of environmentalism, green expertise is not evenly distributed or balanced. There is, at one and the same time, a powerful process of *incorporation* going on, of bringing at least some environmental knowledge and expertise into the political and economic mainstream, while there is also a visible but more marginal process of *resistance*, often combining environmental protest with issues of human rights and social and economic justice.

A central assumption of critics is that contemporary industrial societies continue to be governed by an overriding capitalist or accumulative logic, what Allan Schnaiberg has termed the "treadmill of production" (Schnaiberg and Gould 1994). This logic has led, in many parts of the world, to a process of ecological marginalization, entailing the takeover of local natural resources by powerful external interests, and the subsequent disorganization of the local environments (Kousis 1998). Also important for many critics is the recognition that environmental problems are increasingly linked to issues of racism, justice, equality, and democracy, and that for many of the new protesters solutions have to be more comprehensive than was previously the case. Particularly in developing countries, there is a growing recognition that the corporate quest for sustainable development brings about new inequalities in terms of resource and income distribution, access to knowledge and information, and influence over strategic decision-making (Sachs 1999). In their transfer of responsibility to the private sector, governments and intergovernmental bodies are, perhaps unwittingly, supporting corporate expansion at the expense of local, small-scale initiatives. As the International Society for Ecology and Culture has characterized the situation in a recent analysis, "Small is beautiful, Big is subsidised" (Gorelick 1998). What is needed, according to the diverse collection of critical ecologists, is thus a new kind of politics: new forms of mobilization and opposition to the dominant forces of power.

Building on earlier distinctions between "deep" and "shallow" ecology (e.g. Næss 1973) and between "environmentalists" and "ecologists" (Bookchin 1982), the newer generation of critical ecologists explicitly rejects the incorporation into the mainstream that is so characteristic of corporate, or business environmentalism. Instead, these critics are often seeking to foster new ways of life both in terms of relativizing knowledge claims and in building transnational alliances among representatives of civil society.

As ideal typical counterpoints, or polar opposites, green business and critical ecology have served to bifurcate what in the 1970s could be seen as a somewhat more unified and coherent social movement. While they have developed in parallel fashion, both reacting to a similar set of environmental challenges and political and economic opportunities, and both conditioned by much the same "globalizing" political economy, each of the two main interpretative strategies has tended to develop separate theories and practices. They have seldom informed one another, and they have thus contributed far less than they could have to any comprehensive solution to these serious problems. In the language of Raymond Williams, we can think of them as the responses of "dominant" and "residual" cultural formations, respectively to the emergence of an ecological sensibility, or environmental consciousness (Williams 1977). It seems, therefore, to be increasingly important to delineate a path in between the two polarized positions. As the editors of a recent anthology have put it:

> Transcending this barren modernist/antimodernist, culture/nature dichotomy requires us to find a new set of terms which reflect the co-construction of nature and culture, and which in so doing may provide the grounds for a renewal of public agency and identification with environmental and related public policies. (Szerszynski *et al.* 1996: 5)

It is this bifurcation, or polarization, that has inflicted itself upon both the theory and practice of environmentalism and, in particular, its relations to science, technology, and societal knowledge-making more generally that forms the point of departure for this book. For while both sides propose new kinds of scientific research and technical innovation and new forms of knowledge-making their proposals are all too often incommensurable, based as they are on different kinds of intellectual tradition and the mobilization of very different sorts of cultural and political resource. The green businessmen have their own journals and conferences and networks of communication, and, in most countries, their own sources of political and economic support, while the critical ecologists tend to move in very different types of professional and political circles. By explicitly examining the cognitive praxis of environmental politics in some detail, as well as exploring some of the most relevant historical precedents and formative influences, it is my hope that more synthetic, or bridge-building, approaches to environmental politics might be easier to recognize and strengthen.

Dichotomies of thought

One of the sources of tension that has afflicted the quest for sustainable development derives from the fact that different producers of knowledge, or cognitive actors, take their point of departure, their problem formulation, from different aspects of reality. Whether by choice or by necessity, knowledge-makers identify with different social constituencies and, whether they like it or not, they are often supported by, and must, directly or indirectly, serve the interests of different paymasters. This is not to say that knowledge is bought and sold like any other commodity, but it is to say that the age of the "free-floating" public intellectual is largely a thing of the past (Jacoby 1987). In a knowledge society or knowledge-based economy, thinking becomes a highly valued and valuable social activity.

A basic division that has affected environmental knowledge is between what might be termed cultural and economic approaches to the understanding of human activity. Many focus their attention on the material, or economic aspects, of social life – often reducing those aspects to what companies do – while others focus on the more symbolic, or cultural aspects: what we do in our everyday lives when we are supposedly not pursuing our material interests. As the social sciences became institutionalized in the nineteenth century, the different interests led to different academic disciplines, and, in many countries, to structural barriers between different faculties and types of universities. Economics and management tended to be studied in their own departments and eventually coalesced around business schools and engineering faculties, often at newer scientific and technological universities, while humanists and eventually sociologists and historians tended to consolidate their positions at the older and often more tradition-bound universities, taking over and eventually "modernizing" the medieval subjects of philosophy, rhetoric and theology. In the twentieth century, as separate faculties for the social and human sciences emerged throughout the world, departments of economics and management tended to differentiate themselves from departments of sociology, politics, and government, history, psychology and philosophy, each with their own literatures, theories, methods, and professional rituals and customs of behavior.[5]

The study of society, in more general terms, split into social sciences on the one hand and into arts and humanities on the other, each with different conceptions and ideals of knowledge, indeed, with different conceptions of the truth. And that division has been reproduced in countless varieties over the past hundred years as science has grown into a significant professional activity. The arts–science distinction has served to reinforce the older distinction between the study of nature and the study of society that was articulated in the seventeenth century, between the sciences of nature and the sciences of man, and in the 1990s the bifurcation manifested itself in a number of heated exchanges: the so-called "science wars."[6]

What might be termed the national styles of interaction between the "two cultures" – the natural scientists and engineers on the one hand, and the humanists and social scientists on the other – have, in turn, led to different forms of accommodation in different countries. In some, perhaps in most, countries there have been erected institutional barriers among the cultures; while in others, albeit not very many, spaces for interdisciplinary or transcultural communication have been established where different scholars from different fields can communicate and interact with one another. The science wars were most intense in the United States and Britain, where the old distinctions have been perhaps most rigorously institutionalized; in many European countries, there has been a good deal more interaction between the human/social and the natural/technical sciences, although the forms of interaction have differed from country to country.[7]

In an influential account, Jürgen Habermas argued in the 1960s that the natural, social, and human sciences have different "knowledge-constituting interests" (Habermas 1971). For the natural sciences the central ambition is to achieve technical–practical control over reality, and knowledge is thus developed with an orientation toward use and technical intervention; for the social sciences, the main ambition is to achieve an administrative knowledge that can provide guidance for the effective management and administration of social life; while for the human sciences a reflective interest is paramount, with knowledge primarily pursued in order to increase understanding of the human condition. In later work, Habermas has referred to a communicative rationality in the human and social sciences that is to be distinguished from the instrumental, or technological, rationality that is fundamental to the natural and engineering sciences.

Environmental challenges cannot easily be separated into communicative and instrumental rationalities, however, or, for that matter, into natural, social, and human sciences, and so in the 1970s there were attempts, in what we can term the first "age of ecology," to develop more holistic or comprehensive frameworks of understanding that transcended these historically shaped barriers. Often under the rubric of human ecology or environmental studies, processes of nature–society interaction were studied in a more explicit interdisciplinary fashion. Often, models and theories that had been developed in biological ecology were "transferred" to society and to the understanding of environmental issues. Social relations were reinterpreted, for example, in terms of energy flows and resource use, and economic development was conceptualized in relation to ecological "laws" and processes (e.g. Georgescu-Roegen 1971; Wilkinson 1973). Attention was also focused on the underlying attitudes to nature, and the conceptions of pollution and waste that characterized human interactions with the non-human environment (e.g. Douglas 1966; Passmore 1974). In geography, anthropology, and history, as well as in economics, political science, and sociology, the rise of human ecology had the effect of bringing "nature" explicitly into the frames of understanding, both theoretically and conceptually, of many social science disciplines (e.g. Schnaiberg 1980; Douglas and Wildavsky 1982). In the 1980s, practitioners in the new sub-fields of environmental history, environmental sociology, and ecological and environmental economics began to publish journals and form academic societies.

By the 1990s many of the broader, more interdisciplinary human ecology and environmental studies departments that had been established in the 1970s had fallen on hard times, and their attempts to develop holistic theories and interdisciplinary perspectives had been countered by a resurgence of more narrowly specialized approaches under the general rubric of going "back to basics." Environmental studies were also subdivided into the various issue areas, or sectors, of industrial pollution, agriculture, natural resources, transportation, and energy, which has led to very different forms of scientific expertise that are seldom transferred or translated across the sectors.

The creation of national and international programs in "global environmental change" in the 1980s led to a number of other institutional initiatives which, in many respects, resembled the earlier efforts to develop interdisciplinary environmental studies departments. The result in many universities is that there are small bands of environmental scientists spread around in different departments, at the same time as there are centers of interdisciplinary programs, usually supported on a temporary basis by a company or foundation or international organ. Dialog or communication among the different tribes is minimal, and in many universities there are often now separate and competing departments of environmental studies, with a department in environmental management usually located at or near a business school and a department in human ecology or environmental ethics located at or near the humanities faculty. As such, the understanding of, and knowledge about, the environmental challenges that humankind is facing and the ways that those challenges can best be handled is highly fragmented.

The division that afflicts the contemporary world of environmental knowledge reflects, or reproduces, a number of long-standing divisions that have characterized modern science at least since the seventeenth century. Thomas Kuhn once identified an "essential tension" in modern science between a mathematical and an experimental tradition, each upholding a very different idea of what science was all about and how a scientist went about obtaining truth (Kuhn 1978). Others, like Habermas in our day, have referred to a division of science into instrumental, or positivist, varieties on the one hand, and communicative, or hermeneutic, varieties on the other, what Max Horkheimer and Teodor Adorno in the 1940s called the "dialectic of enlightenment" (Adorno and Horkheimer 1944/1972). Where the positivist tends to seek a specialized knowledge, often based on a thorough investigation of a delimited area of reality, the hermeneutic scientist seeks a general, or critical, understanding of a wide range of disparate phenomena. The specialist values precision and detail while the generalist wants to know a little about many things. They use different research methods, develop different concepts and terminology, and have very different ideals or goals for their research activity. And while the specialist is extremely important for many specific tasks, we also need the fuzzier, but wider range, the attempt to comprehend the *totality*, as Georg Lukács put it, that characterizes the ambit of the generalist (Lukács 1971/1924).

A broader perspective

In my view, if we are to be able to make use of our scientific and technological developments in socially appropriate and ecologically sustainable ways, we must wander outside the confines of any one discipline and any one mode of interpretation into the wider worlds of culture and history. Without adopting a broader perspective, our decision-makers and our opinion-formers will continue to steer developments into trajectories that are too narrow and one-sided, and, as a result, all too often counterproductive. But what does such a broader understanding involve? Let me briefly specify three central elements of the perspective that I will be trying to put to work in the chapters that follow.

First and most fundamental to my understanding of reality is the *historical dimension*, and the overriding importance of historical reflection. Social and cultural changes unfold over time, and if we take reality only as it presents itself to us at any one point in time, or if we consider developments only in a short-term time perspective we can be led to make serious lapses in judgment and profound misunderstandings of the situation. History is important not merely as a narrative chronology of events, as the way things once were, but as an essential component of the present, helping to form or shape contemporary activity. In this respect, history should be seen as a kind of collective memory, as those traditions or legacies of the past which are selectively and continually being mobilized in the ongoing construction of the present (Eyerman and Jamison 1998). Lewis Mumford once likened history to a reservoir of human experiences out of which each generation identifies its own currents and flows.

Without the perpetual rediscovery and reinterpretation of history, without free access to that reservoir, the life of any single generation would be but a trickle of water in a desert. The limited conventions of historians have made us forget, however, that history has an anticipatory side: it is the domain of the possible, the starting point of the ideal . . . The creation and selection of new potentialities, the projection of ideal goals, is, with reference to the future, the counterpart of an intelligent commerce with the past. (Mumford 1944: 12–13)

In the pages that follow, historical reflection will be used to help to identify the roots of contemporary processes, both in terms of precursors and formative traditions, as well as in relation to long-term tensions that have an influence on contemporary events. In order to understand the factors that lead to the emergence of new social actors and processes, as well as the underlying forces of inertia and resistance, historical analysis needs to be given a much more explicit role in our understanding of science, technology, and sustainable development. A historical perspective is also necessary to identify the conditions which serve to differentiate one culture or region from another in its way of "appropriating" technological and other socio-economic developmental processes into the various worlds, or domains, of social life (Hård and Jamison 1998).

Secondly, a broader understanding of the relations between environmental politics and cultural transformation should be informed by a *pluralist, or comparative, sensibility*. The alternative to the dominant technocratic and universalizing conceptions cannot merely be a relativist particularism, such as those proposed by writers identifying with one or another ethnic or "deep ecology" ideology. Both within environmentalism, as well as in the broader discourses of socio-economic development and international relations, it has become fashionable to counter Western, or technoscientific, imperialism by reinventing traditional identities, and although there is much to sympathize with in the writings of many of the new cultural critics, they often exaggerate the contemporary relevance of traditional belief systems (Jamison 1994). A technocratic mindset cannot be adequately challenged by ethnically specific or by explicitly "ecocentric" alternatives. Science and technology are global possessions and they provide humanity, for the most part, with progressive achievements, but what is not to be neglected are the different contributions that different cultures have made, the different "rivers" – in Joseph Needham's metaphor – that have flowed into the ocean of technoscientific knowledge (Needham 1969).

Pluralism means that we give proper recognition to the diversity of technology interactions and, in particular, the ways in which national cultures indigenize international trends, both in relation to ideas as well as artifacts. As Arnold Pacey has argued, innovation in the past has often been shaped by a *technological dialog* among civilizations (Pacey 1990). Techniques have not merely been transferred from one society to another, as the dominant ideology would have it; rather, they have been selectively exchanged and communicated in processes of dialogue and creative interaction. Technological change, we might say, is a multicultural movement of ideas and experiences, and in the contemporary world no policy decisions are taken without reference to contexts which transcend national borders. But neither are policy decisions the result of truly international, or global, processes. Policy-makers and their experts operate in particular national settings at the same time as they belong to transnational, or cosmopolitan actor-networks – academic, economic, civic, and bureaucratic – which share certain common values and ways of life.

The insights of the Latin American *dependencia* theorists have shown us that Western economic development was part of an international process, and that the development of the North was fueled by exploitation of resources and oppression of peoples in the South. Capitalist development was, in large measure, driven by the quest for expansion and domination that characterized colonialism and imperialism (e.g. Frank 1978). Later attempts to reduce economic and political change to the machinations of an all-encompassing world system, or globalization process, however, are not helpful in understanding either the dynamics of scientific and technological, or of social and cultural, change. As Ulrich Beck has recently emphasized, there is a tendency in much of the globalization literature to neglect the complexity of different underlying globalizing processes, and, in particular, to confuse an ideology of globalism with the myriad social and economic processes of globalization (Beck 1998).

What needs to be distinguished within any kind of world system, or globalization, process are the complicated and simultaneous patterns of interaction and competition, of centralization and localization: what Ulf Hannerz has termed "cultural complexity" (Hannerz 1992). Globalization is not of one piece; and to understand what is going on it can be helpful to identify different, and often competing, alliances, coalitions, and campaigns, that are organized into a range of transnational actor-networks. As Edward Said, who has analyzed the role of colonialism in the development of literature, put it:

A confused and limiting notion of priority allows that only the original proponents of an idea can understand and use it. But the history of all cultures is the history of cultural borrowings. Cultures are not impermeable; just as Western science borrowed from Arabs, they had borrowed from India and Greece. Culture is never just a matter of ownership, of borrowing and lending with absolute debtors and creditors, but rather of appropriations, common experiences, and interdependencies of all kinds among different cultures. (Said 1993: 217)

It is well to remember that environmental politics, like all political activities, is the work of people with different agendas, constituencies, and patterns of development, translating or reinterpreting "global" doctrines and approaches into local, or national, contexts. We might well liken the flows of ideas and experiences and policy initiatives to the flows of resources and energy in ecosystems, as different actors seek out particular niches in the diverse landscapes of science and technology and of economics, culture, and politics.

As Karel Kosik once put it, in arguing for the continued relevance of dialectical philosophy, we need to "divide the one" (Kosik 1976), to separate what confronts us as a unified picture of reality into its component parts, and this is a kind of deconstruction activity. In viewing knowledge-production and social development as dynamic cultural processes, we need to understand the ways in which conflicting values, norm systems, and programmatic ambitions come to be combined in the making of "projects" both big and small. Scientists following what they imagine to be their own intellectual curiosity are often more interested in different components of scientific knowledge than are industrialists who are looking for commercially viable new products. The governmental and intergovernmental agencies that have been established to regulate production processes or to improve public health similarly have their own, rather specialized, interests, as do the various groups, organizations, societies, political parties, and just plain concerned citizens who populate the heterogeneous realm of "civil society."

It is important not to lose sight of the conflictual nature of socioeconomic development in general, and of scientific, technological, and other forms of knowledge-making in particular. For while it is widely recognized that there are distinct national patterns of industrial and innovation policy (e.g. Nelson 1993), it is essential to investigate the cultural shaping of these "national systems," the ways in which particular geographical conditions, intellectual traditions, and cultural visions have come into play in the making of regionally differentiated sociotechnological complexes.

In order to better understand these relations, or tensions, it is necessary to go beyond the surface manifestations to the underlying cognitive dimensions of societal interactions, and this is the final, and perhaps most important, element of my approach. Using perspectives from the fields of science, technology, and society studies – and from the cognitive approach to social movements that I have previously developed with Ron Eyerman – I will attempt in this book to elucidate the knowledge interests, or *cognitive praxis*, of environmental politics. This means exploring what we might term the social epistemology of sustainable development, and trace some of the deep-seated assumptions and beliefs – the epistemic commitments – that condition contemporary activities (Elzinga 1985; Jacob 1996). Our actions are informed by ideas and traditions that are seldom brought into the open, and it is important to make those assumptions and proclivities explicit and identifiable. In this respect, a

broader cultural approach, as Kay Milton has put it, can help to "dispell
the myths" that are all too often taken for granted in social and political
interactions, and not least in environmental debates and policy decisions
(Milton 1996).

My own political, or social, epistemology involves an effort to pay attention, serious attention, to oppositional and critical voices. By representing
the responses to, as well as the victims of, so-called modernization, critical and oppositional movements have often functioned as an important
means for reorientation and redirection in the course of scientific, technological, and social development (Jamison 1988). Social movements,
we might say, are a recurrent source for the reconstitution of societies
and their modes of knowledge-production. As carriers of critique and
alternative visions, social movements – from the religious movements of
the early modern era to the labor movements of the nineteenth century
and on to the environmental, feminist, and postcolonial movements of
our own day – have served to articulate alternative criteria for social and
cognitive development. They thus provide an important source of renovation in long-term shifts of societal direction. Taking such critical voices
seriously is not easy; but if our technological advancements are to serve
more than the interests of one group in our societies, it is necessary to
develop new and broader ways of understanding, conceptualizing, and
institutionalizing processes of technological change.

For the analyst, this means recognizing one's own partisanship. Rather
than seeking to achieve a false sense of objectivity and academic distance in relation to the topics that are under investigation, we should
instead try to develop a more conscious sense of our own *intellectual engagement*, combining the detachment of the scientist with the passion of
the participant. As citizens, as human subjects, we are inevitably part of
the processes we study, and our research, whether we like it or not, is
always a form of political intervention. By focusing attention on some
aspect of social reality we also give it form, voice, and meaning, however
scientific and impartial we might try to be. The challenge is to use our
involvement – and our research "role" – creatively, not by dismissing it or
rejecting it, or being ashamed of our own values and beliefs, but by trying
to build those values and normative attachments into our understanding. We have opinions about the things we study, and we should try to
use our engagement in our analyses by being honest about the choices we
make and the sides we take. Here, intellectual engagement means, among
other things, an attempt to put the different sides of the environmental
political debate on speaking terms, and to use the theory, history, and sociology of science to help to fashion a multilogical discursive space and to

build some bridges, and make some connections, across the divisions of environmentalism.

An emerging culture

It will be the contention here that while the dominant, or hegemonic, culture seeks to incorporate environmental concern into its established modes of operation, seeds are also being planted, in the name of sustainable development, for new forms of social solidarity. Almost wherever we choose to look, top-down strategies compete with bottom-up approaches in the integration of an environmental awareness into social and economic life. And while some important attempts have been made to sort out the various theories, or discourses, of the new environmental politics (e.g. Pepper 1996; Harvey 1996; Dryzek 1997; Darier 1999), little attempt has been made to confront an analysis of the discursive "level" with the variety of practical activities that are taking place.

In my view, environmental politics are perhaps best understood in terms of what the literary critic and novelist Raymond Williams once called an "emergent" cultural formation:

> by "emergent" I mean, first, that new meanings and values, new practices, new relationships and kinds of relationship are continually being created. But it is exceptionally difficult to distinguish those which are really elements of some new phase of the dominant culture. . . . and those which are substantially alternative or oppositional to it: emergent in the strict sense, rather than merely novel. (Williams 1977: 123)

As experimental practices, an emergent cultural formation is continually being formed and reformed, and, as Williams also emphasized, it is in inevitable struggle with the dominant culture. In particular, an emergent culture must contend with the complex forms of "incorporation" that the dominant culture develops in response to the new practices and visions. For Williams, what was most characteristic of an emergent cultural formation were the alternative "structures of feeling," the disposition or sensibility or underlying values that are in continuous danger of being destroyed by the incorporating efforts of the dominant culture. But he also stressed that the emergent culture could easily be captured by and retreat into "residual" cultural formations, those traditional ways of life and ideologies that had been overtaken by the dominant culture, but which lived on in the collective memory (Williams 1977: 122–23).

We can perhaps most adequately identify the structures of feeling in the emergent, or what I prefer to call emerging, ecological culture as an ongoing set of social and cultural processes that contain elements of both thought and action, and which are both ideational and material. As Williams put it, they are "social experiences in solution" (ibid.: 133). But they are experiences whose practitioners must wage, as it were, a battle on two fronts: against a dominant, or hegemonic, culture seeking to incorporate them, and against a residual, or reactionary, culture seeking to envelop them. It is this active work of innovation and synthesis, this simultaneous struggle against the twin dangers of cooption and reaction, that is so crucially important to understand.

In order to grasp these processes that are taking place before our eyes we need to fashion a dynamic style of interpretation so that we might be able to explore the myriad types of coalition-forming, network-building, identity-fashioning, and symbol-creating that are often difficult to disentangle and which are seldom examined explicitly. My effort here will draw, somewhat eclectically, on several different academic fields and theoretical traditions, and present findings from a number of recent research projects, to try to grasp what is proving to be neither a particularly straightforward nor coherent process of social and cultural change.

In what follows, I will be considering the ongoing "greening" of our societies primarily as a kind of *knowledge-making*, or cognitive praxis. Like many other social and economic activities, environmental politics contain at their core a cognitive dimension, which we can think of as diverse, and sometimes competing, attempts to construct reality (Berger and Luckmann 1967).

Cognitive praxis is the way that human consciousness is acted out or put into practice; it is knowledge in the making (Latour 1987; Golinski 1998). Like the new "modes" of knowledge-production that have been delineated in the social study of science (Gibbons *et al.* 1994), cognitive praxis consists of both ideas and the procedures that are used to validate them, and of both organizational forms and spatial relations. Cognitive praxis is situationally determined, or context specific, and it consists both of formal and informal types of knowledge making (Haraway 1991). As Michael Polanyi was one of the first to recognize, there is almost always a "tacit" or personal dimension that is of crucial significance in the development of knowledge (Polanyi 1958). In different settings, in different parts of the world, different shades of green theory and practice are being combined in different ways.

My aim in the chapters that follow is to track some of them down, trace their historical roots, and tell some stories along the way. I want to try to identify broader historical patterns in the processes under investigation, and, at the same time, elucidate some of the ways in which different members of the "public" take part in the making of green knowledge. As such, it will be a book of juxtapositions: of past and present, local and global, national and international, academic and activist, personal and political.[8]

NOTES

Some of the formulations in this chapter build on the final report of the project, Public Engagement and Science and Technology Policy Options (PESTO) (Jamison 1999). An earlier version has been published in *Innovation – The European Journal of Social Sciences*, autumn 2000.

1 Betty Friedan's *The Feminine Mystique* (1961) is usually heralded as the harbinger of the women's liberation movement in much the same way that Rachel Carson's *Silent Spring* is seen as the starting-point for environmentalism. The internet grew out of the so-called ARPAnet, which developed as part of the manned space program, and, of course, rock music seems, in retrospect, to have been the main event of the 1960s, soaking up into its many varieties much of the cultural and political energy of that turbulent decade (see Eyerman and Jamison 1998: 106ff for details).

2 Yrjö Haila (1997) makes a distinction between wilderness, which he sees as an ideological construction, and wildness, which can be fostered and revitalized among humans as well as non-humans; see also Turner 1996; Abram 1996.

3 In his book on the toxic-waste movement in the United States, Andrew Szasz shows how NIMBY protests are perhaps more "progressive" than many commentators have suggested. Many of the originally local protests over toxic waste sites grew into broader struggles of environmental justice, he contends; but he also suggests that local protests over pollution were a major source of the "paradigm shift" to preventive approaches that took place in the 1980s. We will return to these matters in chapter 6 (see Szasz 1994).

4 As this manuscript was being finalized, I attended a conference on environmental social science in Finland where I heard a similar, but far more comprehensive, review of these matters by Riley Dunlap. See also Cohen, ed., 1999 and Redclift and Woodgate, eds., 1997.

5 A detailed historical review of these developments, particularly as they took place in the United States, can be found in Ross 1991. The articles collected in Wagner and Wittrock, *et al.* 1991, provide additional insights into the institutionalization of the social sciences.

6 The so-called science wars of the 1990s represented the angry response to the criticism of science from some self-appointed defenders of a traditional scientific faith (e.g. Gross and Levitt 1994), who have depicted science studies and much of the environmental debate, as well, for that matter, as a form of "(higher) superstition". For responses to the response, see the articles collected in *Social Text* 46–47 (1996), which also contains the infamous hoax article by Alan Sokal, in which some of the more exaggerated science studies rhetoric is thrown back at its perpetrators.

7 For some information about European and American institutional processes in the interface of the human and the natural-technical sciences, see the websites and publications of the organizations, 4S (The Society for Social Studies of

Science) and EASST (The European Association for the Study of Science and Technology). In 1995, 4S produced a *Handbook in Science and Technology Studies*, which presents some of the main contributions to the subject area (Jasanoff *et al.* 1995). The bifurcation into "two cultures" was famously identified by the scientist and novelist C. P. Snow in 1959, and his characterization was one of the sources of inspiration for the emergence of a "science of science" and, eventually, a hybrid field of science-technology-society studies (STS) in the 1960s (Snow 1959; Goldsmith and Mackay 1966).

8 In their recent studies of activism in the United States, James Jasper and Paul Lichterman have focused on the individual "life-story" as an important source for understanding protest activity. As Jasper puts it, "Individuals, with their idiosyncrasies, neuroses, and mistakes, are troublesome for social science. . . . But a good social observer, if only to renew her humility, must look at the individuals now and then, to see what motivations and symbols and strategies her models have overlooked" (Jasper 1997: 216). Lichterman has traced what he terms the "search for political community" in the lives of three activists in different environmental organizations in the United States, as a way to relate the individual to the social (Lichterman 1996). As a modest attempt to follow their lead, I will try to bring out some of the personal aspects of the processes I write about.

2 Social movements and knowledge-making

It's where the rivers change direction...
> Kate Wolf, "Across the Great Divide" (1980)

Radical movements may be understood as schools – from which the students graduate not quite the same as when they entered. They also, of course, affect and influence far more persons than their members.
> Norman Birnbaum, *The Radical Renewal* (1988: 140)

From movements to institutions

It is one of the underlying arguments of this book that the political quest for sustainable development is best thought of as an ongoing series of cultural transformations by which the visionary ideas and utopian practices of the environmental movement are working their way into the social lifeblood. From this perspective, the ever more cooperative, or "constructive," roles that many environmental organizations and former activists have taken on can be said to represent a transition from movement to institution, as ideas and activities that were previously considered radical or alternative are now being translated into more acceptable forms (Eder 1996). As the environmental "movement" has come to be redefined, however, and, in the eyes of many, reduced primarily to the machinations of large, "non-governmental" organizations such as Greenpeace and the World Wildlife Fund, something rather fundamental seems to have changed. In the process of winning influence and organizational strength the messages that are being projected and the activities that are being carried out have been transformed in subtle ways. In choosing to join the mainstream there has been a certain narrowing of focus, as well as a kind of professional differentiation, by which the different organizations have divided up what was once a "movement space" into their own specialized areas of operation (Jamison 1996).

Institutionalization has not gone unchallenged, however. In a variety of ways there has been a number of reactions to the new "institutions," both within the establishment itself, as well as among some of the former allies of the institutionalizers, who have begun to identify themselves with some of the losers, or marginalized victims, of the process. A fragmentation, or diversification, of what was once a smaller, but more unified, movement has thus developed. And it has become far more complicated to retain a sense of autonomy and coherence in relation both to the dominant and more residual cultural formations. The challenge has become twofold: on the one hand, not to give in completely to the "rules of the game" of the established social actors, and, on the other, to avoid the ideological simplifications of many of those who are critical of the compromising and conciliatory requirements of institutionalization.

In this chapter I attempt to place these processes in a longer-term time perspective. The general claim is that many social movements of the past, much like the environmental movements of our time, have provided a seedbed, or alternative public space, for the articulation of utopian "knowledge interests" that have then been translated into more socially acceptable forms of knowledge-making (Eyerman and Jamison 1991). Social movements, that is, have periodically served as important contexts for the reconstitution of knowledge.

Francesco Alberoni has distinguished between the "nascent states" of movements in formation and the institutions that movements often become, and has placed their interaction at the center of his theory of social change. As he put it: "It must be remembered that all institutions and all value systems arose originally as a nascent state and often are only a way of channeling and conserving its tremendous energies" (Alberoni 1984: 83). The nascent state, or social movement, mobilizes enormous amounts of human energy and creativity and it is, we might say, only natural that societies have great difficulty in "taming" or institutionalizing those energies. It is also natural that there will be those who object to the efforts by the powers-that-be to bring social movements under control, that is, to get them to stop moving. By exploring some of the historical precursors to contemporary environmentalism, we might be better able to appreciate what is at stake in the contemporary conflicts over environmental politics, particularly in relation to the greening of knowledge. If we can tap into a "usable past" we might even be better prepared to keep the emerging ecological cultural formation from being watered down into meaninglessness and being destroyed by the reactions it unleashes. We might indeed be able to learn something from history.

The scientific revolution as a cultural process

Let us begin with the foundational narrative itself: the making of modern science, which, in several respects, is one of the formative moments of environmentalism. It is fairly obvious that what is commonly referred to as science and technology, and which we might characterize, somewhat more precisely, as the institutions of Western science, emerged as an integral part of a much broader cultural transformation (Huff 1993). For Karl Polanyi, it was simply the "great transformation," while for others it has been termed the "birth of modernity." Whatever it is called it is clear that it included an important and decisive transformation of knowledge-making. In the seventeenth and eighteenth centuries, throughout Europe, something fundamental happened in terms of how human beings go about enlightening themselves: there was a *scientific revolution*, with the simultaneous creation of new theories, methods, instruments, social roles, and organizations for the making of knowledge (Jamison 1989). That the scientific revolution was, in many ways, related to the social and political movements of the times is hard to deny, but such connections are difficult to pin down and, partly because of their intractability, they have only rarely been explored by professional historians. As Christopher Hill put it: "There is a curious academic division of spheres of influence ... as a result of which the history of science and the history of ideas have become something quite separate from 'history'" (Hill 1965: 14).

As it has become an academic discipline – a kind of institution of its own – history, and, more specifically, the history of science, has tended to confine its attention to the *bona fide* scientists of the past and their thoughts and deeds, that is, to a highly circumscribed realm of human cognitive activity. Historical generalists such as Lewis Mumford, Joseph Needham, Michel Foucault, or Carolyn Merchant – or, for that matter, Thomas Kuhn of *The Structure of Scientific Revolutions* – who have tried to describe broader patterns in history, and discern connections between the often hermetically separated spheres of historical specialization, tend to be looked down upon by the professional specialists. As a result, the historical relations between science, technology, and the "rest of society" have been curiously under-examined.

It is only when the social status of science and technology has been seriously questioned, as was the case in the 1920s and 1930s and then again in the 1960s and 1970s, that explicit attempts have been made to relate the history of science and technology to broader social and political movements. At such times, what has been all but ignored by the professional, or specialized, historians has been taken up by "interdisciplinary" generalists and dissenting specialists, who have sought to break down barriers among the disparate disciplines and sub-disciplines, and recombine what we might term the institutionalized compartmentalizations of the past.

In the 1920s the philosopher Max Scheler, in outlining the contours of the sociology of knowledge, used the emergence of modern science as a central example of how changed social practices and social relations had inspired new modes of knowledge production. It had been in the linking of philosophy with work experience that modern science had come into being, Scheler suggested. What had been kept separate in other civilizations – what Edgar Zilsel in the 1930s depicted as the life-worlds of "scholars" and "craftsmen" – were brought together in early modern Europe into a new scientific identity. The experimental philosophers combined scholarship and craftsmanship into a hybrid form of knowledge-making, namely experimentation, as well as into a new social role (Zilsel 1941). In Scheler's sociology of knowledge the "selection of the objects of knowledge" and the development of the "forms of cognition" were made "on the basis of the prevailing social perspectives of interests" (Scheler 1980: 72–73). He was thus one of the first to seek to link changes in the social environment, or societal context, explicitly to changes in the scientific enterprise. Later, in his influential doctoral dissertation of 1938 the American sociologist Robert Merton showed that many of the early scientists in seventeenth-century Britain had been associated with the Puritan movement, but, after the Restoration, and with it, the founding of the Royal Society, they had renounced many of their broader political objectives. His point was that the institutions of modern science had directly grown out of the religious and political struggles of the seventeenth century (Merton 1970/1938).

In the 1960s, in sketching the historical development of the "scientific role," the sociologist Joseph Ben-David returned to some of these perspectives. Ben-David contrasted a "scientistic movement" in the late sixteenth and early seventeenth centuries with the institutionalization process of academy-building that took place in the late seventeenth and early eighteenth centuries (Ben-David 1971). Ben-David drew on a kind of historical detective work, which had identified in sixteenth-century Europe a range of transition figures, such as the enigmatic Philippus Aureolus Theophrastus Bombastus von Hohenheim, better known as Paracelsus (1493–1541). In beginning the transformation of alchemy into chemistry, and in developing the rudiments of scientific medicine, Paracelsus had combined a questioning of established religious and political authority with an interest in nature observation, mathematics, mechanics, and technical improvement. He had an organic view of nature, seeing in the human body a "microcosm" of the "macrocosm" of the heavenly bodies (Merchant 1980).

The teachings of Paracelsus were highly influential in the sixteenth century and influenced many of the early "hybrid" or proto-scientists, such as Tycho Brahe in Denmark, John Dee in England, and Giordano Bruno in Italy. In examining Bruno's "hermetic philosophy" in the 1960s, the historian of the Renaissance Frances Yates argued that:

It may be illuminatory to view the scientific revolution in two phases, the first phase consisting of an animistic universe operated by magic, the second phase of a mathematical universe operated by mechanics. An enquiry into both phases, and their interactions may be a more fruitful line of historical approach to the problems raised by the science of today than the line which concentrates only on the seventeenth-century triumph. Is not all science a gnosis, an insight into the nature of the All, which succeeds by successive revelations? (Yates 1964: 452)

In the 1960s and 1970s the importance of these historical figures was rediscovered, and given a more central role to play in the emergence of modern science. In Ben-David's scheme, for example, Paracelsus and Bruno were part of a movement phase which culminated in the writings of Francis Bacon (1561–1626) with his proposals for new methods of scientific investigation that broke with the "idols of the past." As Bacon characteristically put it in *Novum Organum*, his major philosophical treatise:

It is idle to expect any great advancement in science from the superinducing and engrafting of new things upon old. We must begin anew from the very foundations, unless we would revolve forever in a circle with mean and contemptible progress. (Bacon 1947/1620: 31)

Later, in the revolutionary period from 1640 to 1660, Bacon's writings formed part of what the historian Charles Webster termed the "great instauration," when dissenting groups and other "movement" organizations carried out experiments in agriculture and medicine, and produced a vast amount of popular scientific and technical literature in their pamphlets and informal treatises (Webster 1975). From an environmental perspective, the most interesting of the radical groups was perhaps the Diggers, who planted crops together and developed a "law of freedom" according to which no one person could own the earth (Hill 1975: 128ff). The institutions of science grew from seeds planted by such Puritan activists, who were driven by a millenarian world-view to create a new kingdom of God, and to share the Earth collectively. In recounting that story in the mid-1970s Charles Webster reflected on the way in which historical research itself was connected to contemporary concerns:

It is perhaps only in the most recent phases of acute crisis in science and technology that we have moved into a position whereby a sympathetic estimate of the millenarian worldview can be made ... Environmental circumstances have necessitated reference to an idea of the social accountability of science, analogous to the view which the Puritans more readily derived from their religious convictions...Although the Puritans looked forward to an unprecedented expansion in human knowledge, they realized that it would be necessary to exercise stringent discipline to prevent this knowledge resulting in moral corruption and social exploitation. (Webster 1975: 517–18)

What eventually came to be characterized as modern science represented a form of knowledge production that drew much of its inspiration from earlier and much broader social and political struggles while narrowing, or specializing, the focus and organization of the research activity. The historical project of modernity, we might say, did not begin as a new scientific method, or a new mechanical world-view, or, for that matter, as a new kind of state support for experimental philosophy in the form of scientific academies. It was, rather, a much more all-encompassing project: to "turn the world upside down" as one pamphleteer at the time of the English Civil War put it (Hill 1975). And it was a project, or series of projects, in which "nature," or non-human phenomena, continued to be imbued with meaning and life – either in terms of the magical spiritualism of the Neoplatonists or the more radical "organic" spiritualism of the Paracelsians and the Diggers (Merchant 1980). In the words of Carolyn Merchant:

The pantheistic and Paracelsian ideas...were part of a radical social philosophy that for some groups meant the seizing of common lands and the establishment of egalitarian communal societies like those attempted by the medieval millenarian utopists. Gerrard Winstanley, organizer of the Diggers, who in 1649 took possession of St. George's Hill in Surrey and began to cultivate the commons and wastes, believed that by working together the poor could make the earth 'a common treasury' for all. (Merchant 1980: 123)

As the broader movements gave way to more established institutions in the course of the seventeenth century, political and social experiments came to be transformed into scientific experiments. The political and religious reformation, tinged with political radicalism and filled with mistrust of authority, was redefined and reconstituted as a scientific revolution (Porter 1986). And a broader, open-ended movement of discovery and exploration came to be transformed into the institutions of modern knowledge-making. As Merchant has put it:

From the spectrum of Renaissance organicist philosophies...the mechanists would appropriate and transform presuppositions at the conservative or hierarchical end while denouncing those associated with the more radical religious and political perspectives. The rejection and removal of organic and animistic features and the substitution of mechanically describable components would become the most significant and far-reaching effect of the Scientific Revolution. (Merchant 1980: 125)

The Renaissance had glorified life, and the interest in things technical that spread among scholars during the sixteenth century was meant to enhance man's powers and man's capacities (Rothenberg 1993). In his review of utopian thinking, Lewis Mumford put it this way: "The earlier utopias were concerned to establish the things which men should aim for in life...The utopias of the later Renaissance took those aims for granted and discussed how man's scope of action might be broadened" (Mumford 1922: 106–108).

The Renaissance artist-engineers retain for us an almost superhuman fascination. Michelangelo, Leonardo, Botticelli, Albrecht Dürer continue after half a millennium to epitomize the fullness of human life. Their pursuit of knowledge knew no bounds: science, art, philosophy, engineering, architecture, music, even spiritual and mystical teachings were all reinvented as part of their attempts to infuse new life, a new human energy, into Western civilization. With the turn to the scientific and the experimental, however, the means to that enhancement came to take precedence over the goal of a richer life: the medium started to become the message, and the broader movement, or social ambitions, became institutionalized into scientific profession-building. "Under the new ethic that developed, science's only form of social responsibility was to science itself: to observe its canons of proof, to preserve its integrity and autonomy, and to constantly expand its domain" (Mumford 1970: 115). Ingenuity, we might say, was deflected into narrower trajectories, at the same time as the production of knowledge came to be supported by, and increasingly dependent on, the patronage of the powerful.

Bacon, coming at the endpoint of the Renaissance, can be considered one of the first articulators of an instrumental rationality. But with Bacon the project remained programmatic, visionary, prophetic. Later in the seventeenth century Boyle, Newton, Huygens – the aristocrats of experimental science – linked scholastic interests in understanding nature with practical interests in exploiting nature (Jacob 1997: 73ff). They brought into being a new social role and set of experimental practices, and they defined a new technically oriented mode of knowledge production: experimental philosophy. They developed a range of new scientific instruments, created new social spaces for conducting scientific experiments, and formulated a new philosophy of nature based on the principles of mechanization and human domination (Shapin 1996).

These experimental scientists brought about the "death of nature" that effectively created a lifeless landscape of mechanical, "clockwork," relationships (Merchant 1980). More generally a new form, or mode, of knowledge-making came to be institutionalized. A way of knowing reality was constituted that was mediated through technology (Böhme *et al.* 1978). This was accomplished both by means of new scientific instruments and experimental rituals, as well as through mutual interaction between scientific inquiry and technical improvement, such as took place in the development of steam power, ship-building, and navigational techniques. As the telescope and microscope literally disclosed new dimensions of reality, the clock and the compass provided the scientist and the merchant with images and metaphors within which to recognize the natural world around him (Jardine 1999). And the perfect human construction – mathematical logic – was refined in order to reconstruct reality into forms that were amenable to optimal human intervention.

The new institutions of modern science did not go unchallenged, however. Experimental philosophy was opposed both by the upholders of traditional, religious knowledge and by the marginalized radicals and their descendants (Russell 1983: 136ff). In the later seventeenth and early eighteenth centuries the scientific "aristocracy" that had emerged in London and Paris at the Royal Society and the Académie des Sciences was challenged by dissenting groups and representatives of the emerging middle classes. The Enlightenment also embodied a kind of social movement, or broader-based cluster of social activity. Many of the radical dissenters fled from Europe to the colonies in North America, and some of those who stayed behind established scientific societies, often in provincial areas in opposition to the established science of the capital cities.

Many of the participants in the "radical enlightenment" shared with the academicians and their royal patrons a belief in what Max Weber termed the Protestant Ethic – that is, an interest in the value of hard work and the virtue of making money – and most had an interest in what Francis Bacon had termed useful knowledge. But the new movements that developed in the Enlightenment and helped to inspire the French and American Revolutions objected to the limited ways in which the Royal Society and the Parisian Academy had organized the scientific spirit and institutionalized the new methods and theories of the experimental philosophy (Jacob 1997: 99ff).

The Enlightenment led to a geographical diffusion of the scientific spirit and "academic culture" to places like Sweden and Denmark and North America, where academies of science were created in the early eighteenth century. It also led to new kinds of scientific disciplines, or what Michel Foucault termed a new "episteme," the discipline of ordering, naming, and classifying which is epitomized in the works of Carolus Linnaeus, who was also an important actor in the establishment of the Swedish Academy of Sciences (Frängsmyr 1989). The Enlightenment, in other words, was a new kind of "movement" that also fragmented from its "nascent state" into radical and established, or mainstream, forms.

The various attempts to democratize scientific education in the wake of the French Revolution and to apply the mechanical philosophy to social processes – that is, to view society itself as a topic for scientific research and analysis – indicate how critique and opposition helped once again to bring about new forms of scientific practice (Hobsbawm 1962: 336ff). The revolutionary government was the first to establish a science-based institution of higher education, the Ecole Polytechnique, and it was there that visions of a technocratic order developed in the writings of Count Saint-Simon, and his secretary, Auguste Comte. The institutionalization process included the articulation of new philosophies of science – positivism, in particular – and new disciplines which were related to the emergent needs of an industrializing social order: statistics, geology, thermodynamics, political economy, and the sociology of Comte (Teich and Young 1973).

Out of the "new" social movements of egalitarianism and political democracy, in association with regional, or local industrial development, emerged new scientific institutions and disciplines, new forms of knowledge-making. Adam Smith's science of political economy developed in the Scottish hinterland, and many of the first industrial applications of experimentation and mechanical philosophy took place in the provinces rather than in the capital cities, where the scientific academies were located (Musson and Robinson 1969). James Watt, the innovating improver of the steam engine, was a typical example of the new forms of knowledge-making. He worked as a technician at the university in Glasgow, making scientific instruments for use in academic research as well as taking part in a wide range of infrastructural projects. He brought into the world of scientific experimentation both artisanal knowledge and an entrepreneurial mentality that proved particularly valuable for the industrial breakthrough (Jacob 1997: 116ff).

Social movements and industrial knowledge

Many of the political and cultural currents of the nineteenth century – from romanticism and utopianism to socialism and populism – also began as critical, oppositional, movements that later came to participate in reconstituting the form and content of socially organized knowledge.

A first cycle of social movements began in the early nineteenth century with some of the most dramatic conflicts over technology that have ever taken place: the Luddite revolts. In the newly industrializing districts of northern England there was a series of confrontations, in which craftsmen strategically attacked the machinery that they saw as responsible for their redundancy. In the 1810s, in the name of a mythical Ned Ludd, groups of artisans broke into factories and destroyed the spinning machines that were proving to be so economically beneficial in the textile industry, and the English army came out in force in order to impose the new mechanical order. Later, in the 1820s, bands of peasants and farm-workers followed their own mysterious leader – one Captain Swing – to lead them in attacking the new machines that were forcing them off the land and into the industrial cities with their factories (Thompson 1963; Sale 1996).

In literature, too, the mechanization that characterized the first wave of industrialization was rejected outright by many influential poets and writers. William Blake decried the "dark satanic mills" of the industrial cities and scorned the narrowness of the mechanical philosophy, while William Wordsworth and John Keats escaped from the emerging mechanical world into a world of beauty and passion, countering the coming of the machine with new forms of personal expression (Roszak 1973). Many were the romantics – in art, music, and everyday life, as well as in literature – who turned their backs on industrial society to gain inspiration from the wilderness or from the ideals of earlier, pre-industrial epochs. Perhaps the two most significant "experiments" were those of Mary Shelley and Henry David Thoreau. Shelley's 1819 literary experiment imagined the industrial world-view in the shape of a monster constructed by her mad Doctor Frankenstein; and Thoreau conducted his 1840s experiment in self-sufficiency by building, and living in, a hut at the edge of Walden Pond. He used the opportunity to reflect on the underlying meanings of the emerging industrial order, and provide what would become an exemplary model of ecological behavior (Thoreau 1963/1854; see Marx 1988).

The Romantic "revolt of the senses" – the personal, direct, opposition that was manifested in a range of different forms in the first half of the nineteenth century – was, of course, a broad social and cultural movement, and, like many movements before and since, it included new forms of knowledge-production and organization. In Britain, among the followers of the reforming industrialist Robert Owen, as well as in some of the "utopian communities" of North America, alternative, artisanal forms of production and manufacture were developed (Kingston 1976). In Denmark, the priest and historian N. F. S. Grundtvig initiated a new form of education by starting "people's high schools" in the countryside to provide an "education for life," as he called it, in opposition to the "dead" Latin education at the universities (Borish 1991). And in Britain and many other industrializing countries "Mechanics' Institutes" and adult education centers for studying the sciences were established in order to spread scientific and technical knowledge.

These alternative forms of knowledge production and education that developed in the early nineteenth century were often created in opposition to the professionalization of science and engineering that was taking place at the universities and the new technical colleges (Russell 1983). In many countries there were significant conflicts over how the new universities and technical faculties were to be organized. It has recently been shown, for example, that the founding in 1829 of the Polytechnical University, now Denmark's Technical University, involved a dispute between a science-based educational ideal favored by university professors, led by Hans Christian Ørsted, and an artisanal, "learning-by doing" approach favored by a technical publicist, G. F. Ursin (Wagner 1999).

The alternative technology movement of the early nineteenth century – a kind of artisanal polytechnical cognitive praxis, with links to Romantic ideals and cooperative forms of organization – was largely overtaken, or at least made problematic, by the course that technological development was to take. With the coming of the railroads and the telegraph, it became ever more difficult to escape from, or to develop an alternative to, the dominant industrial society. But throughout Europe and North America, some of the ideas of the "movement" did have impacts on the emerging industrial order and the professionalization of science that accompanied it (Mendelsohn 1964).

On the one hand, a form of romanticism which Alvin Gouldner has termed "popular materialism" became a part of scientific and broader cultural traditions in several European countries (Gouldner 1985). A romantic biology developed in the Germanic and Scandinavian countries, and new kinds of science – cell biology, biochemistry, and ecology – grew in the seeds planted by the Romantic movement. More generally, the very concept of culture, and the various practices of cultural criticism – in journalism, the arts and literature – can be seen as institutionalized forms of the romantic "revolt" (Williams 1963).

Positivism can also be seen as an institutionalization of that aspect of romanticism that glorified the sense perceptions and the experiential relations to nature. The turn to science and the development of an experimental natural science at the universities was, in many ways, an outgrowth of a romantic impulse, and the new "historical" sciences of geology and archeology and eventually evolutionary biology certainly owed something to the interest in the past that was so prominent in the romantic era (Hobsbawm 1962).

It was also under the influence of romanticism that technology was given a central place in the emerging social sciences, as well as in techniques of industrial management and organization. In the wake of the Industrial Revolution, the "machinery question" shook British society and heavily influenced the development of political economy. It has been suggested that economics as an academic discipline, and the labor movement as a political force, were both formed largely as social responses to mechanization (Berg 1980). But in responding to mechanization the new institutions of social science and working-class organization also served to change the nature of the critique. From being a force of the devil and of mankind's darkest emotions, technology became a fundamental economic factor, or productive force, for "scientific" socialists like Marx and Engels, and a potential source for new forms of collective action for others, such as the craftsman revolutionary William Morris in Britain and the populist publicist Edward Bellamy in America.

Marxism and populism

A second wave of social movements in the nineteenth century, with the growth of the labor movement in Europe and populism in America, also had an important influence on knowledge-making. Not only were there inputs to the sciences themselves, philosophically, organizationally, and technically/methodologically, which drew, in complicated ways, on the critiques of socialists and populists (Hobsbawm 1979), but also many of the revolutionary innovations that were to fuel the second industrial revolution (Landes 1969) – electricity, organic chemistry, internal combustion engines, airplanes, moving pictures, the automobile – were motivated by populist or socialist impulses. At the same time, the broader democratic ambition that was so widespread in the 1870s and 1880s led to whole new fields of knowledge, and, in particular, to an opening of the world of science and scientific rationality to new practitioners: women, colonized peoples, farmers, and workers. Perhaps most significantly, however, this second wave of social movements shaped a fundamental new social philosophy that would, for more than a hundred years, lead to a bifurcation of science and politics into the warring worlds of socialism and capitalism. The social movements of the 1870s and 1880s would create not only Marxism (Gouldner 1980), but also the social anarchism, associated with Mikhail Bakunin and Peter Kropotkin, the populist economics of Henry George, the conservationism of John Muir, and the ecology of Ernst Haeckel.

The Marxian contribution would prove to be especially important for the ways in which we think about the processes of knowledge-making and their relations to society. For Karl Marx sought to turn the revolutionary project itself into a science. He brought together the positivist cosmology of Auguste Comte with the technological determinism that was emerging among economists. Perhaps even more significantly in the long run, Marx

articulated and practiced a new kind of scientific role: the partisan intellectual. As he put it in one of his early manuscripts, "the philosophers
have only interpreted the world, in various ways; the point, however, is
to change it." And for Marx, the key resource in changing the world was
a scientific understanding.

The particular scientific understanding that he sought to develop, his
historical materialism, as it came to be called, was a central element in
the transformation of the social movements of the working class into institutions. The scientific socialism that Marx created in the late 1860s
and 1870s helped give political power and, perhaps most importantly,
intellectual legitimacy and credibility to the institutionalizing representatives of the working class. In the transformation of movement to party
in the 1890s and early twentieth century, the theories of Marx would
be enormously influential (Kolakowski 1981). And, as a modest contribution to avoid repeating some of the mistakes that were made at that
time, it might be valuable to look a bit closer at those theories, and, in
particular, at the ideas about knowledge-making.

Marx was nothing if not a believer in science. He viewed the making of scientific–technological knowledge as the central driving force of
industrial development. As he put it, "technology reveals the active relation of man to nature, the direct process of the production of his life,
and thereby it also lays bare the process of the production of the social
relations of his life, and of the mental conceptions that flow from those
relations" (Marx 1976: 493). For Marx, it was technology – changes in
the means, or instruments, of production – that formed the basis for
changes in work organization, social relations, and even for changes in
the "superstructural" ideas of art and science. "Modern industry never
views or treats the existing form of a production process as the definitive one," Marx wrote. "By means of machinery, chemical processes and
other methods, it is continually transforming not only the technical basis
of production but also the functions of the worker and the social combinations of the labour process." (ibid.: 617) For Friedrich Engels, who
supported Marx financially and then served as the main propagator of
the doctrines after Marx's death, "If society has a technical need, that
helps science forward more than ten universities" (Engels 1894 in Marx
and Engels 1968: 704).

The Marxian conceptions have served as points of departure for almost
all subsequent theorizing about technological innovation. In the words of
Nathan Rosenberg, one of the leading contemporary authorities in the
field of innovation economics, "his [Marx's] formulation of the problem
still deserves to be a starting point for any serious investigation of technology and its ramifications" (Rosenberg 1982: 34). As Rosenberg has led

others inside the black box of technological change, he has reformulated the Marxian conception of technology, laying special emphasis on the way in which Marx analyzed what might be called the "internal" workings of technological innovation.

Marx, of course, examined scientific and technological development within a broad political framework. He never lost sight of the consequences of technical change under capitalist society: the destruction and disembodiment of workers' lives, along with the loss of tradition and artisan skills. The ideological point of departure for his analysis of capitalism was the contradiction in capitalist society between the revolutionary nature of industrial development – its technological driving force – and the private-property relations within which its logic unfolded. "This contradiction bursts forth without restraint in the ceaseless human sacrifices required from the working class, in the reckless squandering of labour-powers, and in the devastating effects of social anarchy" (Marx 1976: 618).

The problem, however, is that Marx was unable to bring this social pathos into his analytical framework. In keeping with the rationalistic biases of his age, he sought to develop a scientific understanding of capitalist society, which eventually formed the basis for the ill-fated experiments in the twentieth century with scientific socialism. Marx and later Marxists rejected the insights of the critics of capitalist society, who did not subscribe to the technological imperative and its natural laws of development. Engels called them utopians, and wrote diatribes against them. Marx battled, in particular, with the anarchist theorist Mikhail Bakunin over leadership in the working-class movement and over the role of science in society. For Marx, science, and a scientific understanding of society, followed laws, like physics, while for Bakunin it was all a question of how knowledge was used. "Intrinsically," Marx wrote, "it is not a question of the higher or lower degree of development of the social antagonisms that spring from the natural laws of capitalist production. It is a question of these laws themselves, of these tendencies winning their way through and working themselves out with iron necessity. The country that is more developed industrially only shows, to the less developed, the image of its own future" (Marx 1976: 90–91).

The cognitive praxis of the social movements in the 1870s and 1880s was not, of course, only Marxist. In the United States a home-grown populist movement drew on indigenous traditions of republicanism, self-reliance, and artisanship to fashion an American-style socialism that in the twentieth century has been institutionalized in popular culture, as well as in the religious right (Lasch 1991). In technology, populism has had an enormous impact – from Henry Ford's people's car to the

personal computers of the 1970s. And in the sciences populism has provided, particularly in its religious varieties, an ambiguous counterpoint
to the project of modernity itself. As we shall have occasion to discuss
later on, the populist influence on American environmentalism has been
substantial.

In Britain the working-class movement, as it developed in the 1870s
and 1880s, also drew on indigenous traditions, much to the dismay of
Engels. Of particular significance to the institutions of knowledge-making,
socialism mixed with romanticism to help form what Lewis Mumford
termed the "polytechnic creativity" of William Morris. Both in theory and
in practice, Morris has been an important influence on British society,
and, more particularly, his impact has been widely felt on the emerging
ecological culture (Mumford 1979; Thompson 1977).

Morris – who was an artist, poet, and designer as well as a socialist politician – combined the ideas of Marx with those of John Ruskin
and the Romantic poets into a new synthesis (McCarthy 1994). Morris
was not opposed to technology as such; it was, rather, the effects that
machinery had on human work that he considered to be so problematic. As a craftsman himself, who ran a successful design and architecture business, Morris could criticize, perhaps more colorfully than any
other nineteenth-century thinker, the one-dimensionality of industrial
technology. He wanted machines that would help people to carry out
their "necessary work" and not turn workers into machines or machine-
tenders. "In spite of our inventions," Morris said in one of his socialist
speeches, "no worker works under the present system an hour less on
account of those labour-saving machines, so called. But under a happier
state of things they would be used simply for saving labour..." (Morris
1973/1884: 151).

Even more importantly, perhaps, Morris, with his artistic and romantic background, formulated a vision of an alternative, more human type of
technological society; he sought to apply an artistic sensibility to
innovation processes as he continually tried to specify, for his fellow
socialists, something of the substance of the future socialist society.
He wrote utopian novels, countering the American populist Edward
Bellamy's proto-technocratic vision, *Looking Backward*, with his own
News from Nowhere (1891). But he was even more eloquent in his socialist lectures, as when he envisaged a future society in which beauty and
craftsmanship were given a place of honor. In a lecture entitled "Useful
Work versus Useless Toil" he put it this way:

The factories might be centres of intellectual activity also, and work in them
might well be varied very much: the tending of the necessary machinery might to

each individual be but a short part of the day's work. The other work might vary from raising food from the surrounding country to the study and practice of art and science. It is a matter of course that people engaged in such work, and being the masters of their own lives, would not allow any hurry or want of foresight to force them into enduring dirt, disorder, or want of room. Science duly applied would enable them to get rid of refuse, to minimize, if not wholly to destroy, all the inconveniences which at present attend the use of elaborate machinery, such as smoke, stench and noise; nor would they endure that the buildings in which they worked or lived should be ugly blots on the fair face of the earth. Beginning by making their factories, buildings and sheds decent and convenient like their homes, they would infallibly go on to make them not merely negatively good, inoffensive merely, but even beautiful, so that the glorious art of architecture, now for some time slain by commercial greed, would be born again and flourish. (Morris 1973/1884: 104)

Morris and Ruskin helped to create what came to be called the "arts and crafts movement" – the various attempts around the turn of the century to combine artistic and technical practices in product design. Their critiques also came to influence the "reinvention of tradition" in India, as Gandhi took home from his years in England not only a British law degree but also a grounding in British (counter)culture (Elzinga and Jamison 1986). The critical counter-currents to the emergent technological civilization, which would emerge in the 1920s and 1930s, would not only be European; literary and philosophical "journeys to the east" would provide new kinds of alternative contexts for conceptualizing technological development, as would the prophets of liberation who would emerge in the anti-colonial struggles for national independence (Jamison 1994).

The movements of the interwar years

In the early twentieth century new kinds of social movements developed in the colonies of European imperialism, as well as in the defeated imperialist powers. Then, the movement critique was primarily of the scientific–technological civilization, and what Gandhi in India called its "propagation of immorality." As he wrote in 1908 in his *Hind Swaraj, or Indian Home Rule*, "This civilization is irreligion, and it has taken such a hold on the people in Europe that those who are in it appear to be half mad" (Gandhi 1938: 37). Gandhi was not opposed to technology as such, but to the "disease" of a technological civilization. In the name of modernism, science and technology had come to stand for the future and it had legitimated, in the colonies as well as in Europe, a wholesale destruction of the past and of "traditional" knowledge – the other ways of knowing – that had been developed in other civilizations (Tambiah 1990; Harding 1998).

The critique of the scientific civilization entered into the "reactionary modernism" of fascism and Nazism, and inspired such thinkers of the right as Martin Heidegger in Germany and Knut Hamsun in Norway (Herf 1984). But it also led to new sciences of ethnography and anthropology, as well as to the sociology of knowledge and the history of ideas. Perhaps even more important were the various attempts to combine the artisan knowledge of the past and of other peoples with the modern science and technology of the present in architecture, design and industrial production itself. Many of the regional development programs of the 1930s and 1940s in Europe and North America can trace their roots back to the mistrust of modernism that was inspired by Gandhi and Tagore in India and by William Morris and Patrick Geddes in Britain. Both Roosevelt's New Deal and the Swedish model welfare state can be said to have mobilized critical perspectives in their projects of social engineering (Hård and Jamison 1998).

It seems particularly appropriate to approach the interwar years from a cyclical theory of social change, in which relatively brief and intensive intervals of social movement are seen to be followed by periods of institutional consolidation and incorporation. Ideas or intellectual positions which are combined in social movements are decomposed in periods of incorporation. In this way, social movements serve to recombine ideas that, in "normal" times, tend to be formulated by different types of intellectuals linked to separate, even opposed, social actors and/or political projects. From such a perspective, the 1920s represent a period between movements, that is, between the socialist and populist movements of the late nineteenth century and the mass mobilizations that came in the 1930s in the wake of the Depression. The 1920s, we might say, were a time when the ideas from one movement were transformed into the intellectual seeds of another.

On the one hand there came to be articulated a "technocratic" position that saw in science and technology the building-blocks of a new technological civilization. Opposed to the technocrats were the upholders of traditional values, among not only conservative politicians and cultural elitists but also "populist" intellectuals like Carl Sandburg and Lewis Mumford in the United States and Rudolf Steiner, Elin Wägner, and Romain Rolland in Europe. A basic distinction was between those who would seek to adapt society to the imperatives of the machine – the technocrats and the pragmatists – and those who sought to assimilate technological development into one or another cultural framework. Another debate was between those who sought to counter the emerging technological civilization with "authoritarian" or "democratic" means – the elite traditionalists, who would influence the Nazis, and the more populist-minded humanists, who would take part in the mobilization against fascism (Pells 1973).

Of particular significance for the articulation of a technocratic belief system were the institutional economists Thorstein Veblen and Joseph Schumpeter, both of whom developed economic theories which stressed the central role of technological innovation in the modern industrial economy. For Veblen and Schumpeter, it was the rules of behavior, the legal and organizational structures that govern economic relations – what have come to be called institutions – that were of central importance. Where Marx had emphasized the means of production, giving a role for the state and for planning and for a broader social steering of technology, Veblen and Schumpeter focused attention on the institutional relations of production and on the "entrepreneurs" who were seen as the embodiment of instrumental rationality. Veblen's writings from the early 1920s, *The Engineers and the Price System* (1921) and *Absentee Ownership and Business Enterprise* (1923) provided a view of technology's role in economic life that was influential, particularly in what came to be called the technocratic movement in the United States.

As David Noble has shown, the 1920s were a time when engineers did try to design corporate America in their image, and their achievements are still with us (Noble 1977). One of their main achievements was the development of management science, as well as the emergence of corporate research managers and production consultants. As Noble has put it, "Modern management issued from the requirements of machine production in a capitalist mode and provided the social basis for technical developments designed to reinforce this mode. In essence, it reflected a shift in focus on the part of engineers from the engineering of things to the engineering of people" (Noble 1977: 263–264). In America, the iconoclastic Veblen served as theorist, while Herbert Hoover came to embody the engineer as politician and state bureaucrat. In his activities at the Department of Commerce, Hoover sought to bring technological logic into the center of state economic policy.

In the early 1930s, Howard Scott tried to turn technocracy into a political force, but technocracy was less important as an explicit political movement than as a source of ideas and legacies for corporate managers. What was central to the technocratic position, as it emerged in the interwar years, was a belief in the central role of technological innovation in economic life. The avowed political ambitions of Veblen and Scott faded from the public stage as a more widespread discourse entered into the academic and corporate spheres.

Academically, one of the important figures was Joseph Schumpeter who, already before the First World War, had articulated a theory of economic development in his native Austria. It was Schumpeter who first formulated many of the concepts that are now central to the growing field of innovation economics. Central to Schumpeter's theory was the distinction between inventions and innovations, and the emphasis on the entrepreneur as the key actor in the fostering of technological dynamism. In *Business Cycles*, which he wrote in America in the 1930s, Schumpeter identified innovation as the "prime mover" in the capitalist process. Radical innovations ignited new periods of prosperity after the recurrent depressions that had characterized the capitalist development process. He transformed the Russian economist Kondratieff's statistical analysis of cycles or "long waves" into a theory of continuous reconstruction. In his last book, *Capitalism, Socialism and Democracy* (1941), Schumpeter coined the concept of "creative destruction" in order to emphasize the problematic nature of capitalist society. "Capitalist reality is first and foremost a process of change," he wrote, and then went on to prophesy the eventual replacement of capitalism by one or another form of monopolistic socialism (Swedberg 1990: 157ff).

In the 1920s, a different kind of critique of modern civilization emerged in the United States, from social thinkers like Lewis Mumford, Howard Odum, and other "regionalists" who were ecologically, or biologically, oriented (Thomas 1990). Mumford's activities of the 1920s can be seen as a new form of populism; he defined the community as the antipode to civilization, but for Mumford and Odum, the community or region was not merely historical traditions and memories, it was also a socio-geographic environment, a conditioning place (Jamison 1998). Much like Rudolf Steiner in Germany, and Gandhi's village movement in India, the American neo-populist or communitarian critique would articulate new criteria for technological development and new ideas about diffusing knowledge. Its wrath would be directed both against the undesirable social and human consequences of technology as well as the overextension of instrumental rationality into modern American life. What Howard Odum termed "super-civilization" stood, as he put it, "in many bold contrasts to culture . . . organization over people, mass over individual, power over freedom, machines over men, quantity over quality, artificial over natural, technological over human, production over reproduction" (quoted in Pells 1973: 102). For these "human ecologists," as they would come to be called, culture included social traditions as well as natural conditions; both needed to be mobilized to encourage what came to be called a regionalist approach to development (Mumford 1938).

In the 1930s this populist, or regionalist, position would split into leftist and rightist versions which would become increasingly antagonistic. The "reactionary modernism" of the Nazis, with their backward-looking militant nationalism and their violent hatred of other cultures, would include a certain environmental interest in its eclectic mix of messages (Bramwell 1989). The left-wing populism of the 1930s, on the other hand, would encourage a revitalization of popular art and folk music, as well as new sciences of anthropology and cultural history (Aronowitz 1993). It was in the 1930s that Ruth Benedict published her extremely influential *Patterns of Culture* and Lewis Mumford wrote the two major works that helped to establish the history of technology and planning as academic subjects – *Technics and Civilization* (1934) and *The Culture of Cities* (1938).

Regionalism tended to oppose the more adaptive, or acceptant – what Lewis Mumford termed the "acquiescent" – position emanating from the pragmatism of John Dewey and his disciples in America (Mumford 1926). In Europe, the pragmatic position developed among social-democratic "functionalists" and liberal modernists, both in the arts and sciences. The call, from Dewey as well as from other would-be social engineers, such as the Myrdals in Sweden and Maynard Keynes in Britain, was for a new morality, a democratic gospel, or faith, as a way to respond to the new scientific and technological potentialities. In keeping with William Ogburn's influential notion of the "cultural lag," these latter-day progressive intellectuals sought to reform social institutions to meet the challenges of modern technology. As "rationalizing intellectuals" they served to bring the visions of social democracy into the professions and academic disciplines (Eyerman 1994). In the arts, and perhaps especially in architecture and design, this pragmatic position would become influential. In politics, pragmatism would provide ideas and approaches that would enter into the "new deal order" of the 1930s, as well as into the making of the postwar welfare state throughout Europe.

Social movements and the making of technoscience

In recent decades social movements have also served to reorient science and technology, as well as politics and business, into alternative directions. Out of the anti-imperialist and student movements of the 1960s and the feminist and environmentalist movements of the 1970s and 1980s have emerged a range of alternative ideas about knowledge, in form, content, and meaning, that has given rise to new sciences and technological programs (Eyerman and Jamison 1991; Rose 1994). Out of critique have grown the shoots of new, and often more participatory, ways of sciencing – from environmental impact assessment to women's studies, from postcolonial discourses to renewable energy technology. What were in the 1960s and 1970s protest movements of radical opposition have largely been emptied of their political content, but they have simultaneously given rise to new branches of, and approaches to, knowledge-making. While the more radical, or oppositional, voices have lost much of their influence, the more pragmatic voices have been given a range of new opportunities. This is not to say that there is no longer a radical environmental opposition or a radical women's liberation movement, but radicals and reformists have increasingly drifted apart from one another, and in most countries these groups now work in different organizations, with little sense of a common oppositional movement identity. There has been a fragmentation of what was a coherent movement into a number of disparate bits and pieces (Cramer *et al.* 1987).

This fragmentation, or differentiation, of the new social movements has accompanied a broader change in knowledge-making, namely the emergence of what has been termed a new "mode" of knowledge production, in which science and engineering have converged into *technoscience* (Gibbons *et al.* 1994). From an economic perspective, technoscience represents the merging of academic and industrial research into new hybrid forms, as well as the systematic integration of knowledge-making into the productive sphere: what has been termed a learning, or knowledge economy (e.g. Lundvall and Borras 1998; Archibugi and Lundvall 2001). From a sociological perspective, technoscience involves new forms of transdisciplinary organization and new kinds of hybrid identities and "boundary conditions" that are imposed on the producers of knowledge (e.g. Gieryn 1999). No longer merely industrialized or externally driven, "laboratory life" has become ever more heterogeneous and pluralistic, with research increasingly organized in ad hoc, temporary, networks, determined by the contingencies of particular projects (Latour 1987).

The new social movements rose to prominence in the downturn of a period of scientific and technical expansion and economic growth. They emerged in opposition to the dominant social order and to its hegemonic scientific and technological regime, which had largely been established during and immediately after the Second World War (Jamison and Eyerman 1994: 4ff). That war led to a fundamental transformation in the world of science and technology and to the emergence of a new relation, or contract, between science and politics. Unlike previous phases of industrialization, in which science and engineering had lived related but separate identities, the Second World War ushered in the era of industrialized science (Ravetz 1973). The war effort had been based on an unprecedented mobilization of scientists to create new weapons, from radar to the atomic bomb, and to gather and conduct intelligence. After the war, science and scientists formed a new elite; and there was a massive expansion of funding and manpower. In the process, "little" science was transformed into big science (de Solla Price 1963).

Especially important for the social movements that were to develop in the 1960s and beyond was the fact that scientific research was placed at the center of postwar economic development. Many of the economically significant new products – nylon and other synthetic textiles, plastics, home chemicals and appliances, television – were directly based on scientific research, and the new techniques of production were also of a different type: it was the era of chemical fertilizers and insecticides, of artificial petrochemical-based process industries and food additives (Bookchin 1963; Commoner 1971).

The form of big science also differed from the ways that science had been organized in the past. The big science laboratories – both in the public and private sectors – were like industrial factories, and the "technostructure," as it was labeled by the economist John Kenneth Galbraith, was seen as an important concern for managers and industrial organizers (Galbraith 1967). The use of science in society had become systematized and, as the consequences of the new order became more visible, new forms of mistrust and criticism developed in the public, particularly among the student generation of the 1960s.

Some of the most influential criticisms of the new order were formulated by the émigré European intellectuals who had come to America to escape Nazism. Hannah Arendt, Erich Fromm, Erik Erikson, Herbert Marcuse, and a host of others formulated a wide-ranging critique of mass society, and its "one-dimensional" science and technology. As Marcuse put it:

Technology has become the great vehicle of *reification* – reification in its most mature and effective form. The social position of the individual and his relation to others appear not only to be determined by objective qualities and laws, but these qualities and laws seem to lose their mysterious and uncontrollable character; they appear as calculable manifestations of (scientific) rationality. The world tends to become the stuff of total administration, which absorbs even the administrators. The web of domination has become the web of Reason itself... (Marcuse 1964: 168–169)

Together with Lewis Mumford, C. Wright Mills, Margaret Mead, Paul Goodman and other home-grown products, the émigré, partisan intellectuals mounted a fundamental critique of the scientific-technological state (Jamison and Eyerman 1994). It was the subservience of knowledge-making to the dictates of the "military-industrial complex," the colonization of technological rationality by commercial interests, that was opposed most forcefully (Mendelsohn 1994). In a characteristic statement from the early 1960s, Lewis Mumford put it this way:

A good technology, firmly related to human needs, cannot be one that has a maximum productivity as its supreme goal: it must rather, as in an organic system, seek to provide the right quantity of the right quality at the right time and the right place for the right purpose. To this end deliberate regulation and self direction, in order to ensure continued growth and creativity, must govern our plans in the future, as indefinite expansion and multiplication have done during the past few centuries. The center of gravity is not the corporate organization, but the human personality, utilizing knowledge, not for the increase of power and riches, or even for the further increase of knowledge, but using it, like power and riches, for the enhancement of life. (Mumford 1961/1979: 167)

In his writings from the 1960s, Mumford challenged the domination of the big corporations, with their commercial ethos and their hierarchical logic, over science and technology. Knowledge-making had become authoritarian in its mode of operation, he argued, and the other, more democratic, forms of technics that had existed throughout history were threatened by extinction. Science and technology had become intimately linked to what he termed, in the title of his most controversial book, the "pentagon of power" (Mumford 1970; see Mendelsohn 1990). Together with voices of dissent from other parts of the world, the criticisms of Marcuse and Mumford helped shape what soon became a global student movement. Having grown up in a world of wealth and progress, the students of the 1960s rose up to try to stop the misuse of science and technology, particularly in the war in Vietnam. The student movement was, of course, many things at once, but one of its central components was a mobilization, or re-invention, of the romantic "revolt of the senses," the defense of life against mechanization. As Mario Savio put it in one of the formative moments of the student movement, during the struggle for "free speech" at Berkeley in 1964:

There is a time when the operation of the machine becomes so odious, makes you so sick at heart, that you can't take part; you can't even tacitly take part, and you've got to put your bodies upon the gears and upon the wheels, upon the levers, upon all the apparatus and you've got to make it stop. And you've got to indicate to the people who run it, to the people who own it, that unless you're free, the machines will be prevented from working at all. (Savio, quoted in Marx 1988: 198)

Meanwhile, another wing of the public – particularly in the United States – reacted more specifically to the destruction of the natural environment. In the 1940s and 1950s it began to be recognized that the new kinds of scientific expansion were more dangerous for the natural environment than those that had come before, because they were artificial and thus difficult for natural processes to break down: they were "waste making" (Packard 1960). But it would not be before Rachel Carson's *Silent Spring*, published in 1962, that an environmental movement began to find its voice and its characteristic style of expressing or articulating its message. It was to be by critically evaluating specific instances of industrialized science that the environmentalist critique would be able to reach a broader public. Carson's achievement was to direct the methods of science against science itself, but also to point to another way of doing things: the biological or ecological way (Carson 1962).

In the 1970s a range of "new social movements" emerged throughout the world. Among other things, the new movements of feminism and environmentalism articulated an alternative approach to science and technology, combining the political critique of Marcuse and Mumford with the ecological critique of Carson and Commoner (Dickson 1974). The new movements involved both a rejection of modern science's exploitative attitude to nature, as well as an alternative organizational ideal – a democratic, or participatory ideal – for the development of knowledge (Eyerman and Jamison 1991). There were also distinct forms of collective learning in the new social movements of environmentalism and feminism, as well as grass-roots engineering activities that went under the name of appropriate or alternative technology. In Denmark, experimentation with renewable energy, and in particular wind energy, was a central component of the environmental and anti-nuclear movements. A separate organization for renewable energy was created, which distributed instruction books and manuals and other information, as well as establishing courses and developing workshops and local centers for energy research and development (Jamison *et al.* 1990). Many of these energy offices are still going strong in Denmark, even though wind energy has since become a highly profitable commercial endeavor, and most of the "grass-roots" engineering activity of the 1970s has come to be transformed into professional industrial practice (Jørgensen and Karnoe 1995).

The social movements of the 1970s can be seen to have created an alternative form of knowledge-making that, in many ways, has inspired new sciences – women's studies, environmental studies, cultural studies – as well as the network-based, project-driven, transdisciplinary mode of knowledge production that has become economically significant in recent years, the so-called "mode two" (Gibbons *et al.* 1994). What is striking about the so-called learning economy or knowledge society, from this perspective, is its flexibility and its pluralism, as well as its openness to "tacit" forms of knowledge. But some fundamental transformations have taken place, as the alternative knowledge interests of the new social movements have become institutionalized and professionalized. In the 1970s the environmental knowledge interests, for example, were combined into a central core identity, a *cognitive praxis* which included three dimensions – cosmological, technical, and organizational – which for a time provided a source of collective identity for those who considered themselves a part of the movement. Today, that praxis has largely been transformed and broken down into institutional routines in industry, administration, and everyday life.

The cosmology was primarily the translation of a scientific paradigm into a socio-economic program; in the 1970s, the holistic concepts of systems ecology were transformed into political programs of social ecology – an ecological world view was to govern social and political interactions (*Ecologist* 1972; Commoner 1971). Technology was to be developed under the general perspective that "small is beautiful," as E. F. Schumacher put it, according to the assumption that large-scale, environmentally destructive projects were to be opposed and stopped (Schumacher 1973; Illich 1973). At the same time, new contexts for education and experimentation and for the diffusion of research were created in the form of movement workshops and laboratories and, in the Netherlands, for example, in the form of "science shops," allowing activist groups to gain access to the scientific expertise at the universities (Irwin 1995).

In the 1980s this cognitive praxis came to be decomposed into a disparate cluster of organizations and individuals, networks and companies, academic fields and consulting firms, at both local and national levels, as well as on a "global" level of intergovernmental bodies and committees, non-governmental organizations and transnational corporations. The knowledge interests of the environmental movement came to be transformed into various kinds of professional expertise, which made it possible to incorporate parts of the movement into the established and dominant culture, and shift at least some of the members of the movement from outsider to insider status. Some of the alternative technical projects proved commercially viable – biological agriculture, wind energy plants, waste recycling – and gave rise to a more institutionalized form of environmental politics, science, and technology.

As a result, the confrontational strategies of the past have tended to be supplemented by more conventional, and consensual, forms of activity on the part of many environmental organizations. In several European countries, representatives of major environmental groups are granted access to formal policy bodies and procedures, such as hearings or ministerial committees. Provision of expertise and advice to state agencies and private companies, either through formal or informal channels, has also become increasingly important. In programs of eco-labeling and sustainable transport, for example, environmental organizations often play an important advisory role, as they do in many local Agenda 21 projects. In order to be successfully conducted, these activities require respectability on the part of environmental groups, and a more professional mode of operation (Jamison, ed. 1998).

In the transformations of movements into institutions, a significant channel of cognitive and cultural change can be identified. In the following chapters, we will look more closely into how these processes have affected contemporary environmental movements.

NOTE

This chapter expands on material first published in Jamison 1982; Baark and Jamison 1986; Jamison 1988; Eyerman and Jamison 1991; and Jamison 1998; an earlier version of the chapter has been published in the *International Encyclopedia of Social and Behavioural Sciences* (Elsevier 2001).

3   The dialectics of environmentalism

I've looked at life from both sides now . . .
Joni Mitchell, "Clouds" (1965)

environmentalism is trapped in a tense, sometimes panicked oscillation
between liberal optimism and radical despair, a false choice that has
hobbled the movement for decades if not from its beginnings
Tom Athanasiou, Divided Planet (1996: 104–105)

From traditions to movements

Like many, if not all, social movements, the environmental movements
that developed in the 1960s and 1970s did not emerge from nothing.
Although many of the formative issues were new, and many of the forms
of protest and practical activity were innovative, the substantive content of
the environmental movement was derived from many sources (Eyerman
and Jamison 1991: 66ff). The movements, we might say, served as a
catalyst for the mobilization, or creative recombination, of several distinct
traditions of ideas and practices.

Particularly important in the historical context of the 1960s was the
mixing of inspiration from both the cultural and the political revolts
that had erupted in that turbulent decade. The environmental movement
combined the neo-romanticism of the counterculture, with its questioning of material-based progress, with the political radicalism of the so-
called new left. Many early environmentalists represented a sort of hybrid
hippie–marxist, emphasizing both the spiritual and the political dimensions of the environmental "crisis." But there was also, from the outset, a
touch of practicality thrown in for good measure, a constructive urge that
inspired many a technically minded activist to take part in the emerging
movement.

In many countries there was a significant generational tension between
the new movement, with its youthfulness and radicalism, and the more
staid, established, forms of nature protection and conservation which had

emerged in the late nineteenth century. All of these different motivations eventually led to processes of specialization and professionalization, as well as to the changing strategic orientations, which have given environ-mentalism its characteristic, pendulum-like rotation between fundamen-talism and realism. As Tom Athanasiou, a longtime American activist, put it:

Environmentalists live double lives. As activists and politicians, even as tech-nicians and entrepreneurs, they must think their efforts worthwhile, they must believe they will win. In these roles energy and initiative are essential, and it is op-timism, not any depressive realism, that opens paths to profit and advantage. Yet greens are lost without their darker suspicions . . . It is a movement commonplace that political diversity is crucial, that radicals back up pragmatists, stiffening their spines, and that the two groups combine into a stronger force than either could muster alone. (Athanasiou 1996: 104)

Complicating the picture even more, environmentalists have made use of both political and cultural forms of expression through the years. And they have generated both new aesthetic practices, or cultural impacts – songs, performance rituals, "new age" music, environmental art – as well as the more directly political impacts: green parties, policy initiatives, legal and administrative reforms. At one time, especially during the struggles against nuclear energy in the 1970s, environmental movements in many parts of the world carved out new kinds of public spaces, or alternative public spheres, where the cultural and the political could be combined in popular fronts and mass campaigns. At that time, environmentalism was not merely a political challenge to the powers-that-be but also, for many of its participants, a new "historical project," a vision of a fun-damentally different way of life and knowledge-making. In a number of utopian writings, such as Hazel Henderson's *Creating Alternative Futures* (1971), *A Blueprint for Survival* (1972), Ivan Illich's *Tools for Convivi-ality* (1973), Marge Piercy's *Woman at the Edge of Time* (1974), Ernest Callenbach's *Ecotopia* (1975), as well as in living manifestations of eco-logical, or utopian, communities based on renewable energy technolo-gies and organic agricultural techniques, environmentalism represented a practical utopia, a not-yet-existent realm of harmonious relations be-tween human and non-human nature.

As has been the case with other social movements that have articulated ambitious utopian visions, the diverse mixture of interests and bedfel-lows that were combined in the environmental movements proved to be a rather combustible combination. By the late 1970s, as the struggle against nuclear energy heated up in many industrialized countries, the unity of the fledgling movements was put severely to the test, and deep contradictions emerged (see Rüdig 1990; Flam 1994). Particularly intense have been the recurrent conflicts between the radicals and the reformists, which have developed wherever and whenever political choices have been forced on environmental movements. But there have also been the different personal strategies, or career trajectories, that have led to divisions among activists due to the different opportunities – be they economic, cultural, or political – that have been available.

Over the years, alternative ecological practitioners, rural communards, business-minded scientists and ideologically oriented activists have tended to pursue different life paths. What had once been, or at least felt like, a relatively coherent movement for many of its participants has therefore come to be divided into a wide variety of differentiated organizations, sects, parties, discourses, and practices. Many more people have come to be involved in environmental politics, but the underlying meaning of what they do has changed from a process of collective identity formation to a variety of translation processes: what was once a common message or vision has taken on a wider, and more variegated, range of meanings in different social contexts or life-worlds.

As traditions became the "resources" that were mobilized to meet new social challenges, something significant happened to them. The separate streams or "roads" to (political) ecology were recombined into new and often competing sets of values or projects. The movement drew on many and disparate sources of inspiration to develop its own unique form of collective identity, or cognitive praxis. And as they confronted power, and tried to take part in political decision-making, the movement's members chose different strategies or approaches to pursue their aims. Some wandered down the country roads that John Denver sang about, trying to live more in tune with nature and provide examples, or ecological lifestyles, for others to follow. Others took on the power elites directly and displayed their anger in public by sailing into the radioactive fallout, as the founder of Greenpeace, David McTaggart, did so dramatically in the early 1970s, or by occupying the building sites of nuclear energy plants or airport runways to try to get the wheels of progress to stop. Still others went into business with one or another technical "fix" to the environmental crisis, devising clean machines and greener production processes.

In the ensuing decades, the strategies have led to different organizational choices, different alliances, different campaigns, and, as we have occasion to observe throughout this book, they have come to have competing, even contradictory, meanings in relation to social and cultural transformation. Some environmentalists have become card-carrying members of the establishment, propagating a reformist path to the future ecological society, while others continue to seek to establish a fundamentally alternative society and liberate themselves from the confines and constraints of the dying industrial society.

Besides being interesting in their own right, these dialectical processes perhaps provide an indication of how human cultures change direction, and, more specifically, how societies appropriate new kinds of tasks or projects. The term dialectics refers to the contradictory nature of human development that was first discussed by ancient Greek (and Chinese) philosophers and has since entered social and cultural theory primarily through Hegel and Marx (Kolakowski 1978). What is fundamental to a dialectical understanding, or perspective, is the recognition of conflict as a driving force of social change, and an emphasis on what might be termed the process of recombination: the resolution of contradictory positions into a new "synthesis."

In this chapter I explore the changing relations to the traditions of ecology that have characterized the "life-cycle" of the contemporary environmental movement. In the following chapter, I complicate the story by showing how environmentalism has been affected by national cultures with their own characteristic policy styles and discursive frameworks. What I hope to establish by recollecting these processes is the contextual contingency of environmentalism, and, in particular, its dependence on the broader society. For it is my contention that we must take these broader macro-level processes into more explicit consideration if we are to improve the prospects of ecological-change agents to effect social transformations. In the various struggles to resolve contradictions in both theory and practice, and to transcend the many barriers that have stood in its path, there has emerged an ecological culture that, in many respects, represents a continual synthesis, a bringing together, of its various component parts.

Environmental traditions

In an influential account Donald Worster points to two main historical streams of thought that had come together in the environmental movement, two opposing attitudes to nature that had led, through the centuries, to two different kinds of ecology (Worster 1977). One stream he termed "imperialist," which he traced back to Francis Bacon in the early seventeenth century and the ideas about useful knowledge and the human domination of nature that were so central to Bacon's thought. For Worster, Bacon's philosophy, and the subsequent institutionalization of an experimentally oriented science of nature, had been part of an exploitative ecology through which the non-human environment was portrayed as raw material, or as natural resources for human use and benefit. As Worster put it, "Bacon promised to the world a manmade paradise, to be rendered astonishingly fertile by science and human management. In that utopia, he predicted, man would recover a place of dignity and honor, as well as the authority over all the other creatures he once enjoyed in the Garden of Eden" (Worster 1977: 30).

Carolus Linnaeus in Sweden and Georges Buffon in France were among the most influential scientists in the eighteenth century to begin to give this imperialist ecology a more systematic form and establish its characteristic modes of interacting with nature. It was Linnaeus and Buffon and their many disciples who brought an interest in nature into the broader social processes of colonization, exploration, and exploitation. Linnaeus, for instance, began his career by carrying out investigative journeys of exploration in the Swedish provinces on behalf of the parliament, and he sent his students around the world in search of new species of plants and flowers. From a base in Uppsala, in the remote, semi-civilized periphery of Europe, Linnaeus turned the Baconian vision into a full-fledged classificatory mode of sciencing, an *episteme*. For Michel Foucault, the taxonomic program of Linnaeus was one of the formative elements of the science of the classical age. Observation, classification, naming, and categorizing were the central components of eighteenth-century science. "Natural history in the classical age is not merely the discovery of a new object of curiosity; it covers a series of complex operations that introduce the possibility of a constant order into a totality of representations" (Foucault 1973: 158).

Nature became a system of component parts to be tended, or operated, like a machine so that its productive utilization for human benefit could be made more effective and extensive. Motivated by a deeply felt Christian theology, as well as by an inordinate interest in non-human beings, Linnaeus elaborated an economy of nature in which man was to exploit God's creations as efficiently as possible:

All these treasures of nature, so artfully contrived, so wonderfully propagated, so providentially supported throughout her three kingdoms, seem intended by the Creator for the sake of man. Every thing may be made subservient to his use; if not immediately, yet mediately, not so to that of other animals. By the help of reason man tames the fiercest animals, pursues and catches the swiftest, nay he is able to reach even those, which lye hidden in the bottom of the sea. (quoted in Worster 1977: 36)

This highly utilitarian view of nature came to be promulgated in the eighteenth and nineteenth centuries in philosophy and politics, but especially in the natural sciences, as they took on a more professional and disciplined organizational form. Utilitarianism was a view that fit well with the more general project of industrialization. Science came to be oriented toward the needs of the emerging industrial culture (see Russell 1983). Science became a profession, an integral part of industrial society and, within the sciences, more dynamic, exploitative approaches to nature became the dominant "paradigms" or metaphorical thought-figures.

In many respects, the linking of science with industrial technology was perhaps the most fundamental process of the nineteenth century; it made possible both the consolidation and expansion of a new economic system, as well as the creation of a range of new forms of cultural expression and social interaction. As Alfred North Whitehead once put it, "the greatest invention of the nineteenth century was the invention of the method of invention. A new method entered into life" (Whitehead 1925: 98). And it would be as an experimental, systemic approach to understanding nature that the imperialist road would enter into the science of ecology, when it was given a name and a more formalized identity (by the biologist Ernst Haeckel) in the 1860s.

Opposed to the imperialists were the nature-lovers, to whom Worster gave the label "arcadian" in order to associate their particular version of ecology to the classical "ideal of a simple rural life in close harmony with nature" that had been depicted by Roman poets in the ancient Greek region of Arcady. The back-to-nature folks began to articulate their counter-program at the dawning of the industrial era as part of the Romantic movement. The arcadians shared many of the modernizing, scientific ambitions of the imperialists, but they came to develop a different way of investigating and understanding nature. Tracing arcadians back to the English pastor and writer Gilbert White and especially to his work *The Natural History of Selborne*, originally published in 1789, Worster delineated a stream of experiential, or participatory, ecology that was perhaps most influentially developed further by Henry David Thoreau in the nineteenth century.

One central difference between the two traditions was in the role attributed to the scientist and to his or her expertise. The imperialists were part of a professionalization process, by which science became a vocation, a socially accepted and mandated form of knowledge production. Arcadians, on the other hand, still practiced a "gentleman's" science, and, in the hands of a Thoreau or a Johann Goethe, whose writings have also been an important reference point, they pursued their science in a more engaged and "holistic" manner. The self-imposed limitations that were so central to the Baconians, the narrowing of observation to what could be seen and classified, were rejected by the arcadians. As Thoreau wrote in his first published essay,

The true man of science will know nature better by his finer organization; he will smell, taste, see, hear, feel better than other men. His will be a deeper and finer experience. We do not learn by inference and deduction, and the application of mathematics to philosophy, but by direct intercourse and sympathy . . . The most scientific will still be the healthiest and friendliest man, and possess a more perfect Indian wisdom. (quoted in Worster 1977: 97)

Thoreau and other nineteenth-century arcadian ecologists developed what we might call a different discourse of nature study, a more descriptive and poetic type of knowledge-making that has continued in our day in popular travel and nature literature among other places. In Thoreau's writings, the scientific and the literary are often in an exciting tension, which has led to sometimes heated debates between different environmentalists who lay claim to his legacy.[1]

By the end of the nineteenth century the professional scientist and the nature writer, and with them the broader cultures of science and literature which were still able to be combined in Thoreau, tended to part company. Worster's argument was that the two streams of ecology had both contributed to Charles Darwin's theory of natural evolution, but that they had subsequently given rise, in the course of the twentieth century, to two different ways of thinking about ecology and conducting ecological research. The one was systemic, while the other was individual in focus, and they have fostered an ecosystems-oriented ecology, on the one hand, and an evolutionary, population-oriented ecology on the other, the one taking its point of departure in the systemic relations that exist among species, and the other taking its point of departure in the dynamic relations of one species to its environment (Kwa 1986). What are at work are different attitudes, or conceptions of nature, as well as different methodological and theoretical assumptions about how to investigate, or to interrogate, nature.

In the late nineteenth century, in the making of the conservation movement, the two streams gave rise to two types of conservationism. The arcadian or romantic approach could be seen at work in organizations such as the Sierra Club in the United States, which adopted an approach to conservation that sought to preserve particularly valuable, or striking, landscapes from further exploitation. The imperialist approach came to dominate the development of resource management and scientific forestry, and led to ideas about efficient use and, within science, to the concepts of ecological succession and ecosystems. The opposing programs of Linnaeus and White were reenacted in the so-called preservationism of John Muir, the founder of the Sierra Club, and the conservationism of Gifford Pinchot, the secretary of interior in the "progressive" United States government at the turn of the century (Gottlieb 1993).

Worster's distinction can be considered a first slice of the environmental cake, and like all first slices, it is perhaps a bit too big in the pieces it separates. As with similar dichotomies that have been suggested by other authors – between ecocentrics and anthropocentrics, animists and mechanists, deep and shallow ecologists – Worster's division into imperialist and arcadian roads to ecology captures a fundamental contradiction in contemporary environmentalism. But almost by definition, it also neglects all those approaches that fall in between the two opposed camps. Even more seriously, Worster's scheme, like many of the other dualisms that have been suggested, tends to disregard a third important source of inspiration for the environmental movement. For it was not merely, or even primarily, conservation or nature preservation that provided the focus for the emerging movement. There were also, particularly in industrial cities and urban areas, a number of social problems that had come to be identified in the course of industrialization that were at the center of attention: industrial waste and pollution, automobility, energy use, and, perhaps most importantly, occupational health and safety, the environmental hazards of work. These issues had all been more or less ignored by the conservation movements in the United States, as well as in most other countries, but they came to form an important part of the agenda for the new environmentalism that emerged in the 1960s (Jamison *et al.* 1990; Gottlieb 1993).

In my terminology, what was at work was the mobilization of a third tradition – a tradition of human ecology – that had come with the development of the social sciences at the end of the nineteenth century. Particularly in the United States, in relation to various social welfare and public health projects, a wide range of "human ecologies" emerged both inside and outside the academic world. The settling of the continent and the challenges of taming the wild natural landscape inspired new ideas about the impact of the environment on social and economic development, or what the geographer, George Perkins Marsh, characterized, in his pioneering book from 1864, as the relations between "nature and man." In part motivated by the requirements of engineering and infrastructural development, in part an outgrowth of physical geography and urban planning and, in part, a sub-field of public medicine and public health, human ecologies entered into the new social sciences of sociology and anthropology, of economics and political science, as they became disciplines in the late nineteenth and early twentieth centuries (Ross 1991).

With the closing of the frontier in America, and the colonization of the planet by the European imperial powers in the closing decades of the nineteenth century, the earlier distinctions between nature and society tended to become ever more complicated and mediated. The natural landscape was becoming integrated, as component parts, into the industrializing social order. Fields were becoming food factories, and prairies were becoming sites of animal husbandry. Eventually the forests would become cultivated, as well as industrialized, and many wilderness areas would become parks, at the same time as a new breed of landscape architects like Frederick Olmsted, the designer of New York's Central Park, would selectively bring elements of the wilderness into the urban world. By the early twentieth century it had become apparent to many that a further kind of ecology was necessary – a human, or social, or cultural ecology – that investigated the borderlines and the hybridizations, the multifarious relations between human societies and their natural environs. Particularly in the United States and Britain geographers, sociologists, architects, and planners, as well as socially minded biologists and natural historians, would begin to articulate new conceptual frameworks and terminologies; and these urban and social ecologies would be applied by health officials and town- and city-planners to form, by the 1930s, a recognizable tradition of ideas and viewpoints (Jamison 1998).

Lewis Mumford was perhaps the most visible proponent of what has come to be called a regional approach to social development. Already in his first book, *The Story of Utopias*, from 1922, Mumford outlined the regional, or human ecological perspective, that would come to characterize more than sixty years of writing. Building on the teachings of Patrick Geddes, whom he referred to as his "mentor," Mumford combined elements from history, geography, architecture and urban planning into a synthetic human ecology. Basic to its methodology was what he called, in his first book, the regional survey:

The aim of the Regional Survey is to take a geographic region and explore it in every aspect. It differs from the social survey with which we are acquainted in America in that it is not chiefly a survey of evils; it is, rather, a survey of the existing conditions in all their aspects; and it emphasizes to a much greater extent than the social survey the natural characteristics of the environment, as they are discovered by the geologist, the zoologist, the ecologist – in addition to the development of natural and human conditions in the historic past, as presented by the anthropologist, the archeologist, and the historian. In short, the regional survey attempts a local synthesis of all the specialist "knowledges." (quoted in Jamison 1998: 90)

Mumford's books of the 1930s – *Technics and Civilization* and *The Culture of Cities* – can be considered paradigmatic, or exemplary, works of this

Table 1. *Environmental traditions*

	Conservation	Preservation	Human ecology
Formative influences	Bacon Linnaeus	White Thoreau	Marsh Mumford
Key mobilizers	Odum brothers Brundtland	Carson McTaggart	Ehrlich Commoner
Type of sciencing	experimentation systemic models	natural history thick description	mapping surveying
Relation to nature	management exploitation	participation harmony	planning co-construction
Conception of nature	ecosystem resource base	community locality	region landscape
Ideologies	anthropocentric/ modernism	ecocentric/ deep ecology	pragmatic/ postmodern

human ecological tradition (Guha 1991), which, after the Second World War, has become an important feature of academic life and public policy in both Europe and North America, as well as in other parts of the world. As opposed to the ecological traditions of the natural scientists, the various human ecologies seek to link natural and social knowledges into a coherent whole, usually focused on a particular region or community. Institutionally, human ecology has tended to be practiced in geography departments, but, since the 1970s, it has also been taught in environmental studies departments, and, here and there, in specific departments of human ecology, as well.

To make the story somewhat more complete, it can therefore be useful to add a third tradition to Worster's two ecologies, and to distinguish three ideal-typical traditions that have been mobilized in the making of environmental movements. Each tradition has its own characteristic conception of nature and its own preferred methods of investigation, as well as its own distinct version of an appropriate ecological practice or politics (see Table 1).

The mobilization of traditions

It would be these three traditions and the various sub-sets thereof that came to be mobilized in the 1960s in the making of a new social movement. On the one hand, the imperialist tradition was reinvented, among other places, in the cybernetic language of ecosystems ecology and energy-systems analysis and in the transnational networking of the World

Wildlife Fund. Systems ecology, as developed by Howard Odum's sons, Eugene and Howard, became extremely influential among natural scientists, particularly during the International Biological Program, and, as a new approach to ecology, it would play a major role in the emergence of an environmental consciousness in the 1960s (Worster 1977: 291ff).

The Odums also illustrate the importance of established scientists in the articulation of the new environmentalism's cognitive praxis (Cramer et al. 1987). The environmental movement involved, at the outset, a kind of popularization of science, as well as a translation of concepts and terminology that had been developed in relating non-human nature to society and politics. Eugene and Howard Odum's popular writings provided a scientific legitimacy and authority to the new movement, as well as a powerful terminology and conceptual framework, while the movement helped provide ecological scientists with new opportunities for research, and eventually with a new political mission: ecologizing society (Söderqvist 1986).

In 1962 the arcadian tradition found a contemporary voice in the biologist-turned-science-writer Rachel Carson. After writing two best-selling nature books in the 1950s, Carson had grown extremely concerned about the impact that the new chemical insecticides were having on the forests and on the animals that she loved so much. Her four-year investigation of the environmental consequences of one of those pest-killers resulted in a new form of political broadside, a book of scientific poetry. Silent Spring announced a new kind of arcadian ecology that was to have a major influence on the cognitive praxis of the emerging environmental movement (Jamison and Eyerman 1994: 92ff). But it would also inspire a new generation of arcadian ecologists to reframe their message and challenge the routinized, established approaches of the older conservation movement. To a large extent, the historical dichotomy between the imperialists and the arcadians would be replayed in the conflicts over direction and orientation in the fledgling movement organizations that developed in the late 1960s and early 1970s.

The new human ecologists came from many different directions. Some, like Murray Bookchin, who had been a labor activist in the 1930s, brought a socialist sensibility into the new movement. His book from 1963, Our Synthetic Environment, was one of the first to present the wide range of new environmental problems – occupational health, chemical pollution, household risks, waste disposal – that were to gain increasing public attention in the years to come. Others, like the biochemist Barry Commoner, gave the environmental movement a more technical emphasis; Commoner depicted, in his first book, Science and Survival (1966), the new, subservient role that science was playing in society and production,

Table 2. *Phases of environmentalism*

Period	Emphasis	Examples
(1) **awakening** (pre-1968)	public debate issue identification	World Wildlife Fund *Silent Spring*, 1962
(2) **"age of ecology"** (ca. 1969–74)	organization program articulation	Friends of the Earth *Only One Earth*, 1972
(3) **politicization** (ca. 1975–79)	social movement energy policy	"No Nukes" *Soft Energy Paths*, 1977
(4) **differentiation** (ca. 1980–86)	think tanks "deep ecology"	WRI, CSE, Earth First! *State of the World*, 1984
(5) **internationalization** (ca. 1987–93)	sustainable development global issues	UNCED *Our Common Future*, 1987
(6) **integration** (ca. 1994–)	incorporation resistance	Agenda 21 *Natural Capitalism*, 1999

and suggested new public-service, or critical, activities for scientists to pursue in the emerging movement. The biologist Paul Ehrlich resurrected the Malthusian message of population pressures and resource limitations in his book *The Population Bomb* (1968), and the different perspectives of Commoner and Ehrlich would subsequently combine in new activist organizations and environmental studies departments. Still others, like Lewis Mumford, would provide historical and philosophical perspectives to help understand the new environmental problems. As such, the human ecology tradition was also reinvented, or mobilized, in the 1960s.

Although the actual time-periods in which the different phases took place have varied from country to country, the making of an environmental consciousness can be seen to have gone through six main phases since the 1960s, and it is those phases that will provide the structure for the rest of this chapter (see Table 2).

In the 1950s and 1960s there was an initial period of awakening when the traditions of ecology were given new life. Then came a short-lived "age of ecology," when environmentalism was transformed into a more explicit, programmatic, identity, usually in new organizational settings and with new kinds of institutional frameworks. The third phase was more political, as the struggle against nuclear energy transformed the environmental consciousness in many countries into major political campaigns, which, when resolved, reinforced the processes of differentiation and fragmentation that were there from the beginning, as well as giving rise to new kinds of incorporation pressures. These pressures have had to do with the range of professional opportunities that opened up in the 1980s, with the identification of new kinds of international, or global, environmental issues, and eventually, in the 1990s, with the calls for integrating environmentalism into sustainable paths of socio-economic development. As a result, the emerging culture was subdivided into a range of branches, all drawing on the integrative cognitive praxis that was formed in the 1970s, but increasingly fragmented or differentiated from one another.

The period of awakening

It was in the immediate postwar era that the traditional concerns with nature preservation and resource conservation began to be transformed into a new kind of environmental consciousness. It has become customary to think of this consciousness emerging in the 1960s, inspired primarily by Rachel Carson's *Silent Spring*, but we can actually see the new environmentalism being shaped somewhat earlier by some of the leading figures in the older conservation "movement," particularly in the United States and Britain.

Julian Huxley, a naturalist and the first director of Unesco, played an important part in bringing conservation issues into the United Nations system, and he was also one of the key actors in the creation of IUPN, the International Union for Protection of Nature which, in 1956, would become IUCN, the International Union for Societies for the Conservation of Nature. Meetings arranged by both organizations were extremely important as fora for the articulation of a new environmental perspective to supersede the somewhat more limited nature-protection perspective that had characterized conservation circles since the late nineteenth century (McCormick 1991). The new environmentalism differed from the old both in terms of the issues addressed, but also in terms of the underlying social-cosmological, or world-view assumptions: the way in which nature–society interaction was represented. Particularly important was the recognition that something fundamental had taken place with the emergence of a more active exploitation of the land. What was needed, according to Aldo Leopold, writing in the 1940s, was a new stage in human ethical development to correspond to the material changes: "there is as yet no ethic dealing with man's relation to land and to the animals and plants which grow upon it. Land, like Odysseus' slave-girls, is still property. The land-relation is still strictly economic, entailing privileges but not obligations" (Leopold 1949: 203).

Fairfield Osborn, director of the New York Zoological Society and founder of the Conservation Foundation, was one of the first to put this new ecological perspective into print in his *Our Plundered Planet*, which was published in 1948 and subsequently was translated into thirteen languages (Jamison and Eyerman 1994: 74–82). In 1953 Osborn published *Limits of the Earth*, and he continued throughout the 1950s to foster a more international and ecological perspective among nature-lovers and biologists. He was perhaps the most successful of the conservation movement's new "organization men," people who arranged meetings and research projects, lobbied for funds, and gradually altered the agendas in nature societies and natural history institutions.

In the United States the transformation of conservationism into environmentalism was a gradual process that was brought to a head and to a larger public primarily through the eloquent prose of Rachel Carson. But there were others in the postwar period – writers like Joseph Wood Krutch, activists like David Brower of the Sierra Club, established figures like the American Supreme Court Justice William Douglas, and the nature photographer Ansel Adams – whose activities helped to pave the way (Fox 1985). In particular, the development of a "mass culture" of television and popular science brought the natural world into the home and with it the importance of "saving nature" from further degradation could be spread to a mass audience. In 1961 the World Wildlife Fund was established to give this new conservation message a more professional form in terms of fund-raising, public relations, and dissemination. The WWF was started with the express purpose of bringing more resources into the hands of the nature organizations.

Within the WWF, and then more scientifically in the International Biological Program established in the mid-1960s, the "imperialist" tradition took on a more modern or contemporary manifestation. On the one hand, it became more explicitly international, as scientists and other conservationists came to take part in transnational research and development networks, particularly within the IBP projects (Kwa 1989). On the other hand, the imperialist tradition was brought up to date technologically with the new cybernetic and computer-based approaches to research that were developed by the new breed of ecosystem ecologists led by Eugene and Howard Odum (Taylor 1988). Particularly in the energy-flow schematizations of Howard Odum, the mathematical modeling of nature was presented in an ambitious and sophisticated manner that was to have a major importance on the emerging environmental consciousness.

It was to be the eloquent writings of biologist-turned-science-writer Rachel Carson that would do most to give the arcadian tradition a modern voice. "Over increasingly large areas of the United States spring now comes unheralded by the return of the birds, and the early mornings are strangely silent where once they were filled with the beauty of bird song" (Carson 1962: 97). *Silent Spring* served to awaken the industrial world from its postwar slumbers, and Carson was soon followed by other

writers – Barry Commoner, Georg Borgström, René Dubos, Barbara Ward, and Paul Ehrlich – who, with their scientific authority and sober tone, had a somewhat different impact on the public consciousness.

In the 1960s a new range of environmental problems were identified – industrial pollution, atomic radiation, urban sprawl – that tended to supplant conservation issues from most national political agendas. And as these problems came to be discussed in popular books and the mass media, a new socio-economic developmental perspective gradually came to be articulated: an ecological paradigm in contrast to the industrial paradigm that had guided postwar development (Cotgrove 1982). As more books were published, so awareness grew and diagnoses of the problem became more alarmist, so that by the late 1960s when Paul Ehrlich published *The Population Bomb*, which was an even bigger bestseller than *Silent Spring*, a kind of doomsday, or at least crisis, mentality had emerged, giving the problems a new urgency. When combined with the philosophical critiques of modern technology published by Jacques Ellul, Herbert Marcuse, and Lewis Mumford, as well as the record of their spiritual journeys to the east and beyond by the beat poets and their hippie disciples, environmentalism became a broader movement of social and political opposition.

We can think of this period – from the late 1940s to the late 1960s, with a rather long period of latent interest in the 1950s – as a period of awakening. It was primarily a time of public education, and it took place almost exclusively in the industrialized countries. What was involved was the enunciation by biologists, nature lovers, and writers of a new range of issues and eventually a new ecological perspective. In the 1950s and 1960s a cluster of new societal problems were identified, from chemical risks to automotive air pollution, which gave rise to widespread public debates and eventually to a number of policy responses. The postwar mode of techno-economic development, with its dependence on science-based innovations and its relatively unproblematic view of science and technology, was shown to have serious "side effects"; and the 1960s ushered in a period of questioning, criticism, and reexamination of the dominant doctrines, or paradigms, of socio-economic development, and science and technology policy (Salomon 1977).

The age of ecology

By the end of the 1960s the period of questioning had inspired both the emergence of new activist groups, such as Friends of the Earth (which David Brower, the director of the Sierra Club, created in 1970 as a way to protest against the conservatism of the older organization) and

a process of policy reform and institution-building. In this second phase most of the industrialized countries established new state agencies to deal with environmental protection and other newly identified social problems, and environmental research and technological development were organized in new locations in both the private and the public sectors. Many national parliaments enacted more comprehensive environmental legislation and at the United Nations Conference on the Human Environment in Stockholm in 1972 the protection of the environment was recognized as a new area of international concern.

The manned landing on the moon in 1969 had provided the symbol for the conference, the blue planet viewed from space: small, fragile, and strikingly beautiful in its shape and color. A biologist, Rene Dubos, and an economist, Barbara Ward, collaborated on the book that would set the agenda for the conference. *Only One Earth* made the case for a new kind of environmentalism, combining efficient management of resources with empathetic understanding: "Now that mankind is in the process of completing the colonization of the planet," they wrote, "learning to manage it intelligently is an urgent imperative. Man must accept responsibility for the stewardship of the earth" (Ward and Dubos 1972: 25). In conclusion they noted that the reforms and policy proposals that they suggested would not come easily: "the planet is not yet a centre of rational loyalty for all mankind. But possibly it is precisely this shift of loyalty that a profound and deepening sense of our shared and inter-dependent biosphere can stir to life in us" (ibid.: 298).

In this period there was also, in a broader, and more generalized sense, a reorientation of science and technology policies to what might be termed a "societal" agenda. In the influential report *Science, Growth and Society* of 1971 (the so-called [Harvey] Brooks report), the Organization of Economic Cooperation and Development (OECD) proposed a range of new areas, or social sectors, for state support for scientific research and technological development, as well as a new kind of "assessment" activity that was suggested be included in science and technology policy (Elzinga and Jamison 1995). One of the most important of the new science and technology policy-sectors, as they came to be called, was environmental protection. And many countries followed the lead of the United States in establishing an Office for Technology Assessment.

In the early 1970s there was also a range of "grass-roots" engineering initiatives that emerged in the fledgling environmental movement. In the United States a group of self-proclaimed "new alchemists" moved from the university out to the country to experiment with ecological agriculture and energy technology (Todd 1977). In many European countries, but perhaps especially in Britain, Denmark, and the Netherlands,

a number of research centers and projects in alternative or radical technology were established. At some of the hippie communes and production collectives that developed at the time there was often an interest in renewable energy and organic or biodynamic agriculture, and there were also, among architects and planners, attempts to develop more environmentally friendly approaches and techniques (Dickson 1974; Boyle and Harper 1976).

An interest in alternative technology developed as an integral part of the environmental movement in several countries, and it was given special importance in development assistance, where E. F. Schumacher proposed a new kind of appropriate or "intermediate" technological development that would use modern and traditional techniques in creative combinations (Schumacher 1973). In several United Nations agencies – from UNEP to ILO – appropriate technology became an important priority area, and in countries like India a wide-ranging appropriate technology movement developed in the countryside (Elzinga and Jamison 1986). In retrospect, we can see that the environmental movement opened a public space for experimentation with a collective mode of ecological engineering – or what Ivan Illich called at the time "tools for conviviality" (Illich 1973) – in relation to energy, agriculture, housing, and transportation. The particular technical interests have diffused widely into society – for are we not all a bit more "ecological" in the ways we garden, and decorate our homes, and move ourselves around? – while the collective creativity has largely dissipated. Rather quickly, however, the environmental movement was forced to confront political reality; its visionary outlook, its naïve utopianism was challenged by the coming of the oil crisis, and what might be thought as the age of ecological innocence came to an abrupt end.

Political challenges

It was the first oil crisis, in 1973–1974 that led to a major shift in environmental consciousness, as energy issues moved to the top of many national political agendas, especially in relation to nuclear energy. In several countries the late 1970s were a period of intense political debate and social-movement activity as the pros and cons of nuclear energy, or "hard energy paths" in general, were contested (Lovins 1977). In certain countries, Denmark for example, renewable energy experimentation became a social movement of its own, and led to new industries and government programs. Seen in retrospect, an important result of the energy debates of the 1970s was a professionalization of environmental concern and an incorporation by the established political structures of what had originally been a somewhat delimited political issue. As a result, there was both specialization and institutionalization of knowledge production.

On the one hand new kinds of discipline, or sub-disciplines, developed in many countries. Energy-systems analysis became a recognized field for investigating the costs and benefits of different choices of energy supply and distribution. Human ecology took on the form of a recognized academic field and developed its own theories, based on concepts of entropy and energy flow. In the Netherlands and some other European countries, environmental science, or environmental studies, became a separate field with state research programs providing funding for new university departments and new public research institutions (Leroy 1995). Throughout the world environmental research tended to became a "sector" of its own within the broader systems of research and development.

Within ecology itself, a kind of bifurcation took place between ecosystem ecologists, on the one hand, who were often drawn into larger, multidisciplinary projects, and population, or evolutionary ecologists, on the other, who focused their attention on particular species or ecological communities. There was a still further specialization, due to the range of approaches that emerged in the established disciplines to take on the new environmental and energy issues. As a result of these developments, many of the academic ecologists and other environmental scientists who were active in the formation of new groups and organizations eventually drifted away from activism and the more activist organizations, as opportunities for research careers emerged at the universities (Cramer *et al.* 1987).

On the other hand new kinds of institutional arrangements were created, often from central government. In the United States, for example, there was established both a national government-funded center for renewable energy and an influential Office of Technology Assessment within Congress. In many European countries, new research councils and governmental departments were built up, with ambitions to establish somewhat more policy-related types of research. There were also efforts, in this period, to create new kinds of "service" institutions, linking universities to the environmental movement organizations. In the Netherlands, science students at the universities developed a network of "science shops" to market their expertise more directly to those citizen groups that needed it. There were also self-named "radical scientists" who started to publish journals and arrange conferences. The former included *Science for the People* in the United States, *Radical Science Journal* in Britain, *Wechselwirkung* in Germany and *Naturkampen* in Denmark. And, perhaps the most ambitious of all, environmentally minded engineers and technicians actually constructed their visionary, or "utopian," technologies, such as the world's largest wind power plant at the Tvind schools in western Denmark or the geodesic dome with its self-sufficient ecosystem at the New Alchemy Institute in Massachusetts. When some of these alternative groups gathered at the UN Conference in Vienna on Science, Technology and Development, it was apparent that a new kind of alternative science and technology had emerged.

What, in retrospect, was most characteristic of the period of the late 1970s was the breadth, but also the unity and coherence, of the environmental movement. As a popular front, or campaign, against nuclear energy, the different traditions of ecology were combined into an integrative cognitive praxis, with a visionary ecological philosophy or world-view guiding a range of practical experiments with alternative technology in settings that were largely autonomous and thus outside of the formalized rule systems and organizational frameworks of the larger society. In informal local groups and movement-based workshops and study circles, technical projects and educational activities were conducted with the participation of both "experts" and amateurs. The key point is that for a brief time the movement could provide an organized learning experience in which theory and practice were combined in pursuit of a common collective struggle. These settings would be difficult to maintain for very long, since they were, in many ways, much too fragile for any kind of permanent institutionalization, and when the issue that inspired the movement was resolved, and taken off the political agenda, the different component parts split apart and fragmented (Cramer *et al.* 1987). The unity that had been achieved in struggle simply could not be sustained when the "opportunity structure" was altered, as it came to be throughout the world in the early 1980s.

The challenge to the coherence of the movement was also, to a large extent, a result of the broadening and diversification of environmentalism in the late 1970s. While most activists in Europe were concerned with nuclear energy, which became an issue of major political importance in several countries, other issues were important in other parts of the world. In the United States, the discovery of toxic wastes buried under the neighborhood of Love Canal in Buffalo, New York, inspired a new kind of locally based, working class opposition to environmental pollution (Szasz 1994). It was also in the United States that the new techniques of genetic engineering were critically reviewed by activists for their risks and dangers to the communities in which the laboratory experiments were carried out. In opposing genetic engineering, environmentalists such as Jeremy Rifkin pointed to a new kind of futuristic challenge that made many of the actual environmental problems pale in significance. "Two futures beckon us," Rifkin wrote. "We can choose to engineer the life of the planet, creating a second nature in our image, or we can choose to participate with the rest of the living kingdom. Two futures, two choices. An engineering approach and an ecological approach" (1983: 252).

Meanwhile, in India and other parts of the Third World protests against hydroelectric dams and industrial forestry projects forged new connections among critical environmentalists, scientists, and local populations. In the opposition to the Silent Valley dam, a "people's science movement" came into being with a popular approach to knowledge; while in the Chipko movement, in the foothills of the Himalayas a local ecology of diversified resource use was pitted against the monocultural, managerial ecology of professional forestry (Gadgil and Guha 1992). In India the Gandhian legacy, with its ideal of artisanship and a rural village-based economy, became an important ingredient of the environmental movement, a valuable indigenous tradition that could be mobilized and made relevant to current concerns.

These new forms of environmentalism were difficult to unify in a single movement; rather, in the intellectual and broader political traditions that they tapped into, and in the alliances that they made, sometimes with quite conservative and fundamentalist religious groups, they were often articulating interests and strategies that were diametrically opposed to the positions of "modernist" anti-nuclear activists, as well as many of the professional environmentalists in the think-tanks and the "mainstream organizations". So, while the environmental movement was expanding and diversifying, the seeds were sown for a more explicit process of differentiation in the 1980s.

Patterns of differentiation

When nuclear energy was removed from many national political agendas in the early 1980s, there was a wide range of expertise that had previously not existed. In many European countries, as well as in North America and even some of the larger developing countries, there were university departments and research institutes, as well as substantial state bureaucracies and a wide range of "non-governmental" organizations, which had an institutional interest in environmental and energy issues.

There was also an ideological shift, a veritable counter-revolution in many of the leading industrial nations. Margaret Thatcher in Britain and Ronald Reagan in the United States represented the most visible manifestations of a neo-liberal corporate offensive which opposed much of the substantive program of environmentalism and other "new social movements". In the world of science, technology, and the environment, neo-liberalism led to a change from a social emphasis or policy agenda to a more explicitly economic and commercial orientation. A language of deregulation and strategic research – and new programs that stressed the importance of university–industry collaboration and academic entrepreneurship – came to replace the notions of societal relevance and technology assessment. At the same time, many of the sectorial programs that had been established in the 1970s were curtailed and many of the alternative centers and activities that had flourished were disbanded, especially in Britain and the United States, where the ideological shift was particularly strong (Elzinga and Jamison 1995). The broad public space that environmentalists had carved out was circumscribed and constrained, and broader ambitions to produce both an alternative knowledge and an alternative approach to politics were significantly reduced in scope. What began to emerge instead was a new kind of professional environmentalism, in business and government, as well as in the environmental movement itself, as the neo-liberal ideology spread into the broader society.

On the one hand, there developed in many parts of the world a range of more explicitly commercial activities, such as consulting firms in energy conservation and environmental impact assessment, as well as companies that specialized in new market "niches" such as wind and solar energy, waste recycling and minimization, ecological architecture and design. Many larger companies also began to establish environmental departments in order to develop more pro-active or "preventive" strategies for pollution control. In the United States, in particular, pollution prevention grew into an influential corporate slogan in the 1980s, as the experiments at Minnesota Mining and Manufacturing (3M) indicated that efforts to eliminate pollution at its source could be both effective and profitable (Weale 1992).

A second kind of professionalization that served to alter the character of the environmental movement was the emergence of think-tanks, which were independent of both the private and the public sectors, and which were run on a not-for-profit basis. The Washington-based World Resources Institute, created by one of former President Carter's leading environmental advisors, Gustav Speth, and the Worldwatch Institute established by Lester Brown, an expert in development issues, were particularly influential. In India, Anil Agarwal established the Centre for Science and Environment, primarily as an environmental news agency, which has grown over the years into an influential contributor to international environmental deliberations. These new operations all combined research with investigative journalism, and provided information to the mass media as well as to environmental organizations. Their staff members combined an expertise in specific environmental issues with skills in publishing and communication, and they quickly became significant players in both national and international environmental politics. Because of their proven competence they were able to influence policy agendas more effectively than the less professional activist organizations.

The emergence of these think-tanks was accompanied by the spread of a dramatically innovative and professional environmental activism, spearheaded by Greenpeace and by the reemergence, in many countries, of the older conservation societies. Greenpeace, of course, was a pioneer in a kind of "high-tech environmentalism," making use of computers and sophisticated communications techniques in order to raise awareness about a few highly charged topics: nuclear fallout, seal- and whale-hunting, and oil pollution. As the energy issue lost its media interest, and the ideological counter-offensive of Thatcher and Reagan pushed environmentalists on to the defensive, Greenpeace signaled the coming of a more "radical" and more politically strategic kind of activism (Eyerman and Jamison 1989). The organizational ambition was to carry out a limited number of campaigns that were internationally coordinated and which combined direct, dramatic, forms of action with highly focused information and lobbying efforts.

Finally, the early 1980s witnessed the widespread entrance of environmentalism into the parliamentary arena as green parties, under the inspiration of the West German Grünen, were formed across Europe and North America (as well as in several Asian countries). In most countries the formation of green parties was controversial, and was perhaps the main factor that led to splits and conflicts within most national environmental movements. Many were the activists who contended that movements could not operate as formal political parties, and that the establishment of green parties would be counter-productive. In countries like Sweden, Denmark, and the Netherlands the formation of green parties was opposed by many of the leading activists from the antinuclear movement, many of whom continued to work within the traditional parties as well as within movement organizations (Jamison *et al.* 1990).

By the mid-1980s the environmental movement had thus lost whatever coherence it might once have had. It was divided into distinct branches, or wings, and in most places the branches themselves were subdivided along sectorial lines. In addition to professionalization, there was a kind of specialization process that affected the particular issues that each organization dealt with. This had the consequence of producing project- or topic-specific knowledge in both the think-tanks and the activist organizations. This was one of the factors that made it difficult for environmental organizations to continue to interact with university scientists, whose training was usually less specialized than that of sector activists.

But many academics, under the pressure of liberalization and new professional regimes in the universities, left the "movement" for other reasons at this time. However, links were developed among, for example, academic experts in renewable energy and energy conservation and the commercial firms that emerged out of the struggle against nuclear energy. And in the name of university–industry collaboration environmental concern was brought into university management and engineering departments where it had previously not been significant. It was through such collaborations that many of the innovations in renewable energy and industrial ecology, which would become important in the 1990s, would be generated.

The global agenda

In general terms, it seems appropriate to characterize the first half of the 1980s as a period in which environmentalism retreated from the public stage to establish new institutions and new forms of competence. In the late 1980s environmental concern emerged once again into the broader public sphere, but now in a new more "global" and professional guise. A range of new environmental problems – climate change, ozone depletion, biodiversity – replaced local problems as the main areas of concern, and the solution to these problems came to be characterized in the vocabulary of sustainable development, following the report of the World Commission on Environment and Development in 1987, which drew on terminology previously articulated by the World Wildlife Fund (WWF) in the World Conservation Strategy of 1980.

In the 1980s, in large measure because of deregulation and a weakening of state controls over economic development, a new type of capitalist expansion began to be recognized. Globalization, as it has come to be called, is based on a number of technological innovations in telecommunications and information-processing and distribution, which make it possible to conduct business and financial operations across national boundaries. But it is also based on an ideology, or value-system, that tends to glorify individual risk-taking and entrepreneurship. In the 1980s, this neo-liberal ideology was on the offensive and it strongly influenced environmental politics by shifting responsibility over decision-making directly into the hands of the corporations. No longer would the state seek to regulate the behavior of companies in some kind of socially mandated direction. In Britain and the United States at first, and then throughout the industrialized world, the doctrines of globalization and neo-liberalism led to a fundamental reconstitution of the frameworks of environmental politics and policy-making. The key element in the emerging doctrinal framework was cooperation instead of confrontation. Business and government would work together in order to achieve a kind of socio-economic development that took environmental costs and use of resources into account. A greener, cleaner, mode of industrial production would be a central ingredient in the new doctrine of sustainable development.

The discourse of sustainable development served to redirect environmental politics in three main ways. On the one hand, and most significantly, there was an internationalization of the environmental agenda, and with it an emphasis on trade, foreign aid, and development assistance as well as technology transfer. Secondly, there was an opening up to new actors and political constituencies. The Brundtland Report had been written by a committee composed of scientists and government officials, but also by representatives of non-governmental organizations and business firms. The quest for sustainable development was thus a mission that challenged the sectorial "autonomy" of the environmental movement. In calling for the integration of economics and ecology and for the linking of environmental problems to other issues of income and resource distribution, poverty alleviation, armed conflict, and gender equality, the Brundtland Commission reframed the ecological problematic. Finally, the quest for sustainable development opened up environmentalism to the social sciences. In order to provide a knowledge base for the comprehensive program of global recovery that was outlined in the report, there was call for contributions from many areas of expertise and not only from natural science, which had previously occupied that role.

The internationalization phase can be seen, in retrospect, as a kind of transition period from the oppositional politics of the 1970s to the more diffuse and "constructive" politics of the 1990s. In terms of the mobilization of traditions, sustainable development was a major effort – or perhaps a last attempt – to combine the different ecological traditions into one overall perspective. In many ways, it was inevitable that there would be fundamental conflicts, and that new dichotomies would emerge as the doctrine was put into practice.

Because of its generality and all-inclusiveness, the quest for sustainable development inspired vastly different kinds of social actor, and thus led to a range of different interpretations. The professionals within business and government, as well as within the "mainstream" environmental-movement organizations, transformed the quest into more instrumental terms while, for many local activists and so-called deep ecologists, sustainable development took on rather ethical and moral connotations (Sachs 1999). Soon there would be quite different "discourses" and practices that would emerge as the quest for sustainable development was

appropriated into specific national political cultures, organizational structures, and institutional contexts.

Environmentalism in an entrepreneurial age

In the course of the 1990s, as sustainable development came to be placed
on the international political agenda, other trends were also manifesting
themselves in the disparate worlds of knowledge-making. On the one
hand there has been a general trend towards transnational collaborations and policy-coordination, along with decreasing direct national state
control. In many European countries, there have been significant reduc-
tions in state funding for research and development activities and increased support to programs and initiatives within the European Union.
On the other hand there has also been a growing commercialization and
privatization of research and development activities, and a concomitant
encouragement and fostering of entrepreneurship in universities, government ministries, and local governments. These developments have
been characterized as a new, externally determined "mode" of knowledge production, which transcends traditional disciplinary and institutional boundaries, and which represents a fundamental challenge to the
norm and value systems of universities and knowledge-producing institutions in general (Gibbons *et al.* 1994).

These entrepreneurial approaches to science and technology are not
all of one piece. Entrepreneurs have emerged within both the governmental sphere and the traditional business world. And there have been
many efforts to establish a more explicit entrepreneurial culture, or value
system, within universities by means of new forms of research funding
and external educational programs, as well as in the formation of new
expert identities and roles. Meanwhile, there has been a shift in many environmental "non-governmental" organizations to new tasks having to do
with green consumption, sustainable development, and cleaner products.
A kind of entrepreneurial ethos has made its way into many previously
critical, or even radical, green parties and environmental organizations.
And new types of organization, more exclusively oriented to consulting
activities and advising business firms, have also sprung up: for instance,
the Natural Step, which originated in Sweden, and has now established
branches in Britain and the United States (Dekker *et al.* 1998).

The doctrinal, or discursive, shift in the world of science and technology to the new tasks of sustainable development has come to involve
new combinations of corporate, governmental, and non-governmental
actors. Emphasis is increasingly given in many national and international
research and development (or R&D) programs to the institutionalization

and development of environmental management procedures and so-called cleaner technologies. As such, environmentally oriented knowledge production is no longer the responsibility of a delimited sector; rather, environmental concern has begun to be diffused across the entire realm of science and technology policy in relation to a variety of different, and often conflicting, projects. A growing number of business firms have adopted new methods of environmental management, including environmental auditing, recycling of waste products, and more efficient uses of resources and energy in production processes, while new forms of regulation and policy-making have developed at the national and transnational levels (see Hukkinen 1999).

Ecological modernization, as these entrepreneurial processes are sometimes called, has been the dominant form of integration over the past decade. With its strong faith in technology, its proponents have been led to envision a new age of green engineering and what Amory Lovins, Hunter Lovins, and Paul Hawken have recently termed "natural capitalism." Their argument is that capitalism has failed to deal adequately with environmental problems, because it has not been capitalist enough. The task is to calculate the true costs of productive activities, and increase enormously the efficiency with which resources, physical, human, and social, are utilized. "If there is to be prosperity in the future," they write, "society must make its use of *resources* vastly more productive – deriving four, ten, or even a hundred times as much benefit from each unit of energy, water, materials, or anything else borrowed from the planet and consumed" (Hawken *et al.* 1999: 8). Like the concept of eco-efficiency that is being promulgated by the World Business Council for Sustainable Development, natural capitalism puts the main responsibility for achieving sustainable development in the hands of private, commercial corporations; and, as we shall see, the perspective of green business, or natural capitalism, has indeed served to revitalize many industrial branches and to provide workable solutions for many environmental problems (see DeSimone and Popoff 2000).

But while the advocates of green business attempt to integrate ecology into a capitalist mode of production, critics claim that the continuing operations of that very mode of production are serving to exclude growing numbers of people around the world from productive activity in, for example, matters of food supply (e.g. Shiva 2000). In the name of globalization, resources are continually being expropriated from one part of the world to another, and transnational corporations, with the support of Northern governments and their unlimited faith in "free trade," continue to carry out their activities without paying regard to ecological principles (Gorelick 1998). While one side of the business world speaks with a new kind of green and clean rhetoric, the all-too-brown and dirty reality continues to dominate actual corporate behavior, as well as the policies of such bodies as the World Bank and the World Trade Organization; as the demonstrations in Seattle in November 1999 and after have come to contend, "free" trade is by no means fair and equitable (Agarwal *et al.* 1999). Major reforms in the way in which capitalism operates, and the ways in which capital flows and other financial exchanges are regulated, are perhaps even more crucial than changes in technology and productive efficiency (see French 2000). Thus, even if the utilization of material resources does become more efficient, there remains a continuing and increasing waste and exploitation of human resources due to the very operating procedures of the capitalist system itself.

In a curious kind of cultural dynamic, the solving of material problems tends to create new kinds of human problems. There are always losers, as well as winners, in new outbursts of creative activity and technological innovation. That is why there has emerged an entirely different kind of integration in environmental politics over the past ten years or so – an integration between environmentalism and various struggles for justice and dignity, equity and tolerance, and for the pursuit of sustainable livelihoods. Here, the ambition is to empower human communities to solve their own multiple problems – of resource use, employment, communications, health, education – rather than buying into a global capitalist system that has created most of those problems in the first place. It is these competing and disparate approaches to environmental politics that we will be delineating in the following chapters.

NOTE

This chapter draws on material previously published in Jamison and Eyerman 1994 and Jamison 1996.

1 The exchange between Leo Marx and Lawrence Buell in the *New York Review of Books* in 1999 is a case in point. For Marx, Thoreau was not the ecocentric thinker that Buell makes him out to be in his book on the continued importance of nature writing (Buell 1996), while for Buell it is the very ecocentrism, the rejection of industrial society, that makes Thoreau such an attractive, and relevant, figure. By returning to nature, and propounding an alternative set of biocentric or arcadian ecological values, Thoreau serves as a source of inspiration for what Buell terms "ecocritical" movements.

4 National shades of green

Imagine there's no country, it's easy if you try.
John Lennon, "Imagine" (1972)

Faced with the same "facts" about nature, Americans...fear cancer more than the British, the French tolerate nuclear power better than their German neighbours, and Americans are more receptive to bio-technology than Danes, Norwegians or Germans.
Sheila Jasanoff, "The Songlines of Risk" (1999: 137)

From vision to reality

As we have seen, the environmental movement emerged at a time when many of us could imagine, along with John Lennon, that there was no such thing as country, or possessions, or religion: that there was, or could be, a "brotherhood of man." As those counter-cultural, neo-romantic senti-ments have faded into the collective memory, the dreams, or visions, of yesteryear have run up against a number of very real constraints and coun-terforces, among which the inbred traditions of national political cultures have been among the more intractable. Nationalisms and provincialisms have been reinvented with a vengeance over the past thirty years, and they have twisted and counterattacked everything that has come in their path. In relation to environmentalism, national political cultures have all but obliterated the visionary, universalizing ambitions of the environ-mental movement, and one of the results has been that the emerging ecological culture has been configured into so many national shades or shapes of green.

Whether we like it or not, it has become ever more apparent that there are significant national differences in the ways in which societies function. The idea of national character, which had been so disastrously tainted in the interwar years, when Hitler and Stalin constructed their totalitarian belief systems on the basis of reactionary forms of nationalism, has been rekindled, not the least because it has shown itself to be such a potent force in a supposedly globalized world. National identities exert a powerful hold over people and have become important resources in an age of increasing anonymity and individualization. And, in the social sciences, "theory" has tried to catch up with "practice," as new concepts have been invented to account for the influence of culture on such matters as technological, social and economic development.

In the 1980s, Christopher Freeman identified a particular "national system of innovation" of state–industry collaboration at work in the Japanese approach to technology policy in the postwar era, and Bengt-Åke Lundvall and his colleagues applied the same term to characterize a very different kind of rural "industrial block" as the key to the Danish industrialization process of the nineteenth century (Freeman 1987; Lundvall, ed. 1992). The notion of "social capital" which Robert Putnam derived from his studies of socio-economic development in northern Italy has been recently applied to social life in the United States as well (Putnam 2000). Putnam has argued that regionally distinctive cultural patterns in the form of locally based network relationships and interactions were crucial elements in "making democracy work" in northern Italy, that is, in providing a sense of solidarity and trust that had proved essential for effective governance and economic growth (Putnam 1993). In the United States this type of social capital has been eroding, according to Putnam, as more and more Americans are "bowling alone." The revival of interest in community and "strong democracy" that has been so visible among public-minded intellectuals in the United States in recent years indicates the need for rethinking the role of cultural ties in social life. Throughout the social sciences there has been a growing recognition that "culture matters," that cultural patterns and rituals, national identities and traditions, continue to play a fundamental role in social interaction even in an age of intensifying global reach and economic expansion. From all aspects of the academic spectrum, the identification of cultural factors in political and economic life has become an important concern.[1]

In the particular area of science and technology studies, which is where I have been working, it has become increasingly common, following Freeman and Lundvall, to refer to "systems of innovation" at both the national and regional levels, as important formative influences on policy decisions and technological developmental trajectories (Edquist 1998). But most analysts, for reasons of training and expertise, appear to have limited their interest to the economic, or instrumental, components of policy-making, and have tended to neglect the broader cultural dimensions. It can be argued, however, that contemporary differences in policy-making, and in politics more generally, reflect the impact of somewhat less visible and more long-standing patterns of "habituation," as was already indicated by Thorstein Veblen at the time of the First World War when he compared the British and German paths to industrialization and eventual conflict (Veblen 1915).

In this chapter I want to indicate how contemporary environmental politics have been shaped in significant ways by institutional and cultural patterns, or modes of social capital, that manifest themselves in particular ways in particular national settings. On the one hand, there is what we can call a national policy, or governance, style (see Vogel 1986; Jasper 1990). In this respect, there are major differences in regard to the location of decision-making and the more general sites of politics, that is, whether they tend to be centralized or decentralized, accessible or closed, opaque or transparent. Countries with strong "populist" traditions such as Denmark and the United States provide substantial power to local authorities and comparatively open access to decision-making, while other countries with stronger statist orientations, such as Sweden, France, and China, tend toward less directly accessible and more centralized forms of governance.

There are also differences in relation to what might be termed conflictual or consensual modes of policy-making. Countries with bipolar party systems, such as Britain and the United States, tend to differ dramatically from countries with multiparty systems, such as Denmark and Germany, where there are often governments with broad political representation that leads to a more "consensual" approach to decision-making. In Germany, the influence of the Green Party on national and regional politics has been out of all proportion to the party's electoral support. In the United States and Britain, on the other hand, where representation for small parties is more or less impossible, environmental politics has been channeled more effectively into non-governmental organizations.

There are also significant differences among countries in regard to the kinds of opportunities that are made available for public interest, or social-movement, organizations (Kitschelt 1986; Tarrow 1994). What students of social movements have termed "political opportunity structures" reflect the types of influence that non-governmental organizations can have on decision-making; from a more cultural perspective, we can think of them as the broader set of social contexts within which movements and activist organizations operate, and which thus include opportunities for economic, cultural, and political activities (see Della Porta and Diani 1999).

A second set of conditioning factors are national mentalities, or what the anthropologist Mary Douglas has termed "cultural biases" (Douglas 1978). Because of differences in geographical conditions and attitudes to nature people in different countries have come to think about environmental politics through different linguistic and discursive frameworks (Hård and Jamison 1998). People living in countries like the United States and Sweden, with large wilderness areas and long, relatively formalized traditions of nature conservation, tend to approach environmental politics and environmental knowledge production quite differently from densely populated countries such as the Netherlands and Denmark. These differences are based both on the types of ideas that have been articulated through the centuries by intellectuals of various kinds and on actual developmental experiences in science, technology, and economics. What the economists refer to as "competitive advantage" is based on a long history of social and cultural selection in the realms both of ideas and inventions.

Finally, there are differences that have crystallized more recently in relation to how environmental movements have mobilized and combined the different ecological traditions that we discussed in chapter 3. Most crucial for our understanding of national shadings of greening are the ways in which the formative conflicts and controversies of the 1970s worked themselves out in different countries, the particular social ecological imprints, or legacies, that have been left in the collective memory.

In this chapter, I primarily draw on the historical experiences of Sweden and Denmark and my native United States to illustrate how we might make meaningful distinctions among national shades of green. Having worked in both Sweden and Denmark I have had many occasions to reflect on the differences between these small neighboring lands where many contemporary environmental policy innovations of international significance have first taken place. Since their historical experiences are, in many ways, so similar to one another a closer look at their differences can perhaps give us a clearer understanding of how national peculiarities remain influential in an age of globalization and homogenization. I try to extend the range of my presentation by referring to experiences in other parts of the world, particularly in those countries where I have done some research, such as Vietnam and India. My effort is by no means meant to be exhaustive; I simply want to indicate some of the ways in which national cultural traditions make a difference in the ongoing transformations of environmental politics.

Styles of governance

In academic literature the notion of styles of policy or governance has been given a number of different meanings. Among political scientists, emphasis is often given to structural factors, such as institutional frameworks, formalized decision-making structures and, more generally, to the ways in which the organs of government interact with one another. Distinctions tend to be made between centralized and decentralized forms of policy-making, between open and closed states, and between degrees of formality and informality – what is sometimes called the degree of transparency – in governance procedures.

In science and technology policy there has been a strong interest in recent years to identify "national systems" of research and development, or innovation, as well as to characterize different types and degrees of state involvement in policy-making. Often, attempts to identify styles of policy have been made for advisory reasons, that is, in order to help to improve interaction among different bodies and to fashion hybrid networks and institutions that can better mobilize the particular national resources that are available (e.g. Nelson 1993). In environmental policy there has been a tendency, particularly among political scientists, to focus on forms of institutionalization: the ways in which legal, financial, and regulatory institutions have been put in place to create a particular national policy "capacity" for environmental protection, or, more recently, for ecological modernization (e.g. Jänicke and Weidner 1997). In general it can be argued that for most political scientists, policy-making, or governance, is usually seen to be a matter of form rather than content; of mechanisms, or instruments, rather than dynamic, cultural processes.

In my research projects – on the cultural dimensions of science and technology policy in developing countries, and on public participation in environmental science and technology policy in Europe – I have tried to develop a somewhat different meaning of policy style derived from the theory of science, cultural studies, and intellectual history. For me, a style of governance is something that has emerged over time in the patterns of interaction among the various "policy cultures" that can be said to represent the different constituencies or "publics" that are involved in the making of policy – bureaucratic, economic, academic and civic (Baark and Jamison 1995; Jamison ed. 1998). The style is more like a set of working relations, or mode of interactive behavior, than a fixed system or formal institutional framework.

Let me briefly illustrate policy styles in operation with reference to the countries that were involved in the project on public participation (better known, perhaps, as PESTO). In Sweden, for example, the powerful state bureaucracy that was established in the seventeenth century and the legacy of the nineteenth-century industrialization process, dominated by large mechanical firms (Ericsson, ASEA, Alfa-Laval), together have served to constrain recent efforts to reconstitute environmental science and technology policy in more sustainable directions. The recent conflict over nuclear energy, which deeply affected Swedish society during the 1970s, was particularly important in constructing contemporary policy tensions. The "dilemmas" of polarization are very much alive in the current debates about sustainable development, roughly dividing Sweden into two antagonistic camps: one remains firmly committed to large-scale, environmentally problematic industrial development, and the other promulgates more ecological paths to socio-economic development.

In my terms these camps consist, in large measure, of alliances between representatives of the economic and bureaucratic policy cultures, on the one hand – policy entrepreneurs in business and certain branches of government – and between civil servants in other branches and representatives of civil society, on the other – what might be termed the "leftovers" of the Swedish model in the social democratic party and public-interest organizations. The style of governance is highly polarized and often conflictual, as the two camps counter each other's initiatives and seek to incorporate the quest for sustainable development into their own "cultural" preferences and interests. ASEA, now fused into ASEA Brown Boveri, is a particularly important agent of globalization, of course, and, while talking up a new green rhetoric, continues to support the nuclear energy that it played so important a role in developing. The former opponents of nuclear energy have meanwhile attained influence within both the ruling social democratic party, which has recently begun the controversial process of closing nuclear plants, and, perhaps most crucially, at the local and regional level of government. The result is a curious combination of government-sponsored "activism" and corporate-sponsored resistance (Jamison 1997).

Denmark (and, in a similar vein, the Netherlands) has developed very different kinds of cultural tension around sustainable development. The "consensual mode" of policy-making, and stronger civic traditions, have led to a greater public acceptance of sustainable development programs in both countries, as well as a more active combination of economic and environmental policies. The problem for these front-running countries is in finding market niches for the new cleaner and greener products that their industries are starting to produce while, at the same time, not neglecting the older, more traditional concerns of environmental protection, particularly in relation to agriculture. The so-called greening of industry, which has been particularly influential in Denmark and the Netherlands, has also led to tensions between the emerging green experts and the more activist wings of the civil society (Baark 1997; Andringa and Schot 1997).

In Britain the quest for sustainable development has been less pronounced due to other policy priorities being higher on the political agenda as well as to stronger forces of both resistance and inertia. Here the legacy of Thatcherite neo-liberalism has been marked; also significant is the continuing and all-but-hegemonic hold of the representatives of academic culture over the realm of science and technology policy-making in general. Not surprisingly, in the country where the institutions of modern science were first established, it has been more difficult for the civic culture to play a particularly active role in green knowledge-making. In any case, environmental organizations have been much more militant in Britain than in most other European countries, and it is in Britain that the new wave of radical environmentalism has been most pronounced (van Zwanenberg 1997).

The Lithuanian experience is especially interesting because the environmental issue, as in many other countries of eastern Europe, emerged as part of a struggle for national independence and, when that struggle was won, other economic priorities have been seen as more pressing and urgent (Rinkevicius 1997). An emerging economic culture has been relatively weak, and the previously strong alliance between the civic and academic cultures, which was a constituent part of the independence movement, has been diminished as new external actors – non-governmental organizations, international organizations, transnational firms – have entered the country in a more active way (Rinkevicius 2000).

If we look outside of Europe we see still different patterns or styles of governance at work. Vietnam, for example, provides a very different kind of experience, in that the civic culture has been given a very small role to play in the quest for sustainable development. Alliances between the hegemonic bureaucratic culture and an emergent economic culture have tended to overwhelm initiatives from the civic culture, and have kept environmental issues from becoming a central policy concern. As in eastern Europe, it has been the influence of transnational non-governmental organizations and, to a certain extent, intergovernmental organizations such as the United Nations Development Programme (UNDP) that have brought environmental concern on to the policy agenda (Bach 1998).

India, meanwhile, is a country where conflict among the policy cultures has been accompanied by conflict among regions as well as among people with different religious affiliations. The existence of a dual society of urban and rural life-worlds has also meant that policies in the environmental field, as in most other policy areas, have had highly skewed impacts. The relatively high level of democracy and of democratic institutions – in comparison to most other developing countries – has also meant that a wide range of groups and organizations seeking to represent a large and variegated civil society have been able to play a significant part in environmental policy-making in relation to many specific controversies and decisions. The openness of the political culture has also led to a number of innovative links between the academic and civic cultures, both on the individual and the organizational level (Gadgil and Guha 1992).

In these terms the United States is a country in which the bureaucratic policy culture is a good deal weaker than in most European countries, while the economic culture and the civic culture have long histories of influencing policy-making in the environmental field, as well as in most other areas of public policy. In the name of American exceptionalism, the state has had a much more limited range of functions than in most other parts of the world (Jasanoff 1990). Through powerful public interest organizations and think-tanks, both the economic and civic cultures exert pressure on the bureaucratic culture in order to achieve their ends. In the environmental arena this has led to a number of pitched battles through the years, but also to a rather large gap between federal and local decisions and policies. The gap has fostered highly fragmented responses to environmental challenges from the private sector, or economic culture, as well as from the environmental movement representing the various publics of the highly diverse civil society (see Dowie 1996). The style of governance is not so much oriented to the shaping of consensus, or even to the coordination of effort, as much as to a balancing of interests. In many aspects of the quest for sustainable development, particularly after the Reagan administration had "de-regulated" so much of the state policy apparatus, it has been the economic culture that established priorities, constituted programs, and provided the main support for projects and initiatives, but often in a rather decentralized and highly differentiated manner (see Vig and Kraft 1999).

Discursive frameworks

Policy style – or the interactions of the policy cultures – is perhaps the most obvious or visible way in which national cultures can be seen to influence environmental politics. Under the formal surface of policy-making, however, there are a range of somewhat more elusive factors which have to do with national "mentalities," or ways of life. They are often difficult to identify in any rigorous fashion, but there can be little doubt that people in different countries are affected by different "mindsets" or discursive frameworks.

In an earlier comparison of national components of Swedish and Danish science and technology, I suggested that because of different geographical conditions, as well as different vocabularies or representations that have developed over time, "nature" has come to be given somewhat different meanings in Denmark and Sweden. By roaming freely in the historical and ethnographic literature, I tried to identify a *national metaphysical bias,* or cosmology, a particular way in which the exploration and investigation of nature and natural resources had been conceptualized in each country.

In Sweden, with its vast expanses of forests and mountains, nature was, from early on, a rather forbidding place, both in theory and practice, harsh and threatening and somewhat mysterious, and the task for science and engineering was to bring it under human mastery. Not for nothing has Carl von Linné, or Linnaeus, as he is known outside Sweden, been called the initiator of an imperialist attitude to nature and the instigator of a managerial approach to ecology. Linnaeus, as we have seen, conceived natural relationships in a mechanical, systemic way, believing, as Donald Worster has put it, that the "Creator had designed an integrated order in nature which functioned like a single, universal, well-oiled machine" (Worster 1977: 39).

What is intriguing, however, is that many other Swedish scientists and engineers have shared this imperial, or mechanical, attitude to nature that is so characteristic of Linnaean taxonomy. Throughout Swedish history we find systematizers, catalogers, system-builders, modelers, not only among scientists and engineers but also among philosophers and theologians, for example Emanuel Swedenborg in the eighteenth century and the extremely influential Christopher Boström in the nineteenth century, who developed a kind of systematic philosophy for the civil service. Swedish history, in other words, has given rise, and a certain dominant cultural position, to a systemic mentality. In the words of Sten Lindroth, the Swedish historian of science: "The average Swede undoubtedly has an appreciable aptitude for organization and order, and this desire for description and classification has found purposeful expression in the natural scientists" (Lindroth 1952: 31).

While the systemic, or imperialist, attitude to nature has been the dominant one throughout Swedish history, there has also been a minority position, an alternative attitude to nature, that can be found in Sweden as well as in the other Nordic countries of Iceland, Denmark, Finland, and Norway, and extending on into Russia and Alaska. Reaching back to the pagan, pre-Christian past, a kind of animism, or naturalist belief system, has been kept alive among poets and artists through the centuries, as well as in some of the customs and rituals of the popular culture. It has often stood for an emotional identification with non-human nature, leading to a primitivism or spiritualism in which nature is not so much exploited or even understood so much as listened to and lived with in a state of mutual respect and non-verbal communication (Haila 1999).

In the twentieth century we can see the tradition being mobilized in the films of Ingmar Bergman and the nature poetry of Harry Martinson, as well as in the "deep ecology" of Arne Næss and Georg Henrik von Wright's philosophical critique of modernism. And we can also hear it in the recent wave of electrified folk music that has attracted a good deal of international attention. It has provided environmentalism with a radical, often extremist, component that continues to characterize at least some activism in Finland, as well as in Sweden. In both countries there has been a remarkable rise in "animal liberation" protests, particularly among young people, that is much more prominent than in most other European countries (see Konttinen *et al.*, 1999).

The systemic, ordering, bias, or mentality, was perhaps encouraged by the geography, but already in the seventeenth century the copper and iron mines of northern Sweden gave early impetus to the consolidation of particular national scientific–technical interests in mechanics, chemistry, and metallurgy. And it was the further development and "technification" of those interests that would play a major role in the country's industrialization process. In Sweden a number of large engineering firms emerged in the 1870s, and industrialization was largely based on the handful of companies that grew up at that time – Ericsson, ASEA, Alfa-Laval, Nobel, Bofors – all big, export-oriented firms that drew on the Swedish mechanical and chemical heritage, and which derived their strength from a basic engineering competence. These by-now transnational corporations in the twentieth century came to include the automotive manufacturers, SAAB and Volvo, and they have exercised both a doctrinal and functional hegemony over Swedish research and development that is central to the "national system of innovation" (Edquist and Lundvall 1993).

The general public has historically been poorly represented in this Swedish national political culture. In the nineteenth century, as elsewhere in Europe, popular movements emerged among the farmers and members of the industrial working class, but in Sweden these movements rather quickly became institutionalized in the form of political parties: the Center party represented the farmers and the social democratic party represented the industrial workers. It has been primarily through the formalized parliamentary system that Swedish democracy has offered opportunities for public participation in policy-making. The Swedish legal framework has ensured public access to nature, and, for that matter, to the state bureaucracy, both as a way of guaranteeing public acceptance and support and as a means of legitimizing a strong state role in economic affairs. The ombudsman, serving to mediate between the state and the public, is a uniquely Swedish institution, as is the tradition of *allemansrätt*, the officially sanctioned free access to nature that dates back to the early modern era. The notion of the "people's home" that was adopted as a kind of slogan by the social democratic prime minister Per Albin Hansson in the

1930s similarly rests on a long-continued pattern of self-conscious paternalism in the state's dealings with the citizenry (Elzinga *et al.* 1998). The state bureaucracy in Sweden has sought to serve as the public's protector, first against the landed aristocracy and in the twentieth century against the modern version of the aristocracy, the large corporate industrial firms.

The cultural legacy is quite different in Denmark. To begin with we find that the image of the workshop is a recurrent theme in the national attitude to nature. The natural environment was to be worked with pragmatically, not through theory or systemic distancing, but by a kind of organic interaction, or experimentation. Already in the Middle Ages there was a noticeably practical bent among Danish philosophers and with it an identification with an organic, experimental relation to nature (Jamison 1982: 197ff). A good example is Tycho Brahe who, almost alone among the great men in the history of science, gained his reputation for practical work, for instrument-building and precise observations, rather than for theorizing. Again, in the nineteenth century the fame of Hans Christian Ørsted rested on a practical discovery (of electromagnetism) rather than on a theory. Ørsted was an impassioned believer in the practical value of understanding nature's secrets; almost uniquely in the Europe of his time he combined a romantic nature philosophy with a technically oriented utilitarianism. He wrote about the spirit in nature and gave lectures to industrialists about the importance of science.

Other particularly influential components of the Danish national identity are the People's High Schools that were developed in the nineteenth century and then spread to the other Scandinavian countries, as well as to the United States at the Highlander School in Tennessee, which has played significant roles in both the Civil Rights Movement and the new social movements of feminism and environmentalism (see Eyerman and Jamison 1998). The schools not only came to represent a unique expression of the national character of the Danish people but also helped to mobilize the rural population to take part in the industrialization process. So, too, the system of technical consultancy that was so important in the development of the dairy and food-processing industries can be said to be derived from a rural populism that was articulated by Grundtvig and others in the nineteenth century (Edquist and Lundvall 1993).

It is also worth noting that Denmark was one of the few countries in Europe to accomplish a peaceful transition to the parliamentary system. The mobilization of farmers by the Liberal Party (*Venstre*) in the late nineteenth century created a viable opposition to the political dominance of the landowners' Right Party (*Højre*), which increasingly came to represent the new class of industrialists based in Copenhagen. The strength of the liberals and, during the early part of the twentieth century, of the

Social Democrats led to a distinct tradition of the delegation of administrative tasks to regional or local government. Combined with the cooperative movement that relied on local entrepreneurship and educational institutions such as the People's High Schools, which aimed to provide both training in practical skills for young people in the countryside and to offer opportunities to participate in political decision-making, the Danish style of decentralized administration has helped to shape a "populist" political tradition that has been extremely important in recent decades, perhaps especially in regard to environmental issues.

It may be useful to say something about the American discursive framework and attitudes to nature. The nation developed by taming its vast natural expanses, conquering a rough nature through ingenuity, technology, and hard work. But the experience of conquest and domination gave rise to two rather different conceptions of nature, one which might be called "romantic" and the other which might be called "utilitarian." Where the first tended to respect nature, at times even to glorify the beauty and tranquility of certain natural areas, the other saw nature as a kind of enemy for human development, a foe to be outwitted and exploited for economic benefit (Worster 1993).

Both images helped to give nature a place in the national identity, and protection of nature an importance in the industrialization process. But they provided those who would protect nature with rather different kinds of argument to justify their activities (see Fox 1985). The romantic, or pastoral, image led to ideas of tending and cultivating the natural environment, and eventually to living in "harmony with nature" and preserving parts of nature from further human encroachment. The pragmatic, or frontier, image on the other hand came to justify exploitation, even domination, of nature, setting the rugged individualist, first the woodsman and then the inventor and entrepreneur, the task of taming a wild, belligerent natural landscape.

In time utilitarian exploitation turned into efficient management, but the underlying image remained largely the same, as the ending of the first phase of exploitation of the frontier led to the identification of what Vannevar Bush, in 1945, called the "endless frontier" of science and technology (Jamison and Eyerman 1994). The images have coexisted uneasily throughout American history, sometimes contending with each other for the allegiance of scientists and other intellectuals, at others combining in new constructive syntheses. In the battle between the images we can see the roots of the conflict between culture and civilization and, even more perhaps, a tension between a puritan "work ethic" and community spirit and sense of limits, on the one hand, and a militaristic ethos of growth and expansion on the other.

At the turn of the century, in the so-called progressive era when Theodore Roosevelt was president, conservation became institutionalized in federal agencies for national parks, fisheries, wilderness, etc. and conservation itself came to be justified on pragmatic grounds. Preserving natural resources became a part of the progressive era's "gospel of efficiency" but, by the 1920s, short-term gain and exploitation had once again come to characterize the dominant American attitude to nature (Hays 1959).

The 1930s were a period of active reform and marked something of a return to the earlier progressive principles. Among the activities of the so-called New Deal era some of the most lasting were the efforts made to preserve nature. The area set aside for national parks was substantially increased, and access to the parks was considerably improved. There was also a growth of membership in hunting and fishing organizations, and for many members of the National Wildlife Federation – which is still today the largest environmental organization in America – there emerged a concern with rational "game management" (Gottlieb 1993).

It should not be surprising that the science of ecology found fertile soil for its cognitive growth in the United States. In the 1930s, ecological approaches came to be quite popular among both biologists and other natural scientists, but also, as we have seen, among social scientists. The notions of regionalism, an important part of rural reconstruction schemes, and urbanization, a central aspect of social planning doctrines, as well as the managerial conservationism that was fostered by governmental programs, were all based on ecological ideas.

It was a different ecology from the one that emerged in the 1960s, however. In the 1930s nature was still something "out there," separate from society, and, as such, it was primarily to be managed and controled. The huge hydroelectric dams on the Columbia River that Woody Guthrie was asked to write songs about served as the symbol for a progressive use of nature's bounty, and the Tennessee Valley Authority, with its community control of resources, became a model of ecological engineering. Natural beauty could inspire the poet or the artist but in the 1930s, had little political impact. In keeping with the pragmatic orientation of American history nature was something to be used by man for his pleasure, benefit, and wealth. It was only when that ambition proved to have such disastrous consequences and implications – first with the atomic bomb and then with the suburbanization of postwar America – that a new way of thinking, a new environmental consciousness, emerged.

That consciousness, as it spread around the world, interacted with other discursive frameworks and broader mentalities. In a country like India, as we have seen, the influence from indigenous religious and philosophical traditions has been especially important. Vandana Shiva, for example, has continually emphasized in her writings how "feminine principles" are central to Indian attitudes to nature. In her words, "Contemporary Western views of nature are fraught with the dichotomy or duality between man and woman, and person and nature ... In Indian cosmology, by contrast, person and nature are a duality in unity" (Shiva 1988: 40). For Shiva, a compassionate or caring attitude to nature is part of an Indian identity, which is perhaps one of the resaons why Indian environmentalists have played such a central role in international environmental politics.

Following on from the ideas promoted by Gandhi and Tagore in the interwar years, Indian environmentalists have come to articulate an alternative belief system to dominant Western attitudes that has proved attractive and relevant for many non-Indians. Throughout Indian environmental politics the Gandhian emphasis on non-violence and on moral protest – as well as the interest in craftsmanship and traditional skills and knowledges, epitomized by Gandhi's own personal simplicity in his mannerisms and way of life – have been particularly influential (Elzinga and Jamison 1986). Gandhi's practice has served as a frame of reference for almost all Indian environmentalists and, in its international influence, indicates how particular national discursive frameworks need not degenerate into "nationalisms."

However, in the 1990s the influence of Gandhi's non-violent and secular "discourse" over Indian society has weakened considerably (Akula 1995). As religious fundamentalism has flourished, and a neo-liberal economic policy has been promulgated at the national level, the Gandhian discursive framework has been challenged by both explicitly ethnic traditionalisms as well as by a global cosmopolitanism. Where the one has pulled environmentalism into a locally based populism, the other has countered the environmental message with a new kind of economic development discourse. For both the populists and the cosmopolitans, the Gandhian discourse, and such movements as the Chipko tree-huggers, who won such international renown in the the 1980s, are seen as less relevant and less exemplary at the present time (Rangan 1996; Gooch 1998).

Movement legacies

A third set of conditioning factors to consider are the more recent experiences in relation to how environmental movements have developed. Again, let me illustrate what I have in mind by referring to Sweden, Denmark, and the United States, since they provide a useful and varied range of experiences – and, for personal reasons, I have some first-hand knowledge. In Sweden, the environmental movement has primarily been a reactive force. Swedish political culture, with its strong state and bureaucratic institutions, has left a strong imprint on the way in which environmentalism has developed. In particular, the hegemony of the Swedish Social Democratic party has been decisive. Although environmentalism has been a very important political force in Sweden, the comparatively early incorporation of an environmental consciousness into the established political culture has made it difficult for an autonomous environmental movement to develop (Jamison *et al.* 1990: 13ff).

During the 1970s the environmental debate in Sweden was dominated by the issue of nuclear energy, and the transformation of the environmental movement into an anti-nuclear opposition was, in what might be termed typical Swedish fashion, largely taken over by established political actors. Nowhere else in Europe was anti-nuclear sentiment so deeply "parliamentarized" as it was in Sweden. In particular, the Centre Party's identification with an environmental and anti-nuclear position meant that anti-nuclear protest in Sweden, almost from its beginning, was a parliamentary affair. The environmental movement, as a result of internal splits and external pressures, fragmented during this period of anti-nuclear opposition. In the 1980s, as in other countries, a new cluster of transnational non-governmental organizations – from Greenpeace to the World Wildlife Fund – came on the scene, and there emerged a parliamentary Green Party that now provides crucial support for the ruling minority Social-Democratic government. Most significant, however, was the renovation of the older conservation society, the Swedish Society for Nature Protection, which has become a key actor in many of the programs of sustainable development and ecological modernization. In recent years, the society's expert staff has played a central role in a number of new activities, from eco-labeling to sustainable transport policy-making. In relation to local Agenda 21 activities, the society has served as a national coordinating body, filling in when decreased funding has kept the state Environmental Protection Agency from playing an active role (Andringa *et al.* 1998).

In Denmark the environmental movement has been much more characterized by local experiments, and a booming wind-energy industry is one of the most visible results (Jamison *et al.* 1990: 66ff). Environmental issues lay dormant in Denmark for much longer than in Sweden, and became more directly associated with the alternative political ideologies that grew out of the youth rebellion and the student movement of the late 1960s. The most important organization in this connection was NOAH, started in 1969 by biology and architecture students in Copenhagen, which soon developed into a national organization of environmental activism. NOAH utilized scientific information and cooperated with scientists who served as "counter-experts," particularly in relation to the media. In this way, the first efforts at creating public awareness of environmental problems in Denmark were carried out by an alliance between students and the media that was highly critical of the "establishment."

The activist approach of NOAH drew on the Danish tradition of participatory democracy associated with the cooperative movement and the People's High Schools and, more generally, on the populist political tradition of the nineteenth century. The social movements like NOAH that emerged in the 1960s contributed to a new civic policy culture for environmental science and technology that was to grow stronger over the following decades. In Denmark the public debate on environmental issues was not so easy to incorporate as in Sweden. And, in contrast to other countries, the "grass roots" dimension became more important as environmentalists took part in the struggle against nuclear energy and the search for alternative means of energy supply. The opposition to nuclear energy was coordinated by an independent Organization for Information about Nuclear Power (OOA), which so effectively mobilized public resistance and pressure that the Danish government abandoned its nuclear plans in the late 1970s. In addition, the popular debate on alternative energy sources and various public awareness and information campaigns encouraged movement organizations to foster local practical initiatives that gradually became incorporated into Denmark's environmental policy.

In the United States the environmental movement of the 1970s rather quickly divided into what have come to be called the "mainstream" organizations that have become highly professionalized, and various voluntary local groups and networks that have tended to develop around particular issues, from nuclear energy to toxic waste, from climate change and biodiversity to animal rights (Dowie 1996). Where the romantic, or arcadian, tradition received a new lease on life with the counter-culture of the 1960s and then with the emergence of "new age" politics and the widespread movement "back to the country," the managerial, or imperialist, tradition has come to play a significant role in public policy-making and, perhaps especially, in the making of green business.

The mainstream organizations have become active both in programs of sustainable development and in new-issue areas like biotechnology and climate change. Also influential in the United States has been the role of "movement intellectuals," or experts, like Barry Commoner, Amory Lovins, and John and Nancy Jack Todd, who have established alternative research centers and contributed to the innovation of many environmentally friendly techniques and scientific-technical concepts (e.g. Commoner 1971; Todd 1977; Lovins 1977). Thus the environmental movement in the United States has been highly diverse, with much less common ground among local protesters, professional experts, and mainstream organizations than in many European countries. Also in the United States the commercialization of environmental politics has been particularly intense, with the Reagan administration representing a veritable "counter-revolution" in relation to a great many of the achievements of the 1970s. The need for an active private-sector involvement thus became particularly crucial for the environmental movement of the 1980s, as government support to local initiatives turned into a highly visible "backlash" (Rowell 1996).

In the United States of recent years the emergence of a vocal anti-environmental movement is very noticeable (see Luke 2000). For many right-wing populists environmentalism has come to be a part of a global conspiracy of free-traders and internationalists, and the defense of the exploitation of nature has been coupled to the defense of personal freedom. And there has been a pronounced influence of such viewpoints on the role that Americans have played in the new kinds of transnational environmentalism. Local communities in the United States have done much less than many of their European counterparts to implement Agenda 21, for example (Lake 2000). American officials have been unwilling to enter into international agreements that would affect the possibilities for American business firms to operate in the global marketplace (see French 2000).

Sweden in the 1990s

The transformation of environmentalism from a loosely organized activist movement in the 1970s to an ever more differentiated array of "non-governmental organizations" in the 1990s has taken place in every country of the world. But obviously the role that environmental organizations and other social actors have played in the quest for sustainable development has differed dramatically from country to country. In Sweden there has emerged a new rhetoric of "environmental adaptation" and an ideological effort by the ruling social democratic government to create a "green" welfare state (Hermele 2000; Lidskog and Elander 2000). At the same time, however, the main responsibility for environmental research and development has shifted over the past ten years from the public to the private sector. Although Swedish industry was comparatively late to take up the new ideas about pollution prevention and cleaner technology that have been widely propagated in other European countries, much of the Swedish approach to sustainable development has been devoted to environmental improvements in industry. In 1993, a new Foundation for Strategic Environmental Research (in Swedish: *Stiftelsen för strategisk miljöforskning*, or MISTRA) was created to support large-scale projects involving collaboration between universities and industry in the area of sustainable development.

At the same time, several other foundations were established with money taken by the then conservative government from the controversial wage-earner funds, which the Social Democrats had created in the 1980s. These foundations are charged with funding strategic industrial research and technological competence-building and are run as private foundations, with decisions taken primarily by representatives of industrial firms and engineering or technological sciences. One small foundation supports the International Institute for Industrial Environmental Economics at the Technical University in Lund. And at other technical universities and business schools a number of projects and courses are being instituted in environmental management and economics, many with the support of the new foundations. At both the Chalmers Institute of Technology in Gothenburg and the Royal Institute of Technology in Stockholm there are courses and research programs in environmental management, as well as at a number of the newer regional colleges that have been established. At the latter, efforts in environmental technology and management are often carried out in collaboration with local industry, and tend to have a highly practical orientation.

Compared with many other European countries, however, these initiatives have come relatively late, and have had trouble integrating with established disciplines and institutions. The example of the institute in Lund, which lies outside of the traditional disciplinary structure and has its own outside funding, is typical of the Swedish transformation process. For, at the same time as there are new initiatives of "green business," environmental policy continues to be filtered through the Environmental Protection Agency (EPA) and the other sectorial bodies – energy, transportation, waste treatment, occupational health, regional planning, construction, and so on – that were created in the 1970s. As things stand now, the environmental science and technology "system" is certainly growing, but it still has relatively little impact on the main priorities of Swedish science and technology development, which, as in most other countries, are focused on the so-called advanced or "high" technologies: information technology, biotechnology, industrial materials. Meanwhile, conservative politicians and economists have compared the ideas of a green welfare state to the social engineering that was so prominent in the 1940s and 1950s, when suburbs and the modern infrastructure were established in Sweden by means of strong centralized planning that has since gone out of fashion. That kind of planning, it is argued, can no longer function in a society that is so strongly integrated into the international market.

The government has not managed to convince Swedish industry with its proposals to rebuild Sweden.While the issue of nuclear energy probably contributed to the lack of consensus about sustainable development, different opinions about economic policy seem to underlie the conflict between government and industry. According to critics, the Social Democratic policy – with large-scale state measures and an expansive short-term employment policy – lacks a comprehensive long-term strategy, and is simply a return to the good old days of the Swedish model, when the state supported large infrastructural projects of "social engineering" in construction, housing, transportation, and energy. The argument is that such approaches are no longer relevant, and that the new plans will not be successfully implemented (Berggren 1997).

In many respects, the efforts to propel Sweden into more sustainable directions have been constrained by the legacy of the past (Lundqvist 1996). The first wave of environmental science and technology policy brought into being a system of "end-of-pipe" competence, that is, an addition to normal operations, integrated into Swedish industry that has tended to dominate both the theory and practice of environmental engineering ever since. The specialized competences of environmental control and waste treatment have been difficult to transform into a more general expertise in pollution prevention, cleaner technologies, or sustainable development. The fragmented orientation of Swedish (environmental) science and technology policy has meant that environmental issues have had difficulty leaving their sectorial isolation and entering into broader discourses about industrial and economic development. But, of course, the problem also has to do with the structure and emphases of Swedish industry. The large corporations that were built up in the late nineteenth century were based, to a large extent, on the exploitation of natural resources in the mines and the forests, and environmental consequences and impacts were evaluated accordingly. It has proved difficult to restructure Swedish industry and to incorporate an environmental concern into the characteristic forms of economic activity. But, after some delay, there are nonetheless indications that the systematic Swedes are beginning to consider a broader environmentally oriented transformation process. In late 1998 a new Social Democratic government, governing with the support of the Green Party, formulated the notion of a "Green People's Home," mobilizing the rhetoric that had been so much a part of the earlier Swedish model (Elzinga *et al.* 1998).

A Danish model?

Denmark seems to have had greater success than Sweden or many other European countries with introducing cleaner production processes and environmental management systems into industry. For Denmark the problem has been to bring an environmental consciousness to the important agro-industrial corporations, and, even more seriously, to the rural population that, as in other parts of Europe, has come to be affected by an influential populist reaction. Denmark has had a gradual and deepseated realization that "end-of-pipe" solutions are not sufficient and new approaches that stress a change in productive technology are called for.

Given the perceived limitations of supply of energy sources – further reinforced by the decision to abandon nuclear power as a result of the intense public debate of the 1970s – the Danish government has emphasized the transition to renewable energy sources. On the one hand this led to the establishment and rapid growth of the Danish wind-turbine industry and, on the other hand, to a diversified regulatory framework in the energy sector to encourage energy-efficient technologies. The attention gradually shifted towards identification of solutions that could be integrated earlier on in the cycles of production and consumption. The relative effectiveness of economic incentives in improving the technological and organizational capacity for saving energy has inspired similar initiatives in the environmental field: a move from end-of-pipe solutions to a model that emphasizes preventive solutions including the development and diffusion of cleaner technology. Beginning in 1986, the Danish government has launched a series of major support programs in cleaner technology. Compared to most other European countries, the Danish efforts have been substantial, and have spread the various preventive technical approaches to environmental problems throughout Danish industry (Remmen 1995).

In the first phase, from 1986 to 1989, the effort was concentrated primarily on investigating the potential for cleaner technologies in different branches of the economy, and in conducting demonstration projects in particular firms. The general approach followed similar "national programs" in technology development that had taken place in the 1980s in relation to information technology and biotechnology and that were based on the long-standing Danish emphasis on demonstration projects in technology policy. The second phase of the cleaner technology program, from 1990 to 1992, involved a more active broadening of focus, as well as increased competence-building and information dissemination. Courses were held at engineering colleges and associations, handbooks were written, and special consulting schemes in cleaner technology were established in four particular areas: furniture-making, meat-processing, fish production, and metal-working. At the same time environmental management systems were instituted in a number of small and medium-sized companies with governmental support, and major efforts were made to document experiences with cleaner technology by means of a number of technology assessment projects at the technological universities. From 1993 onwards the efforts have expanded as the environmental administration has adopted a more flexible, interactive, approach, seeking to pass responsibility and policy initiative from the public to the private sector (Remmen 1998).

The new attempts to alleviate the problems of environmental degradation are, to a significant extent, based on a dialog between public and private interests that has characterized Danish approaches from the beginning, and a new ideology of commercialization and the use of market forces in regulation (Andersen 1994). In the political atmosphere that prevailed in Denmark during the 1980s, when the government was usually based on a combination of parties from the center to the right of the political spectrum under the leadership of the Conservative Party, there was a strong leaning towards liberal economic policies and indirect instruments of regulation, that is, small government. Even in areas where the government was unable to secure a majority of votes in the Parliament for its policies – as the case was for much of the environmental legislation which was dominated by the so-called "green majority" (social liberals, social democrats, and two left-wing parties) – the subsequent implementation of policies tended to be framed in the manner of indirect regulation.

The actual administration of policies that related to environmental science and technology was typical of an economic policy culture and paid more attention to ensuring the cooperation or even the promotion of business interests, for instance in connection with the growth of the environmental consulting engineering firms and the establishment of a competitive industry for the production and exports of wind turbines. In fact the case of the wind-turbine industry in Denmark illustrates the extent to which a combination of innovative policies, local industrial entrepreneurship, and a set of priorities evolving from the political pressure of public debate can contribute to the shaping of new technologies (Jørgensen and Karnoe 1995).

This shift in awareness and attention to a wider economic perspective was reinforced by the initiatives which sought to integrate technology assessment more directly into policy-making procedures. In many ways a particular Danish style of technology assessment found its application in the policy debates related to areas such as biotechnology and cleaner technology (Jamison and Baark 1990).

One of the most important aspects of Danish environmental science and technology policy in the 1990s has been the effort to move beyond the sectorial perception of environmental problems to ensure that areas such as energy, transport, agriculture, and industry would integrate environmental concerns into their activities. The actual policy-making and administration is still split up according to the sectorial responsibilities of ministries, but the Ministry of the Environment and Energy is attempting to provide overall coordination of the activities in each sector. However, a problem is that influential agricultural and agro-industrial interests still remain outside of the emerging consensus.

The process of policy integration and cooperation among major actors is particularly evident in efforts to promote cleaner technology. On the one hand the government initiated a program of support for cleaner technologies in an attempt to reduce the costs of compliance with existing emission standards and to achieve future standards for emission of heavy metals, for example. On the other the EPA has become increasingly forthcoming in entering into active dialogs with individual firms to find solutions to their problems. In many cases the new approach to interaction between business and public authorities has also been associated with the methodology of Life Cycle Assessment (LCA) or "cradle-to-grave" analysis for products. In the case of LCA, for instance, business firms have sought to develop a better environmental image for their products by examining the "environmental load" of each of the components that enters into the production process; frequently they have discovered that there were substantial cost savings associated with "greener" production methods and naturally this has created a substantial amount of goodwill among business interests. The problem for Denmark, however, is that the world outside remains stubbornly anti-ecological and in order to compete in an international marketplace Danish companies cannot move too quickly. There is thus, particularly in agriculture and the food processing industries, a resistance to many of the new ideas and programs that might grow more serious in coming years. A populist anti-Europeanism, which is a strong political force in Denmark, is not particularly interested in ecological transformations if they are to challenge traditional values and interests.

In the 1990s Denmark became one of the most active countries in Europe in pursuing the new ideas of pollution prevention and cleaner production. Indeed, the environmental minister Svend Auken proposed on a number of occasions that Denmark should seek to provide an exemplary model for other countries to follow. As in the nineteenth century

when traditions of popular participation were mobilized in the industrialization process, and in the twentieth during the Second World War,
when resistance to the Nazis drew on national cultural traditions, Auken
has argued that the strength of both Danish democratic institutions and
not least grass-roots movements is an important factor in explaining the
relative success of Danish environmental policy (Miljø-og energi minis-
teriet 1995).

However, it is somewhat premature to view Denmark as a model of ecological modernization or of a new economically oriented environmental
policy. While there can be no denying that the Danish environmental
movement struck especially deep chords within society in the 1970s, and
played an important role in preventing parliament from approving the
development of nuclear energy, it can be questioned how deeply the new
ideas of sustainable development have actually ingrained themselves in
the Danish political culture. In 1998 a political scientist mounted a widely
reported media attack on environmentalism, and many of the ecological
modernizers were thrown on the defensive (Lomborg 1998). And there
is a strong agricultural industry and a highway lobby, both of which are
rooted in the rural districts, that has little interest in Denmark becoming a green idyll. As elsewhere, ecological transformations are filled with
contradictions, but there is no question that Denmark has played a pioneering role in many areas, from energy to agriculture, and it might
be valuable for those experiences to be given more attention by other
countries in the years to come.

American shades of green

When we turn our attention to the United States we see much more clearly
than in any other part of the world a commercial environmentalism that is
slowly but surely winning terrain and influencing people. With the end of
the Reagan–Bush era environmentalism received a new lease on life and
during the Clinton–Gore administration a number of important changes
took place in American environmental politics.

The rhetoric changed dramatically as "green speak," and an interest
in sustainable development and environmental technological innovation,
entered the federal government. The vice-president was a prominent
environmentalist and his *Earth in the Balance* was one of several programmatic books to signal the coming of a new global environmental
agenda. In the 1990s there have been a number of important efforts in
energy, transportation, pollution-prevention, and, not least, in environmental management and "eco-efficiency" that to a certain extent represent a "greening" of industry and technology (Commoner 1991; Hawken
et al. 1999). These efforts have of course been dominated by private

corporations, pursuing the so-called "win-win" strategies of trying to turn a healthy profit while also contributing to sustainable development. There has also been an organized opposition, a green backlash, particularly in the older industrial branches.

Perhaps even more importantly new forms of local politics and community empowerment have developed in the name of sustainable development and environmental justice (Harvey 1996; Gould et al. 1996). A number of projects in devastated urban areas, hit hard by the effects of globalization and the transfer of many traditional kinds of industrial production from the United States to Asia and Latin America, have made use of environmental issues to mobilize resources, human, financial, and material, for environmental improvements. These projects of "civic environmentalism," as they have been called, are still quite limited and, as we shall see in chapter 6, many of them are temporary and poorly funded (Shutkin 2000). But they are a significant part of what has been termed "fourth-wave" environmentalism, a new era of locally based activity that is highly diversified but has nonetheless been growing during the 1990s encouraged, no doubt, by the sympathy of the federal government and the support of many state and local authorities (Dowie 1996).

Intriguingly, we may see in the United States as well as in Sweden and Denmark the mobilization of national cultural traditions in the making of different national shades of green. In Sweden there is the ambition to become once again a "model" for others to follow, a great power. In Denmark, the populist heritage is being revived as the country's own room for maneuver is constrained by the project of European integration.

In the United States the historical battle between the exploiters and the preservers is being reenacted in the world of environmental politics. In the nineteenth century populism developed as an indigenous movement of opposition to the "frontier capitalism" that spread across the continent. It drew on "old-time religion" but also on certain republican values that had characterized the revolutionary legacy (Lasch 1991; Kazin 1995). The capitalists, however, also had "God on their side" as they built the railways, the highways and automobiles and airplanes and factories, and eventually colonized space with their machines and powerful science-based instruments.

What is striking about the new environmental politics is that the emerging ecological culture is seeking to mobilize both traditions. On the one hand there is an effort to make capitalism more ecological, or natural, as former activists advise corporations on how best to clean their production processes and manufacture greener products (Frankel 1998; Hawken et al. 1999). On the other, local activists are reinventing populism as they mobilize their lay knowledge and experiences to oppose the further con-tamination of their communities (Edelstein 1988; Szasz 1994). Whether the capitalism can become "natural" and whether the communities can become less contaminated will depend on the ways in which the different sides interact with one another. The battles of Seattle and Washington in 1999 and 2000 point to deep contradictions in the American, and, for that matter, the global quest for sustainable development. In what follows I look more closely at some of the underlying tensions on both sides of the "dialectics of environmentalism."

NOTE

This chapter draws on material previously published in Jamison and Baark 1999 as well as earlier comparisons of Sweden and Denmark in Jamison 1982 and Jamison *et al.* 1990.

1 The academic interest in culture ranges from the conservative ideas of Samuel Huntington, who sees cultural differences causing what he has termed the "clash of civilizations," to the radical views of people like Edward Said, who argues that cultural representations are crucial ingredients in the imperialisms of both the past and present. For a wide range of reflections and perspectives on culture in relation to globalization, see Jameson and Miyoshi 1999.

5   The challenge of green business

Imagine a world that gets progressively cleaner...
Vivendi advertisement (1999)

... the fundamental assumption [is] that economic growth and the resolution of ecological problems can, in principle, be reconciled ... ecological modernization suggests that the recognition of the ecological crisis actually constitutes a challenge for business. Not only does it open up new markets and create new demands; if executed well, it would stimulate innovation in methods of production and transport, industrial organization, consumer goods...
Maarten Hajer, The Politics of Environmental Discourse (1995: 26, 32–3)

From opposition to coop(era)tion

As I suggested in chapter 1, it is possible to place the different strategies, or approaches, in the world of environmental politics along a continuum between two poles, or opposing "cultural formations". On the one hand there is the dominant formation of green business, or commerce, which seeks to divert environmentalism into profit-making directions, integrating the quest for sustainable development into processes of global corporate expansion. On the other hand there are the various "residual formations" of *ecological resistance*, or critical ecology, which tend to draw environmental struggles into all sorts of political and social campaigns: for justice and equity, community and consumer empowerment, as well as for cultural survival and local resistance to the various effects and repercussions of globalization. In this and the following chapter I explore the relations between the emerging ecological culture and these two contemporary poles of environmental politics by means of illustrative examples. I begin by examining the challenge of green commerce and in chapter 6 I look at some of what I term the dilemmas of activism in the world of ecological resistance, or critical ecology.

The oppositional stance that tended to dominate the political discourse of environmentalism in the late 1960s and early 1970s has come to be

supplemented in the 1990s by what has been termed the discourse of ecological modernization (Hajer 1995; Mol and Sonnenfeld 2000). Whether
we see it as cooperation or cooption, as seeking greater influence or simply
selling out, there can be little denying the fact that much of what was once
a movement composed primarily of voluntary activists has gone to market. During the past fifteen years environmentalism – or a large number
of people who are involved in environmental politics – has come in from
the cold, and many are the efforts to redefine environmental politics as a
"positive-sum game" in which economic growth can be combined with,
or even reinvigorated by means of, environmental improvements. Business leaders who banded together after the Exxon Valdez disaster in 1989
to form a World Business Council for Sustainable Development identify
"eco-efficiency" as a new driving force for industrial progress (DeSimone
and Popoff 2000). Former activists such as Amory and Hunter Lovins
and Paul Hawken speak of a new age of "natural capitalism" in which economic activity can be adapted to ecological laws and principles (Hawken
et al. 1999). And on our television screens we are treated to advertisements in which leading oil and automotive companies, previously openly
antagonistic to environmental measures, proclaim their change of heart
and tell us, among other things, how they have recruited environmentalists to help them save the earth.[1]

   While there can be no doubt that many corporate officials and business
leaders have come to acknowledge the need to pay more regard to the
environment, many of the actual practices of the companies they run
and/or represent all too often continue to follow "business as usual."
The precepts of deregulation and privatization that were put firmly on
the policy agenda in the 1980s have tended to infect many ecological
transformation processes with what might be called a commercial virus.
It is not that the companies are doing nothing, for many are indeed doing
a great deal; it is rather that the quest for sustainable development is being
reduced or limited to those activities that can turn a profit. All too many
efforts, whether it is appropriate or not, are determined by relations of
competition and marketability.

   The institutional mechanisms by which programs are selected and corporate strategies are designed tend to combine environmental objectives
and economic objectives without taking care to distinguish among the
very different criteria of evaluation and means of implementation that
come into play (Hukkinen 1999). Of course, in some companies, the for-
tuity of circumstance can make an environmental project also a money-
earner. But after more than a decade of chanting the mantra of ecological
modernization – "pollution prevention pays" – there is little evidence that
environmental improvements *in general* are good for business. There are

simply too many other factors at work; and in recent years there have also developed a number of other commercial options in information technology and genetic technology that have drawn capital, as well as ingenuity and creativity, away from the green marketplace. And there are always competitors who remain obstinately anti-ecological.

At the same time the underlying instrumental mindset – and with it the belief in what the Finnish philosopher Georg Henrik von Wright has called the "myth of progress" – has not been sufficiently modified by those who propound the virtues of eco-efficiency and natural capitalism to take into account less acquisitive values that the ecological culture envisions and represents (von Wright 1993). Under the assumption that "you can have your cake and eat it, too" environmental concern is instead being reinvented as a kind of enlightened consumer behavior. An inherently collective vision of solidarity with non-human nature – a "partnership ethics" – has, like so much else in our societies, been turned into a pursuit of market shares and economic gain (Merchant 1999). However, self-interest works both ways, as the protests by farmers and truck-drivers against environmentally motivated tax increases on diesel fuel that took place across Europe in the summer of 2000 so visibly demonstrated. There is no indication that consumers in general are willing to pay more for environmentally friendly products, nor is there any evidence that green products can be as cheap to produce as the products that propelled the environmental movement in the first place. What is economically beneficial for some tends to be costly for others, which is why cultural transformation – an underlying change in beliefs and values and knowledge – is such an important part of any meaningful environmental politics. In order to change behavior people need a reason to believe and, even more crucially, they need a motive that is relevant for them. And we should remember that however valuable specific technical and managerial improvements might be for an individual branch or company, what is done by any one firm tends to be cancelled out by the continuing expansion of production as a whole (Pellow *et al.* 2000).

Take the efforts to control the automobile, for example. In the 1960s the automobile was shown to be "unsafe at any speed," as Ralph Nader put it, as well as being the major cause of air pollution (Nader 1966). A broad public debate ensued and a number of alternatives were proposed and tested, ranging from non-polluting automobile engines to new-fangled safety devices and imaginative forms of public transit. At the first Earth Day in 1970, when the ecological culture began to manifest itself, a few cars were buried as a way to symbolize the message of the movement. The car was not merely to be improved or made "environmentally friendly"; the task was to do away with it altogether. As one "radical technologist"

put it in the mid-1970s:

the accent must be far more on *reducing* the amount of travel than on looking for the technological 'fix'. The crucial changes must be *social* rather than techno-logical. We shall have to live closer to our work and shop locally, buying locally grown food and locally made goods consisting far more of local materials . . . In short, the key to alternative transport lies in the alternative *to* transport. (Rivers 1976: 227).

Soon, however, not one but several "technical fixes" had been developed – the catalytic muffler as a filtering device for automotive air pollution, airbags and better seatbelts to improve the chances of surviving crashes, unleaded and more energy-efficient fuels, as well as electronic instruments of production and distribution – that more or less ended the debate until the late 1980s, when it reemerged in relation to the new discourse of sustainable development. As part of the new doctrine trans-portation was also to become environmentally friendly and many were the plans in the late 1980s and early 1990s to reorganize transportation systems along more sustainable lines. The auto companies, as Mitsubishi put it in a widely disseminated advertisement, refocused their research and development efforts with only one ambition in mind: to "save the earth." Environmental think-tanks, such as the World Resources Insti-tute, set out to count the "real" costs of transportation. Amory Lovins, who had been actively involved in the energy debates of the 1970s, de-veloped the notion of the "hypercar" to show how new production meth-ods and management techniques could allow companies to make cars that were cleaner and less damaging to the environment. The Business Council for Sustainable Development, the World Bank, and many other governmental and intergovernmental bodies, set up committees and re-search programs to develop criteria for sustainable transportation. And even Greenpeace announced plans to develop a green car (Jamison 1995).

Again, however, business interests have gone on the offensive and be-come dominant, largely turning the quest for sustainable development into the acquisition of market niches. The automobile manufacturers have developed electric cars for some, "cleaner and leaner" production pro-cesses for others, and moved much of their marketing effort to the rapidly "modernizing" developing countries, where there is less of a public debate to respond to. But while the technical fixes have been coming fast and furious, there has been relatively little attention paid to how all the new technologies can be used most appropriately. As Amory Lovins and his co-authors put it, "the car is being reinvented faster than the implications of its reconception are being rethought" (Hawken *et al.* 1999: 47). The fact that green cars, or hypercars, do little if anything to improve the environmental and social costs of automotive transportation without a fundamental change in thinking about mobility is obvious; and yet it is against their interests for car-makers to challenge the ruling value system with its belief in progress and, more specifically, in the "love of the automobile" (Sachs 1992). In the projects of sustainable transportation it is often the car-makers who, by virtue of their greater resources and "expertise", assume responsibility and end up setting the agenda and the terms of implementation (e.g. Hajer and Kesselring 1999). But overall responsibility for sustainable transportation cannot be given to business, however green its representatives claim themselves to be. In this as in so many other areas there needs to be a coordination of different efforts; otherwise high-speed trains and hypercars are cancelled out by increases in consumption and transport and by the innovative products that sidestep the pollution and safety regulations, such as the not-so-small trucks that are becoming an increasing part of the idea of the good life – at least for a certain section of the market. As long as mobility itself is not understood and transformed into more ecological patterns the individual technical fixes will continue to propel the "treadmill of production" (Schnaiberg and Gould 1994).

Networks of green commerce

Over the past twenty years, while the broad social movements of environmental and anti-nuclear opposition have tended to lose their significance in many parts of the world, a new range of organizations has entered the world of environmental politics. On the one hand there are the transnational corporations themselves as well as new configurations, such as the World Business Council for Sustainable Development, which seek to provide a corporate presence in environmental politics, and new intergovernmental initiatives, such as the Global Environmental Facility (GEF), the European Environmental Agency, the environmental activities of the World Bank, regional development banks and trade organizations (see Gan 1995; French 2000). And then there are the activities of transnational non-governmental organizations such as Greenpeace and the Worldwide Fund for Nature (WWF) which have been central formulators of the global environmental agenda and key participants in the quest for sustainable development (Jamison 1996).

On the other hand there are a number of actors from within the separate domains of government, business, academic life, and civil society, as well as between and among the domains, who have come together in looser, hybrid formations, coalitions, and networks. For while the 1990s has witnessed the emergence of a new discourse of environmental politics in the guise of ecological modernization there has emerged also a cluster of networks that have tended to fill, or replace, the public spaces that were once occupied by environmental movements and movement organizations.

These networks share many of the assumptions and ambitions of the environmental movements of the 1970s, but they nonetheless reflect the changing times and contextual conditions in their language and rituals and in their theory and practice. By leaving the "movement space" behind and linking up with more established social actors these new networkers have sought to translate the environmental message into terms that their new partners can understand and find acceptable.

To improve our understanding of what is taking place, and, in particular, to separate the rhetoric from the reality, it is useful to take a closer look at some of the cognitive dimensions, or learning processes, that are involved in green commerce (Rinkevicius 1998). There are new systems of accounting and organization, new kinds of technological and production paradigms, new management procedures, new economic theories, new business strategies, and new kinds of relations among universities, state agencies, and business firms. There are also new "pro-active" forms of public relations and marketing – as well as a more active collaboration with the more commercially minded non-governmental organizations – that many companies are pursuing.

If we think of green business in cognitive terms we must look at the kinds of human agency that are involved in these various "learning processes": companies, universities, public authorities and non-governmental organizations. We should also consider the hybrid forms of interaction that have developed among these domains. I take as my point of departure one particular agent that has tried to involve all four central constituencies, namely the Greening of Industry Network (GIN). In the openness of its operations and the variety of its participants GIN offers, for my purposes, a useful window into the world of ecological modernization. All too often these developments are discussed primarily in programmatic or rhetorical terms as new kinds of management doctrine or ideology, or as new kinds of technical paradigm or policy instrument. By examining the actual cognitive praxis of specific network formations like GIN we might be better able to evaluate the potential, as well as the limitations, of ecological modernization and of green business generally. I do not claim that GIN covers the total picture of green commerce or ecological modernization. But a closer, more intimate examination of one network and its members may help to bring to life some of the underlying tensions that are at work in the emerging ecological culture as a whole.

This "case study" of GIN traces three dimensions of cognitive praxis – cosmological, technological, and organizational – from GIN's "roots" in the environmental movement of the 1970s to its recombination in the late 1980s and to its growing separation in the course of the 1990s. Like so many other examples of ecological modernization GIN has come up against the power of possession and the logic of commercial enterprise: the all-too-familiar principles of business as usual. Ecological modernization, or sustainable development, is in danger of being reduced to salesmanship – to products to sell and market shares to acquire – as the dominant culture seeks to incorporate the values and practices that have emerged in the environmental movement.

The roots of the network

The Greening of Industry Network, like many of the other agents of ecological modernization or green commerce, can trace its roots back to the experiences of the 1970s when, as we have seen in chapter 3, the various traditions of ecology were mobilized in the making of a new social movement (Hajer 1995: 73–103). From an "imperialist" or managerial tradition there was the influence of systems thinking, which made perhaps its most visible public appearance in the *Limits to Growth* report to the Club of Rome of 1972 (Meadows *et al.* 1972). Here was a new breed of managerial ecologists who used computer projections of economic trends and a cybernetic language of feedback mechanisms to interpret interactions between natural resources and socio-economic development.

Like the ecosystems ecologists who had been so influential in the late 1960s, systems analysts were an outgrowth of the diffusion of computers and cybernetics, particularly in American society, but they were also responding to a new phase in the human interaction with non-human nature (Cramer *et al.* 1987). As material production in the postwar era became ever more dependent on science-based invention, the means of regulation and control also needed to change. In particular there was a need for more sophisticated conceptual tools to bring resource and energy flows into the models of the ecologist. By linking cybernetics with biology, systems ecology was a crucial component of the new environmental consciousness (Jamison 1993). Further, the imperialist tradition inspired energy systems analysts, like Amory Lovins, who would play such a major role in the energy debates of the late 1970s.

From the arcadian tradition came an interest in moving back to the land. The arcadian tradition also inspired a concern with local, or indigenous, forms of knowledge and an identification with history and traditions as part of the environmental movement. Arcadianism received its paradigmatic expression in *A Blueprint for Survival*, also from 1972, a program for a community-based ecology that was decentralized, autonomous and participatory (*Ecologist* 1972). But it can be suggested that it was more in the spirit of the movement, in the emphasis that was placed on local groups and "consciousness-raising," that the arcadian tradition had its most profound impact. Indeed, many environmentally minded biologists and engineers "dropped out" in the 1970s and formed rural, experimental, sites for their research activity, such as the Rocky Mountain Institute in Colorado and the New Alchemy Institute in Massachusetts. In many so-called developing countries, like India, a number of scientists and engineers left the cities in the 1970s to form centers for "appropriate technology" in the countryside (Elzinga and Jamison 1986).

It was mainly in this way that the pragmatic "human ecology" tradition entered into the movement with its experimentalism, its "do-it-yourself-ism," which tended to manifest itself most visibly in an interest in alternative, or appropriate technologies. At that time environmental technology, as we have noted earlier, was articulated primarily in "utopian" terms, that is, as not-yet-existing visionary alternatives, but, here and there, centers and communes were established to construct living examples of what ecological technology might look like – a kind of utopian practice (MacRobie 1981).

The main idea in those days was to develop criteria for scientific and technological development that responded to the objections of the activists. An ecological technology was thus the polar opposite of the large-scale, non-renewable, environmentally destructive technologies that the environmental movement had emerged to oppose. Robin Clarke published a widely disseminated list to characterize alternative technology; he also set up a Centre for Alternative Technology in Wales (Dickson 1974: 103). For several years workshops, courses, journals, and informal study groups developed archetypes or designs for alternative, radical, or appropriate technology (for experiences in the US see Pursell 1993). A major effort was undertaken by shop stewards at Lucas Aerospace Corporation to develop an alternative corporate plan by which the interests of the environmental movement could be operationalized within the context of a major industrial firm (Wainwright and Eliot 1982).

For a short time the different branches coexisted within one movement, carving out a cognitive space, a new kind of social or political ecology which combined the systemic, the experiential, and the pragmatic. In particular in the struggles against nuclear power, the traditions informed and interacted with one another in a synergistic fashion in order to strengthen each other's various arguments and approaches and to develop a broad-based and coherent alternative vision of an ecological society.

The cognitive praxis of the movement thus represented a recombination of the three ecology traditions. Managerialism provided much of the cosmology or world-view assumptions through its systemic holism, its one-earth-ism that was so characteristic of the political ecology of the 1970s. The arcadian tradition provided much of the organizational ambition that colored the movement, the effort to escape from the confines of industrial society and create "liberated zones" in the countryside from where different forms of exemplary action could be mounted against destroyers of the environment. The human ecology tradition provided a connection between the imperialists and the arcadians by offering practical–technical substance in its propagation of, and experimentation with, appropriate small-scale non-polluting technologies.

Eventually, however, unity broke apart, but the visionary seeds that had been planted continued to grow and stay alive in the collective memory. Already in the heat of the energy debate of the late 1970s renewable energy technologies became the focal point of the alternative technology movement and gradually, after the political battles had been resolved in one way or another, a number of companies emerged to commercialize what had been unleashed: wind energy, solar energy, and other forms of environmentally friendly energy technology. In the 1980s several new "branches" of industry developed out of the alternative technology movement, such as wind energy and organic foods industries in Denmark, as well as various consulting firms in energy conservation, non-waste technology, ecological design, etc.

In addition to the development of new industrial branches, there was also a gradual shift, in several countries, in the way in which environmental technology and environmental regulation came to be thought about by policy-makers (Weale 1992). Originally, environmental technology was generally viewed as something to be placed at the end-point of a production process as a control or filtering technique, such as the catalytic mufflers that were added to automobiles in response to the pollution-control legislation that was enacted in many countries. The technology came, as it were, at the "end of the pipe" as an addition to normal operations. But here and there a few companies, under the influence of the environmental movement, started to experiment with environmental technology that was more process-oriented and that attempted to prevent pollution or waste at their source.

By the early 1980s the notion of pollution prevention had begun to be discussed among environmental consultants and gradually the experiences of such pioneering companies as Minnesota Mining and Manufacturing (3M) began to be referred to as examples to emulate. By the late 1980s several consulting firms and industrial research organizations, both in Europe and the United States, were carrying out projects in pollution prevention or waste-reduction technology (e.g. Buriks 1988). The efforts made by the Dutch research organization the TNO Center for Technology and Policy, the cleaner technology programs initiated by the Danish Environmental Ministry, and the pollution prevention activities, sponsored by the United Nations Environment Programme were particularly important. In the late 1980s and early 1990s these efforts came to be consolidated in the form of new networks of innovators, and it was at that time that GIN was initiated.

The making of a network

In 1989 a young Dutch historian traveled around the United States in search of kindred souls. Not yet 30, Johan Schot had already set out on an unusual personal trajectory, combining an academic interest in the history and social study of technology with professional consulting in environmental management. After a first degree in history from the Erasmus University in Rotterdam Schot had obtained a job at the TNO Center, a private research institute in Apeldoorn, as a consultant in the area of environmental technology. TNO had been one of the first research organizations in Europe to take the ideas of pollution prevention seriously, and it was as part of that interest that Schot traveled to the U.S. to visit some of the companies where the ideas had first developed.

Schot gave a talk on constructive technology assessment to an academic conference in California that was organized by the Society for the History of Technology. In his presentation he applied some of the new conceptual tools of evolutionary economics and innovation theory to technology developments in the environmental field. By reflecting on technological development in this more proactive way, Schot argued, technology assessment could be integrated into the construction, or design, process, thus making many production processes more appropriate and responsive to societal needs (Schot 1992).

Schot characterized three elements of constructive technology assessment, which he has continued to develop in the years since he first presented his paper (1998). On the one hand, he contended, there was the element of expectation or anticipation; CTA sought to identify and articulate the ideas, visions, and goals of particular projects as an explicit part of the technological development process. Secondly, there was the element of reflexivity, of building processes of dialog and interactive communication into the design and construction of technology. And, thirdly, there was the element of contextual, or social, innovation: technology development, or construction, was not merely a matter of ideas or communication, it was also a matter of connecting people, of establishing what Schot called a "technological nexus" for bringing different "actors" or participants together in the co-construction process. To a large extent, GIN is an example writ large of what Schot discussed in his conference paper.

Schot then toured the US, and eventually met up with Kurt Fischer at Tufts. Fischer had worked in a number of different companies but was back in academia, and trying to get his fellow academics interested in the environmental changes which were taking place in the business world. Like Schot, Fischer was also working in the not-yet-existing intellectual terrain of environmental management, and, also like Schot, he was interested in creating new channels of communication and interaction not just within academia but in business, government, and "non-government." Together, Schot and Fischer thought up the idea of a transatlantic meeting, bringing together a coterie of Americans and Europeans from different social domains and areas of concern in order to develop a new environmental management agenda. And so GIN was born.

The first GIN conference in the Netherlands in 1991 was kept small by design but the second, held two years later in Boston, attracted 166 participants, with Dutch and Americans making up well over half the number on both occasions. Thereafter the network expanded rapidly, and a pattern was set, which continued throughout the 1990s, of having a conference one year in North America and the following year in Europe. The network has enrolled substantial numbers of participants from Denmark (Copenhagen, 1994), from Canada (Toronto, 1995), Germany (Heidelberg, 1996), California (Santa Barbara, 1997), and Italy (Rome, 1998). In 1998 a node was established in Asia, with a network office in Bangkok inaugurated at an ambitious launch meeting in July. In addition to the conferences a number of workshops have been held on particular themes that have attracted local participation. A series of publications have drawn not only on conference papers, but have included substantive bibliographies of relevant literature.

Members of the network

According to an internal evaluation report written in 1998 the geographical and professional backgrounds of the network participants have become ever more diverse, atthough there has continued to be a larger representation from academia than from any other societal domain (Brand and de Bruijn 1998). At the first meeting in the Netherlands in November 1991 29 of the 68 participants were Dutch, with 14 of them from the research community. Fifteen participants were from the United States, 10 from research institutions. By the time of the fifth conference in 1996 the Dutch contingent had expanded to total 51, and the American contingent totaled 30; the overall number of participants reached 379. And participants from academia had increased from 53 to 76 percent of the total. Let us take a closer and admittedly personal look at some of the "core" actors.

Many members of the network have a cross-disciplinary education, which may combine natural or engineering sciences with social sciences or humanities. Interdisciplinary fields such as science and technology studies (STS) and environmental studies have been well represented at Greening conferences, although the traditional management disciplines have usually provided the largest contingents of academics. Affiliations of the participants tend to reflect the hybrid character of the "greening of industry" in both organizational and disciplinary terms. Many participants come from independent or semi-independent research institutes, often with a non-governmental identity, and many come from new centers or departments of environmental management that have only recently been established at universities.

Many of the participants have an activist background although they might no longer be identified with *bona fide* activist organizations. Jacqueline Cramer, who co-authored the first conference report with Fischer and Schot, had been a leading environmental activist in the 1970s, and had served as chairman of the Dutch Friends of the Earth, as well as taking active part in the creation of the Amsterdam Science Shop. She had recently joined Schot at TNO after several years at the Department of Science Dynamics at the University of Amsterdam. Peter Groenewegen of the Free University in Amsterdam had also worked for a time at Science Dynamics and was active in the development of science shops, as well as in the environmental movement. Another veteran of the Science Shops movement was Philip Vergragt who had long been working in STS in the Netherlands. In addition to his involvement in GIN Vergragt would initiate the Sustainable Technology Development Program, a collaborative venture among several ministries that would be an exemplary case of Dutch-style "ecological modernization."

There were activists or former activists from other countries at the first meeting – Jack Doyle, a leading critic of agricultural biotechnology, and a long-time environmental activist from the United States; Alan Irwin from Britain, who had worked with environmental groups for many years, as had Per Sorup and Susse Georg from Denmark, who had both served as editors of *Naturkampen* (Nature Struggle), the Danish "radical science" journal.

In addition to their multidisciplinary and activist orientations many of the participants had been at the forefront of developing environmental management research and education programs. Donald Huisingh, one of the first to work with pollution prevention technology when he was in the US, and who is now professor at the International Institute for Industrial Environmental Economics in Lund (as well as one of the organizers of the Cleaner Production Roundtable and editor of the *Journal for Cleaner Production*), was at the first meeting and has taken part in several meetings since. Nicholas Ashford from MIT, another pioneer in environmental management, was at the first meeting and organized the second conference in 1993. Ken Green from the Manchester School of Management, who has been active in developing environmental management research in Britain, joined the network at the second conference and has been one of the core members ever since.

A third constituency that has continued to be active in the network is made up of what might be termed "progressive" business people. Already General Electric and Dow Chemical Corporation were represented at the first meeting, and in the years since companies like Polaroid, Novo Nordisk, General Motors and Sun Computers to name just some of the more actively interested companies, have made presentations at conferences as well as contributing to funding the network. Business representation has not been large in absolute terms, but it has been significant throughout the life of the network. The involvement of Harry Fatkin, who is responsible for environmental affairs at Polaroid, has been perhaps especially important as he has served on the advisory council and helped to plan conferences.

Since the initial meeting there has been the steady participation of a number of environmental officials in both governmental and intergovernmental bodies. Representatives from national and state environmental protection agencies, as well as from the United Nations Environmental Programme, have taken part in all of the conferences, and on selected occasions, members of other ministries or governmental departments, such as industry, finance, and research, have contributed. In addition to the official representation at international conferences workshop activity has often taken the form of collaboration with local governments and environmental authorities in different parts of Europe and North America.

The network in action

The Greening of Industry network is neither a non-governmental organization nor a business firm. Nor is it an academic society or an intergovernmental body. While attracting participants from all of the four types of policy cultures or domains that I characterized in chapter 4 – business, government, academia, and civil society – GIN is something different and autonomous. It is in principle not reducible to any one set of values or organizational pattern. In a sense, then, GIN draws on resources, ideas, and interests from all four domains and makes them into something new. Its leaders continually combine the various sources of influence and inspiration into new packages, which is both the charm, but also perhaps the source of the dilemma of the network.

GIN can be considered as an agent of ecological modernization in that its participants strive for an integration of environmental concern with economics. The point here is that environmental problems are not to be seen as side-effects of industrial development, as they were viewed in the early days of environmentalism in the 1960s and 1970s. Rather, they are to be seen as intrinsic to industrial development; and if these problems are to be solved or at least dealt with more effectively they need to be incorporated into industrial development in a fundamental sense. Industry, in short, has to be "greened" through various preventative measures and approaches. But environmental discourse must be translated into the language of business and economics.

The notion of "greening" is, of course, multifaceted and can be thought of as an application of the concept of sustainable development to the economic or corporate sphere. In the report from the first GIN conference it is put this way: "Companies must attune their managerial attitudes and practices to the goal of sustainable development." The goal of the network's first conference was "to improve our understanding of how companies act on environmental issues and under which conditions companies are becoming 'green'" (Cramer *et al.* 1991: 1).

"Greening of industry" is a processual term; it focuses on the dynamic elements of change rather than on what might be termed the substantial elements, and it was thus no easy matter to carve out the particular discursive space in which the network could operate. From the outset it was clear that GIN was not trying to develop a new academic discipline; rather, greening was to be seen in interdisciplinary terms and the subject-matter was primarily to be company behavior and procedures, both in theory and practice.

In keeping with the belief system of ecological modernization, the cosmology of the network also includes a strong emphasis on dialog, cooperation, communication, and networking. As a social process, greening is seen to necessitate new forms of institutional and organizational "learning," and, from that very first conference, a good deal of the network's attention has been devoted to learning theories, particularly in management science, and to innovation theories. Greening was defined as a process of changing behavior among business managers, but also among engineers, consumers, and public officials.

Here, however, we can see a rather clear development over the past ten years, a gradual shift of focus from the hardware side to the software, or organizational, side of company behavior. At the early conferences there were a number of papers on technological innovation and significant representation from those academics who work in the field of science and technology studies. By the time of the Rome conference in 1998 the technological emphasis had largely faded from the program; there was a plenary session on "Can technology save the earth?" but there were few other sessions on science- and technology-related topics.

At the same time participation from academics in the field of science and technology studies was much smaller as a proportion of the whole. At the first conference about half of the number of academics could be characterized as science- and technology-oriented, and half could be characterized as management-oriented. At the Rome conference in 1998 there was only a handful of academics in science and technology studies among the several hundred participants, and they were mainly academics from management departments and business schools.

In this respect the shift in focus can be viewed as a process of specialization. While other networks and organizations have developed in the areas of cleaner technology and energy-efficient technology, and even sustainable technology, GIN has become more oriented to the study of business management. The result is not only a narrowing of the technological dimension of the network's cognitive praxis, but also a sharpening of the contours of the network's identity.

The character of the organizational dimension has also changed or, rather, expanded in a number of ways since the network was first established. The original idea to hold conferences led to a range of other activities that included projects, publications, and workshops. The network's founders have devoted significant attention to reflecting on the network's organizational form by formulating strategy documents and interacting on a regular, less formal basis with some of the network's core members, particularly those in the corporate sphere. Kurt Fischer and Johan Schot, and, more recently, Theo de Bruijn have visited a number of companies involved in the network and have proposed specific activities that companies can take part in and support, such as the survey of members that was conducted by General Motors in 1998 and reported to the Rome conference.

As befits a "movement" in a commercial age, a good deal of energy within the network goes to fund-raising, public relations, and marketing. As the conferences have become bigger (from sixty-eight participants in 1991 to more than 400 in 1998) so the organizational challenge has grown. The general principle, however, is that the conferences should pay for themselves through (rather high) registration fees, although there is a great deal of sponsorship of particular sections of the program by local firms.

A characteristic of the network conferences on the organizational level is the continual commitment to innovation and interaction. Plenary debates are sometimes carried out in a mass-meeting format, with a moderator (such as the longterm member Eric-Jan Tuininga) circulating in the audience with a microphone and quizzing the panelists and the audience much like a television talk show host (which he has been). What makes GIN conferences interesting is that they are explicitly meant to be innovative meetings, reducible to neither trade fairs, academic conferences, organizational meetings, nor policy deliberations. What GIN tries to produce are events that are both memorable in their own right and are also part of a process of network-building. The conferences are supposed to be noteworthy and informative but also catalytic, providing opportunities for people to meet across the normal societal domains and to catalyze initiatives across the different areas of society, and the world.

The catalytic nature of the network is not just confined to the conferences. Several attempts have been made to formulate research agendas and to use conferences and workshops for projects and publications. The network has established relations with a journal, *Business Strategy and the Environment*, which publishes contributions to the conferences both in theme issues and separately; and with a publisher, Island Press, where several volumes have been produced (Fischer and Schot 1993; Groenewegen *et al.* 1996).

One of the special features of GIN is its transnational quality. While it is a central "discourse coalition" in regard to ecological modernization, what gives it a good part of its special identity is the confrontation and/or dialogue that has been established between North American and European variants of eco-modernism. To compare the two conferences that I attended, Santa Barbara in 1997 and Rome in 1998, provides a way to explore the differences between these variants and reflect on what the differences depend on. For while both the Santa Barbara and Rome conferences were organized around similar topics and themes – pollution prevention, environmental management, sustainable transport, etc. – their presentation differed in intriguing ways.

To begin with the emblems were different: the Santa Barbara conference was entitled "Developing Sustainability: New Dialogue, New Approaches" and there was an emphasis on terminology, on ideas, on values – on what might be termed the ethics of greening. The American presence was as usual quite strong and the plenary sessions sometimes had the tone of a camp meeting, with different preachers, ministers, "believers" promulgating their new ideas on the eco-modernist discourse. The emblem of "responsibility" was significant and, like a new denomination, the Coalition for Environmental Responsibility and Sustainability (CERES) also had its day, with plenaries and parallel "break-out" sessions, one of which I chaired.

The religious tone was hard to miss, especially since CERES' new executive director had been recruited from the Harvard Divinity School. He spoke of the values and the ethics of the sustainability transition and the greening process. CERES has a list of principles that companies are encouraged to sign, a kind of "ten commandments of greening," and these principles are urged as the way to alter the values of the firm.

The emblems in Rome were quite different. Here, the business of greening was in the hands of a new national actor, the co-host Legambiente, an NGO-cum-think-tank-cum-consulting firm which has all but replaced the public authorities in Italy, and which is secular, rational, and pragmatic in its presentation of the green message. Entitled "Partnership and Leadership. Building Alliances for a Sustainable Future," the Rome conference emphasized the business of greening, the process of operating: in short, green entrepreneurship. There were sessions on financing and marketing, on substance chain management, and on life-cycle analysis. The emphasis was on the mechanics of greening. The session I chaired on Local Initiatives in Sustainable Development became a kind of marketing session where we discussed techniques to mobilize local activists. A leading member of Legambiente spent some time in defending his own organization's activities; like a salesman for a particular business concept he stressed the significance of strong leadership and professional management skills in the taking of local initiatives.

I took part in a plenary session on technology organized by Johan Schot, which included a representative from General Motors. Johan Schot had prepared a multi-media show with film clips from newsreels from the 1939 World's Fair. In his speech he criticized some of the technocratic dreams that had been so prominent at the fair and which had reappeared in the 1990s among many ecological modernists. My own comments stressed the continued hold of the "myth of progress" over the environmental agenda which was, of course, disputed by the corporate representatives on the panel. We ended up disagreeing about the role of technology in the greening of industry. Minds had not met: they had stated opposing positions.

A broad social assessment of technology, which had been one of the prime concerns of GIN when it was brought into being, had become marginal at best and highly suspect at worst, for many of the influential members of the network. As cleaner technologists moved their products and their product concepts closer to the commercial marketplace, the "space" for critical discussion and reflection seemed to be getting smaller. The marketers of cleaner and greener products apparently no longer needed the benefit of an open-ended public arena; rather, they increasingly joined more focused and specialized fora for exchange and communication, such as the Cleaner Production Roundtable, national and international industrial branch associations, and the commercial trade fairs at which they could sell their products without the scrutiny of academic critics.

From network to business

The Greening of Industry network provides a window onto the changing world of ecological modernization. Emerging in the late 1980s as part of the quest for sustainable development, ecological modernization has developed into one of the ruling doctrines of environmental policy in the late 1990s. But it has also lost a good many of its original ambitions along the way.

On the one hand ecological modernization has tended to fragment into a number of different sub-areas or special interests. Most noticeably the proponents of environmental management have developed a discourse or sub-discourse of their own which has separated out from a technical, or engineering, discourse of cleaner production and green technology. In relation to GIN the management "wing" of eco-modernism has tended to take over, and the engineering, or science and technology, "wing" has tended to move on to other fora and organizational locations, and the environmental activities of engineering associations, both nationally and internationally.

This has meant an increasing specialization, but also a narrowing of the original ambitions. Over time the focus has become more oriented to the business world, and, even more narrowly, to the world of business education. It is indicative of this development that the 1999 conference was held for the first time at a business school, at the University of North Carolina, and that the meeting was framed in a much more explicit managerial language than previous conferences had been. In this respect GIN is part of a larger and more widespread process of managerial "reductionism" that has afflicted ecological modernization as a whole (see Mol and Sonnenfeld, 2000). Greening of industry, as a phrase or slogan, has tended to be supplanted by more explicitly business-oriented terms and conceptual frameworks – strategic niche management, environmental management systems, life-cycle assessment, industrial ecology, cleaner production, product chain management, extended producer responsibility.

Even more serious is what might be called the closing of the autonomous space that the network has represented throughout the 1990s. GIN has been both open and open-ended, which has meant that anyone who wanted to could present a paper, but also anyone who wanted to could be involved in its operations. As Kurt Fischer put it, "you're a member if you do some work." This quality is perhaps what most resembles that of a social movement, and it is something that seems to be challenged by the new kinds of activity that the network is taking on: the expansion to Asia, and the interaction with General Motors in surveying members' interests and in developing further programs.

There has always been a tension in the network among those who were most interested in what might be termed the project of greening – primarily environmental activists and former activists – and those who were most interested in the specific forms of greening industry – primarily business people and management experts. For most of the 1990s, it was a fruitful and creative tension, and the success of the network in holding memorable conferences and in producing interesting literature has been, in large measure, a result of the mixing or recombining of perspectives. With a sharper emphasis on doing business and influencing the world of business, and a more ambitious agenda that will require increasing efforts in fund-raising and acquiring corporate assistance and support, it is an open question how long the network can remain "movement-like."

The changes that can be seen in GIN are in many respects representative of the dilemmas that have confronted green business in general as its proponents have sought to put their visions into practice. Ecological modernization, we might say, has been seriously constrained by the logic of commercialization. As economists and engineers have developed the concepts of environmental management, cleaner production, eco-efficiency, and industrial ecology among many others, they have been forced to seek out market niches in the global economy. The original ambition of "greening" industry has thus been transformed into the business of greening. Members of the network, as well as members of many other such groups, have become competitors, selling their own particular concepts, their own particular expertise, in what has increasingly become a highly competitive market.

From movement intellectuals to network brokers

In terms of social agency the making of green commerce can be seen as representing a shift within the emerging ecological culture from a voluntary array of "movement intellectuals" to more professionalized and institutionally circumscribed forms of brokerage. Social network analysts use the concept of brokerage to characterize the kinds of things that networkers do: linking different actors together in common projects, promoting technical and social innovations, transferring ideas and inventions from one social sphere to another. Like the buying and selling that takes place on the stock market, or the fixing and negotiating of investments and loans, brokerage involves acquisition. In the world of green business the acquisition need not be purely monetary, but it tends to be directed to acquiring shares of a market, be it an academic, economic, or symbolic market. In the shift from activism to brokerage an entrepreneurial value system has been "imported" into the environmental movement, thus colonizing the ecological culture with a commercial mentality or mindset.

In the research project on Public Engagement and Science and Technology Policy Options (PESTO), my colleagues and I identified four main types of brokerage that had been especially prominent in the quest for sustainable development in Europe in recent years (see Jamison 1999). Visiting a wide range of companies that had instituted environmental management systems and cleaner technology programs, and a variety of university departments and governmental agencies that had conducted research in environmental science and technology, the emergence of an entrepreneurial "ethic" was quite noticeable. New kinds of professional roles and, with them, new kinds of skills and competences were crucial for the implementation of the various activities.

The kinds of skill and knowledge that are valuable in most of these undertakings and types of brokerage are strikingly different from those that come into play in "movement" settings. The organizational competence that is intrinsic to network-building tends to be operational, while the movement intellectual tends to be more inspirational, even charismatic, in his or her way of functioning. Making a network like GIN is a matter of fund-raising, public relations, negotiating, and enroling other people into one's particular organizational concept. A movement intellectual is more an articulator of a not-yet-formulated vision (Eyerman and Jamison 1991). Rather than possessing organizational skills, the movement intellectual has what might be termed "synthetic skills," fusing disparate knowledge forms into new combinations. Both are "hybrids," or transdisciplinary, but their motivations and criteria for success tend to be somewhat different.

The translator type of brokerage that is performed in networks is also different from what might be called the "interpreting" that goes on in movements (Bauman 1987). Translators usually have a particular, often highly specialized, technical competence which they transfer from one type of organization to another (from universities to businesses, from non-governmental organizations to governmental agencies, etc.). A translator broker is a kind of transfer agent, much like the "social carriers of techniques" that have been identified in relation to international transfer of technology projects (Edqvist and Edquist 1980). Donald Huisingh, for example, has been a tireless proponent of pollution prevention and cleaner production for some fifteen years now, and has carried the concept from North America to Europe where he has established networks and educational programs, as well as projects at companies in a number of different countries.

In movements interpretation tends to be a far more flexible or general kind of activity, and the competence that is required is that of the popularizing intellectual generalist – a Barry Commoner or a Ralph Nader, for example – for getting the message out to a broad audience and mobilizing the participation of voluntary activists. Interpretation involves making an issue relevant to different kinds of "publics," reframing or appropriating a concept or approach into other contexts. Intellectuals in the anti-nuclear movement, for instance, devised ways to relate the issue of nuclear power to a range of different life-worlds in order to mobilize a mass movement of activists. Translator brokers have much more specific "clients" and more circumscribed audiences for their intellectual activity.

Project-making is also somewhat different in the realms of movements and networks. There is some similarity as both movements and networks need to be managed and planned and implemented effectively, but there is a world of difference in managing paid employees and coordinating the efforts of volunteers. Skills and competences that are required are also different, as a movement intellectual attempts to coordinate different kinds of "lay" knowledge or local knowledges, while the professional project-maker needs to manage and combine more formalized types of competence.

Finally, the entrepreneurship that is to be found in a non-governmental organization like Natural Step, or an academic institution such as the International Institute for Industrial Environmental Economics in Lund, Sweden, is very distant from the "resource mobilization" that is carried out by movement intellectuals. Where one accepts the rules of the game in order to win influence and contracts, the other is constantly breaking the rules or, at least, is trying to establish a different set of rules. Entrepreneurship involves developing and then selling a concept or approach to paying clients, whether they be companies looking for advice or students looking for career opportunities. The movement intellectual takes part in what Ivan Illich in the 1970s called "conviviality" – sharing experiences and knowledge in a friendly, altruistic manner: the idea is to share one's knowledge and apply it to a collective task (Illich 1973). The entrepreneurial broker, on the other hand, is, to all intents and purposes, a salesman. The Natural Step, for instance, which was started by the Swedish medical doctor Karl-Henrik Robert in the late 1980s, and has since expanded to the United States and Britain, operates much like a consulting firm, and its success is measured in terms of how many companies are willing to pay for its services (Nattrass and Altomare 1999). It is also worth noting that Robert's "product" is not based primarily on scientific research – the Natural Step is not a scientific finding, but is rather more like a commercial organizational innovation. The procedures that are sold to clients are applications, or operationalizations, of scientific concepts into marketable commodities. The institute in Lund is also in a kind of business, namely that of selling an instrumental training, and, with it, a particular approach to environmental management and sustainable development. The graduates of the institute are often referred to in Sweden – both by institute officials and the media – as "missionaries" for the concept of cleaner production, rather than activists participating in an egalitarian and voluntary movement.

In terms of intellectual roles as well as specific forms of knowledge-making, there is a clear difference between what goes on in voluntary social movements and in the more professional, business-oriented networks. Movements and their intellectuals tend to play a primarily educative function in society, articulating new problem areas and envisioning new kinds of cultural values. Intellectuals of the environmental movements in Sweden, Denmark, and the Netherlands in the period of activism and public mobilization in the 1970s were, among other things, popular educators, grass-roots engineers, critical scientists, and utopian theorists (Jamison et al. 1990). They took part in an open public space of "critical discourse" or dialogic communication, whereas the new kinds of network broker operate in more limited arenas. While movement intellectuals attain the status of intellectuals within the movement, often developing their skills and knowledge as part of a collective learning process, brokers attain their status on the basis of the intellectual capital that they have acquired outside of the networks in which they operate. In movements, the individual is shaped by the social, or collective, identity in formation; in networks individuals construct together an operational, or instrumental form of interaction, or identity, in order to fulfill individual interests.

In relation to knowledge-making, the transition from movement to network has led to a shift from collective creativity to corporate learning. As a result, for many people a concern with protecting the environment has been both privatized and commercialized, and integrated into corporate strategy and marketing. It is the subsequent mixing of motivations that is most problematic, as companies combine what are two rather different behavioral motives into one. Profit-making and environmental improvement can be combined, but it is certainly not obvious, or even logical, that they can be combined in all cases. Indeed, as Janne Hukkinen has argued, in many real-world cases the two objectives need to be clearly separated and choices need to be made between them. The proper identification of what he terms the different "time-scales" for different types of technological development projects and a "sensitivity" about the specific, local conditions of "institutional design" is especially important (Hukkinen 1999).

Perhaps the main dilemma of green business is that there are no universally applicable solutions. What seems to be appropriate in one setting is often counterproductive in another. What we might call the "institutional logic" of one company is often incompatible, or incommensurable, with the operational logic of another. In this, as in so many other areas of social life, a specific, processual, and cultural focus can be extremely useful. If green business is to make any real contribution to the ecological transformations of our societies its modes of operation need to become more culturally sensitive and contextually informed. As the authors of a paper on "cleaner production and organizational learning" have put it, after reviewing a number of experiences in different companies, there needs to be "more fundamental questioning of existing technological trajectories and the corporate interests and socio-economic assumptions which underpin them. The recognition of limitations to firm-based organizational learning as a route to sustainable industry, given that business survival and profitability is the core concern in a competitive, globalized economy, reinforces the need for creative thinking and experimentation..." (Vickers and Cordey-Hayes 1999: 90).

NOTES

This chapter draws on the case-study of the Greening of Industry network that was conducted as a part of the European research project, Public Engagement and Science and Technology Policy Options (PESTO), for which the author served as coordinator (see Jamison ed. 1999). In addition to the participatory observation of network conferences discussed here, the case study involved interviews with Kurt Fischer and Johan Schot as well as a background report on the network written by Jose Andringa as part of her work in the project.

1 The Shell advertisement I saw frequently in 1999 was particularly striking. A former activist is shown lying on his back staring into space in a dramatic natural setting. The camera zooms in and he tells us why he has decided to work for Shell and help them to save nature by developing renewable energy.

Also worthy of note are the frequent automobile advertisements with a green message; for example, Mitsubishi has recently run one to tell us that it has been producing a new engine for only one reason: "the earth." Meanwhile a new Toyota, powered by a hybrid motor, is depicted in one advertisement as a small, marginal presence amid a forest of giant trees. "Don't think about the environment," the advertisement tells us, "Let Toyota do it for you" (*Sydsvenska dagbladet*, 19 October 2000).

6   On the dilemmas of activism

Finally the tables are starting to turn...
Tracy Chapman, "Talkin' 'Bout a Revolution" (1988)

With prevailing economic systems in various degrees of disarray, the worldwide environmental movement seems uniquely positioned to serve as a vehicle for a civilization ordered on a new basis. It is clear now that both capitalism and socialism, in all their experimental forms, have failed to create ecologically sustainable economies.
Mark Dowie, Losing Ground (1996: 262–263)

From critique to resistance

With the coming of green business, or ecological modernization, or whatever it is we choose to call it, the more radical, or critical, components of the ecological culture have tended to be marginalized. And yet everywhere we look there are signs of resistance, of activism, some new and some not so new, some merely updating the environmental critique of the 1970s to changing times, and some contending that they represent a new movement, or a new generation, or a new strategy, or a "new age" altogether.

There are those who foresee the abrupt demise of green businessmen and the coming of a grand synthesis of, among others, deep ecologists, ecofeminists, the "left" and "true democrats" (Dowie 1996). There are those who are aggressively "reclaiming" the streets on behalf of a generally vague sense of dissatisfaction with the workings of transnational, corporate capitalism (Wall 1999). There are those who are trying to bring it all back home and turn environmental politics into urban renewal or the reinvention of community in places that are threatened by the myriad forces that are trying to sustain the unsustainable (Shutkin 2000). There are those who hear the call of the wild and beckon us to renounce the civilization that most of us clearly are unable to live without (Turner 1996). And there are the realists, with ever more sophisticated brands of green expertise, who continue to try to reform the system into greener and cleaner directions (e.g. French 2000).

All of these strategies – and there are a great many others, as we shall see in this chapter – make it obvious that the ecological culture is very much alive today. The difficulty in assessing these strategies is that they are so diverse and, in many ways, so contradictory: sometimes explicitly, sometimes not, they are in competition with one another. They compete for public attention, for official favor, for funds, for moral support, for interest and engagement; in short, they compete for our trust, allegiance, and participation.

If there is to be any meaning in the quest for sustainable development, the several varieties of ecological resistance, or critical ecology, must find ways to articulate the rudiments of a common agenda, and to create spaces for working out their disagreements. We need to strengthen what Douglas Torgerson has termed a "green public sphere" (Torgerson 1999). Forces of incorporation are strong, especially the commercial forces of green business; but in relation to activism it is the "residual" cultural formations that can be most difficult to deal with because they tend to operate in such subtle ways. Old ideologies and allegiances may turn the protests and the projects of the emerging culture into particular, and often quite destructive, directions. Thus what is progressive can become regressive, collective actions can become extremist reactions, and visions of a new age are translated into old-fashioned and all-too-familiar dogmas. As Murray Bookchin wrote in the 1960s when the new left was so quickly starting to grow old, "all the old crap of the thirties is coming back," by which he meant Marxist dogmatism and Leninist "strategy" and an avowed communist ideology (Bookchin 1971: 173ff).

Currently there are signs that the "old crap" from the 1960s is coming back in the name of anti-globalism (so much like the anti-imperialism of the 1960s and early 1970s); there is a sense of despair among green activists that may seriously weaken the "new wave" of environmental politics that has been on the rise for some years. In recent campaigns against globalization, for instance – the battles of Seattle and thereafter – we see intransigence and extremism that is counterproductive. All too often, the arguments against globalization are framed without reference to ecological concerns; the struggle against globalization tends to be "reduced" to old-fashioned ideology, even when it is obvious that far more than the old class of national or material interests are at stake. If globalization is to become greener we need greater awareness of its ecological and cultural dimensions. And, I contend, we need more self-criticism, more reflection about the forces that have brought us here and the various attempts that have been made over the past few decades to develop a more ecological society. As Torgerson puts it, "An uncompromising green politics intent on ecological resistance threatens to succumb to a kind of resentment that, in the end, could undermine not only the intrinsic value of political action but anything further one might hope to gain from politics" (1999:168).

As a modest contribution to the making of a green public sphere – the "resilient green politics" that Torgerson and so many others are seeking to foster on the theoretical level – I will consider the dilemmas of resistance in terms of cognitive praxis, so that we may better be able to distinguish the emerging culture from the residual cultural formations that threaten to capture or contain it. While the dominant culture with its commercialism and its acquisitive values tries to turn us all into salesmen and entrepreneurs, the residual cultural formations try to pull us back into older ways of practice and thought that are no longer relevant. We need to distinguish between the innovative mobilization of traditions and the reactionary fundamentalism of traditionalist belief. The use of traditions is always selective and requires, like the rest of social action, that we become conscious of our criteria of selection and reflective about our processes of knowledge-making. In what follows I try to draw out some of the key points of convergence and divergence among the world's critical ecologists in the hope that such an exercise might improve our mutual understanding of what it is we are trying to accomplish.

The varieties of activism

A first step is getting a somewhat clearer idea of who the critical ecologists are. As I argued in chapter 1, there are serious problems with the ways in which environmental politics are usually examined and reflected upon. There is a gap between theoretical and empirical work, there are disciplinary divisions, and there are differences in knowledge interest. But, perhaps most seriously, there are too many categorizations at large, too many mutually incompatible ways to characterize the emerging ecological culture and who is involved in it.

The groupings that I propose here are based on different forms of practice, and, more specifically, on different forms of cognitive praxis. They divide the emerging ecological culture into four ideal-typical types, which I have adapted from the work of Bronislaw Szerszynski at the Centre for the Study of Environmental Change in Lancaster, Britain. What I have learned from his work and from the work of CSEC in general is the need to combine our eclectic tendencies in a creative way. In many respects, CSEC can be considered as a kind of green public sphere, created at the interface between the academic and the activist worlds. In Szerszynski's case the academic discourses of religious studies and sociology have been combined with environmental politics in order to differentiate forms of what he has termed ecological "piety" (Szerszynski 1997). He distinguishes between purposive and principled action, the first aiming to change political decisions or achieve direct political results, the second concerned to modify values or behavior. Szerszynski further distinguishes between counter-cultural and mainstream forms of practice.

Thus we have, first, what Szerszynski calls a "monastic" piety, which is principled and counter-cultural and characteristic of closely linked groups that develop common "lifestyles" and attempt to practice an ecological way of life often in production collectives of one kind or another. There is here an attempt to withdraw from the larger society, to establish an enclave, a liberated zone, outside of the dictates of consumerist capitalism. As in the monastic tradition as it developed historically in Christianity, this is a "piety of self-enunciation – the giving up of self-serving desires, or the surrendering of the individual to the collective" (Szerszynski 1997: 40).

Secondly there is "sectarian" piety, which is purposive and counter-cultural, characteristic of direct action protest groups, such as those opposing motorway construction and animal experimentation, and, more generally, reclaiming the streets. By characterizing them as sectarian, Szerszynski links them to the sects of the Protestant Reformation, stressing the sense of moral, personal, "witnessing" against evil, as well as the feeling of urgency and personal commitment that the eco-warriors share with the Protestant sectarians.

Thirdly, there is "churchly" piety, which is purposive, but also established, and is characteristic of groups such as Greenpeace or the Worldwide Fund for Nature (WWF). Here, one participates in environmental politics by paying one's dues to a professional organization: a green church:

Just as membership of the church became disconnected from any need for conspicuous displays of personal piety and commitment, Greenpeace accommodates itself to worldly existence by constructing a passive identity for its supporters entirely compatible with a non-heroic world of employment and family. And whereas the 'community of saints' in one of the small direct action groups such as the Dongas or Earth First! is experienced by each of its members in the form of face-to-face affectual relationships, the community that is Greenpeace is thus experienced, like that of a church, more in the imagination, as a quiet confidence in its ongoing activity. (Szerszynski 1997: 45)

Finally there is a "folk piety," which is principled and mainstream and characteristic of less organized, more personal forms of participation in environmental politics, such as green consumerism, waste recycling, and energy conservation. Here membership, or activism, is much more "part time" than in a social movement, and it is also highly flexible in its criteria for involvement. Szerszynski names it "folk piety" in order to underscore its similarity to the "religion of the peasant majority of late medieval and early modern Europe, which was dismantled by the forces of the Reformation and Counter Reformation in the sixteenth century." Like peasant religion, the folk piety of green consumerism involves the "ritual-isation of the everyday," and, in the emerging rituals and taboos, serves to "affirm the identity of the individual, and their social bonds with others, as much as to navigate around a risky world" (Szerszynski 1997: 48–49).

My own categorization, which is inspired by Szerszynski's, takes its point of departure in the actual development of different types of green knowledge-making. There are dynamic relations among the different types and, as we shall see, significant personal trajectories, or life-histories, that enter into the world of ecological activism. There are both relations of cooperation and of a common, collective identity, as well as relations of competition, as the different types of critical ecologists propose and develop different tactics, values, beliefs, and practices. Of particular im-portance is the specific type of cognitive praxis that characterizes the vari-eties of environmentalism, the approaches to knowledge and the ways in which knowledge production and dissemination are constituted. Adopt-ing Szerszynski's method I employ four categories which I call commu-nity, professional, militant, and personal. Presenting the categories like this may provide some new ways to consider what they represent and the dilemmas they present.

Community environmentalism

Community environmentalists and professional environmentalists are the purposive activists in Szerszynski's terms. What they share is a secular, or instrumental, emphasis, a focus on results, on changing policies and polit-ical decisions rather than on changing beliefs. Some of them retain in their own persons something of the spiritual, or ethical, motivation that played such a strong role in the early days of environmentalism, but in most of their activities the spiritual side is toned down. In terms of their rela-tions to knowledge, both community and professional environmentalists tend to favor the factual, the empirical or scientific–technical approaches over the normative, or moral–philosophical; and their practices or dissem-ination strategies are more argumentative and rational than exemplary and ethical. In many countries, environmentalists have emerged from a common "movement" origin but as the years have progressed have tended to drift apart. The community environmentalists have tried to uphold the original strong democratic ambitions while the professionals have responded to an expanding range of opportunities that have opened up (see Fischer 2000). As we saw in chapter 3, in the 1970s at least some activists found ways to turn their environmental engagement into professional careers, and the career trajectories have diversified and multiplied ever since.

Community environmentalists emerged from the largely decentralized groups that oppose particular cases of environmental destruction and develop alternative initiatives for environmental improvements in their communities. Their work thus consists, in large measure, in the mobilization of "local" knowledge and experiences. There are, of course, many different kinds of such groups around the world, but what they all have in common is the ambition to empower local groups or communities by providing some new factual information. The information is primarily of two main types: empirical details about particular environmental problems (factories discharging effluents into the air or water, plans for new projects, and so on) and information about solutions to problems that are already known (how to recycle or distribute waste matter, how to calculate environmental impact or "ecological footprints," how to change projected plans or halt projects by suggesting alternatives). Community environmentalists thus produce and disseminate information. What is involved for them is local research and promotion of their findings.

Until the 1990s most of this community environmentalism was technical or medical, a kind of grass-roots engineering and lay epidemiology, or what Alan Irwin has called citizen science (see Irwin 1995). The idea was to disclose the hazards, risks, and environmental dangers that were lurking behind the scenes in the local community and to develop ways of mobilizing local skills in the creative resolution of those dangers. And while there are many amateur and now highly competent citizen scientists working throughout the world to identify problems and develop solutions, what has been added in the 1990s is an ambitious and much broader social agenda. For sustainable development is not merely about environmental problems: it is also about local governance, about making democracy work. So the knowledge and skills – the cognitive praxis – that are involved have become much broader to include techniques of communication, the translation of concepts, and, most crucially, combination, or synthesis. Community activism today is about synthesizing local knowledge and experiences with global challenges, and it is important that we understand the difficulties involved. No longer "environmentally centered," the challenge for local activists is to create processes of dialogue and facilitate what might be termed "social innovations of strong democracy."

In Europe it has been primarily under the rubric of "Local Agenda 21" that such groups have been given both a mandate and an ever more influential role to play in environmental politics and policy-making in recent years (O'Riordan and Voisey eds. 1997). Many of these activities were started in the aftermath of the Brundtland Report of 1987, *Our Common Future*, which was the work of an international commission headed by the former Norwegian prime minister (and environmental minister) Gro Harlem Brundtland, presently the director of the World Health Organization (WHO). In the Scandinavian countries as well as in Germany and the Netherlands substantial "follow-up" programs were established after publication of *Our Common Future*. In Denmark there have been a large number of local projects in urban ecology so residents have been given the opportunity to propose and develop environmentally friendly improvements in their neighborhoods: collective gardens, the installation of solar heating panels and wind-power plants and, perhaps most significantly, the creation of new procedures for energy conservation and recycling of household waste (see Holm 1999). In many of these programs particular techniques have been developed for taking into account an individual's or a family's ecological impact in terms of energy use and food consumption. The idea is that a community, or neighborhood, or region, can calculate its "ecological footprint" and on the basis of such information may devise local agendas for reform and strategic improvement (for details on these developments in different European countries see Lafferty 1999).

In Norway, Brundtland's home country, there has been, as might be expected, a somewhat more organized effort to respond to the call for sustainable development than in many other countries (see Aall 1999). A campaign for environment and development was launched in 1987 and, after a round of planning and preparations, the parliament established a new kind of "umbrella" organization in 1990 to operate at a local level with various kinds of initiatives in sustainable development. The Environmental Home Guard, as the organization has come to be called, was formally created in 1991 and to date it has some 75,000 members. As with similar activities elsewhere in Europe the Home Guard operates through specific agents who work in offices at the municipal level, but it is the voluntary involvement of people in specific activities with which the organization is most concerned. The activities are often carried out in cooperation with schools or daycare centers and involve attempts to produce various kinds of change toward more environmentally friendly behavior and consumption. One important feature of the Home Guard is its close alliance with the main environmental organizations in Norway to provide expertise in specific topic areas, but also channels of dissemination and communication.

In 1992 the United Nations Conference on Environment and Development in Brazil produced an ambitious political agenda for the twenty-first century, the so-called Agenda 21, which formulated a large number of specific tasks at different levels of society as a way to implement more sustainable paths of socio-economic development. In many European countries laws were passed requiring all municipalities to produce their own Local Agenda 21 documents, with various plans and projects for implementation. One criterion for these plans has been the participation of members of the public in measures to achieve sustainable development. But interpretation of what public participation means in practice has varied enormously from municipality to municipality and from country to country (see Jamison ed. 1998).

A comparison of three municipalities in Sweden gives a good indication of the range of interpretations of "public participation" (Andringa *et al.* 1998: 90–98). Malmö, the largest of the three, has also had the most diverse activities. There, the "official" Local Agenda 21 activity consisted primarily of the drafting and eventual negotiation of a formal planning document, of general principles and aims for the achievement of sustainable development. At the sub-municipal level, however, Agenda 21 program funding made it possible for particular neighborhoods to carry out projects in urban renewal. Perhaps the most innovative result has been the establishment of a Green House in Malmö, where the different local activists can exchange experiences and discuss common problems. It should be noted, however, that of the three municipalities Malmö provided the least amount of funding per inhabitant. And it can be questioned how sustainable the overall development strategy for the municipality is in light of the massive highway expansion that has been carried out in connection with the recent construction of the bridge to Denmark.

In Lund, Local Agenda 21 appears to have had a greater impact on local government and public administration. For one thing, those who were hired to carry out the general operation of the activity were located physically in the municipal government building, and they were given resources to organize a number of thematic study groups around the town in collaboration with environmental experts at the university. Many more people were thereby involved in the actual formulation of a Local Agenda 21 document, and thus there were a number of specific proposals in relation to transportation and waste recycling that were able to be implemented more or less immediately.

Finally in Växjö, the third municipality, a significant amount of new productive industrial activity was directly stimulated by the Local Agenda 21. As a kind of "pilot" project, the national conservation society placed one of its own experts in the town and helped to bring together, in the process, people from different social constituencies. In particular local businessmen, interested in developing the commercial use of "wood chips" for energy production, were given the opportunity to meet informally with representatives of local environmental organizations as well as with the local governmental authorities. One result has been a new kind of renewable energy technology that has great potential in areas that are surrounded by forests, such as Växjö, where wood chips are an inevitable and often under-utilized waste product from the lumber industry (see Löfstedt 1996).

In other parts of the world similar projects of community-based environmentalism have been stimulated by the calls for sustainable development that have emanated from international conferences and national governments (see Low *et al.* 2000). William Shutkin has described how in the Dudley area of Boston local residents have teamed up with former New Alchemist John Todd to develop plans for community gardening and ecological food production (Shutkin 2000: 143ff). In Oakland, CA, Shutkin also reports how plans for revitalizing the downtown area have been developed in conjunction with the improvement of the local collective transportation system's station facility. Further north, much like many of their counterparts in Europe, local government officials have formulated a plan for a "Sustainable Seattle" with a system of indicators of sustainability by which people can be made accountable for their actions (Connelly and Smith 1999: 300–305).

In Southern Europe (Greece, Spain, and Portugal), community-based environmental activism in the decades following the collapse of dictatorial regimes made significant steps towards the amelioration of environmental problems. These advances were mostly urban, defensive, and exposure-related forms of resistance which transcended the political traditions of the past and, when needed, established networks with national as well as international professional environmental organizations to try and solve serious environmental problems at the local level. Official responses to these local citizen and environmental activists, however, have been primarily negative (Kousis 1999).

In many developing countries there is a substantial community-based environmentalism that is often supported by development-assistance organizations in the industrialized countries. These efforts at "ecodevelopment," or green development, as William Adams has called them, were, at an early stage, stimulated by the training programs and other activities of the United Nations Environment Programme which was established after the UN Conference on the Human Environment in 1972 (Adams 1990; Sachs 1994). Over the years involvement of non-governmental development and environmental organizations in these projects has increased to the point where many environmentalists have developed an expertise in both project management and particular techniques of public participation and collaboration (Chambers 1997).

Ideas and procedures of "participatory rural appraisal" and the concept of sustainable development itself, both linking environmental protection to economic production, were born out of these experiences. In the 1970s WWF, IUCN, and UNEP together formulated a World Conservation Strategy which criticized the relegation of environmental protection to a special and often marginal sector in the world of "development" (Sachs 1999). What has changed over the past thirty years is the involvement of the private sector. Now, as elsewhere, there is often a commercial interest in many of these projects. As development assistance has been linked in many countries to the needs of the national industry it is sometimes more difficult than before to see who is actually benefiting from specific sustainable development projects.

Many of the programs that have been established in the 1990s follow the precepts of ecological modernization, or green business, in trying to "economize" ecology and translate community activism into new forms of management and engineering. As such, the meanings of participation are highly varied, and often incompatible. The participation of a local government official is very different from the participation of a potential consumer of the products from a "cleaner" local factory. While empowerment is the aim for all participatory activities of community environmentalism it is important to recognize that empowerment is not without its contradictions. In the words of Robert Chambers, "whether empowerment is good depends on who is empowered, and how their new power is used. If those who gain are outsiders who exploit, or a local elite which dominates, the poor and disadvantaged may be worse off" (Chambers 1997: 217).

In many respects these new kinds of activity may be considered as an outgrowth of the environmental activism that first manifested itself in the 1960s and 1970s. It was primarily as a collection of specific local groups, with specific local grievances, that an environmental movement emerged in many parts of the world, and this category of resistance thus represents a kind of continuity across the decades. What has changed and developed is what might be termed the social or political consciousness among them.

The NIMBY, or "not in my backyard," label came into use in the 1970s as this kind of environmentalism took on a greater political significance, particularly in the United States, in the so-called "toxic waste" protests that began in the Love Canal area of Buffalo, New York, when local citizens discovered poisons buried under their communities (Szasz 1994). Like most such labels NIMBY was coined by the opponents of the resisters and so undercuts the true meaning of community-based environmental activism (Dowie 1996: 126–140).

In general, these kinds of protest have a number of common features that are useful to characterize. They have been mobilized by concerned citizens, often new to politics, who have reacted to particular local problems. They have been specific in the sense that they have focused on particular cases of environmental degradation. And they have been temporary. Sometimes there have been recurrences, or remobilizations, and in many cases expansions, extensions, or even institutionalizations, in terms of forming local parties or alliances with similar groups. But the actual process of resistance has been difficult to sustain or to make into a permanent feature of community life.

In some European countries community-based environmentalism has been, to a large extent, state supported, and organized through particular projects and local initiatives: what Carlo Aall, writing about the Norwegian case, has termed "sustainability light" (Aall 1999; see also Bovin and Magnusson 1997). In Denmark a special "green fund" has been created, by which resources are allocated through the Ministry of the Environment to local projects in sustainable development, and there has been a program for "green guides," people who have been placed in municipalities and business firms on a temporary basis, to serve as catalysts for activities in energy conservation, urban ecology, transport planning, etc. (Læssøe 1994; Holm 1999). The critical, and oppositional, elements of environmental activism – and knowledge-making – have inevitably tended to be toned down and the result, in many countries, is a kind of popular science activity in the name of ecology that serves as a complement to official research and development programs. What has emerged is thus a kind of surrogate and highly circumscribed movement which receives public support for its activities, but, on the other hand, is given little role to play in official decision-making processes (see Læssøe 1999).

Professional environmentalism

The second category has, to a large extent, evolved out of the first; as we have seen, the rise of an environmental movement in the 1970s created a vast range of opportunities for new kinds of professional to emerge within its ranks. And in many countries, as the movements fell on hard times in the period of "counterrevolution" of the 1980s, it was the professionals who kept the emerging ecological culture alive. In countries like Britain and the United States, where the neo-liberal backlash was particularly intense, many of the environmental protest activities were incorporated into what came to be referred to as mainstream environmental organizations. But at the same time sources of tension developed between those ever-more professional organizations and the local activist groups, who often felt that they knew more about their situation and their particular struggle than the campaigners, or fund-raisers, or experts, from the professional organizations.

In many European countries the professional organizations – especially newer ones like Greenpeace – tended to "take over" the mantle of the movement, both in terms of media attention as well as in regard to general public interest (Eyerman and Jamison 1989). But, even more importantly, Greenpeace and the WWF, as well as the national conservation societies, became the agenda-setters, the agents who formulated the strategies for the culture as a whole, and who took on the responsibility of representing the broader interest in the environment. Together with the green parties that started to win their way into local government and even into some national parliaments in the 1980s, professional organizations became the "stand-in" for the broader public as well as being the form of agency through which civil society was offered opportunities to participate in what came to be called "sustainable development." It is no accident that the term itself was originally formulated by the WWF in the World Conservation Strategy, produced together with the UN Environment Program and the International Union for Societies for the Conservation of Nature (IUCN) in 1956.

We should remember that many of these organizations predated the environmental movement of the 1960s and thus embody traditions and "residual" cultural formations that have been difficult for the organizations to transcend. As conservation societies and ornithological associations, as tourist organizations and rural preservation councils, as wildlife federations and wilderness clubs, these organizations became a part of the political cultures of most industrialized countries in the early twentieth century, and many of them extended their reach into the so-called developing countries in the immediate postwar era, when the former colonies began to win their independence. There are thus discursive frameworks and organizational experiences – a kind of traditional knowledge – that many of these organizations are able to build upon and mobilize in their contemporary activities. But it also becomes difficult for them to escape from the limits of their histories, to transcend their traditions.

Already in the 1960s these "first wave" organizations, dating back to the nineteenth century, came to be complemented and, in some places, challenged by new organizations that were reacting to the new kinds of pollution and urban environmental problems that had been identified in the public debate. As we have seen, NOAH in Denmark and the competing national federations of local groups in Sweden came into being at that time. Many of their founding members were young people who had been associated for a time with the older organizations, but who now found them too staid and "established." In North America Friends of the Earth and Greenpeace were formed in the early 1970s for much the same reason, and they soon grew into international alliances as the UN Conference in 1972 helped to transform this new environmentalism into a global movement (McCormick 1991). In the 1970s a number of other national organizations and green parties emerged in many countries to coordinate the efforts of the predominantly local action groups that sprang up to oppose nuclear energy and other types of environmental destruction.

By the 1980s the new and the old organizations, those of the first and second waves, had become ever more professional, and, particularly when new forms of "grass-roots" protest started to emerge in the late 1980s, it became increasingly common to refer to the larger organizations as "mainstream" environmental movements that, in many respects, had come to have interests of their own. According to many observers they had become institutions, rather than movements, more like bureaucratic organizations than local activists (Eder 1996; van der Heiden 1997).

In the United States the mainstream organizations grew into a significant political force during the Reagan years as they made use of the "opportunity structures" of the American political culture to take active part in political lobbying and consultation in order to defend what had been achieved in the 1970s. But, as Mark Dowie has put it, by the mid-1990s they were "losing ground"; they had become too enmeshed in Washington politics, in litigation, and in compromise, and had lost a good deal of their active support at the "grass-roots" level (Dowie 1996: 63ff). In a similar vein Mario Diani and Paolo Donati have recently characterized environmental activism in Europe in terms of a transformation from participatory protest organizations to public interest lobbies (Diani and Donati 1999). Organizations like Legambiente in Italy and the WWF are more like business firms than social movements. In individual countries as well as at the inter-governmental, European Union level, and, perhaps most especially, with regard to international environmental negotiations, professional organizations have been given a range of new opportunities that have affected their orientations as well as their mode of operations (see Bichsel 1996; Jordan and Maloney 1997; Dekker *et al.* 1998; van der Heiden 1999).

Throughout the world the activist or social movement organizations that were so prominent in the 1970s, when environmentalism represented for many young people around the world an alternative way of life that was based on an ecological "world view" and oppositional forms of political action, have in the 1990s been displaced by a differentiated realm of so-called non-governmental organizations, or NGOs, with an international reach (Jamison 1996). Among other activities NGOs provide advice for business firms, government agencies, and public education programs, lobby for legislative and policy reforms, and take part in a wide variety of international development assistance projects (Runyan 1999; Kellow 2000). They also play key roles in many countries in local, regional, and national sustainable development activities, and, after its adoption in Brazil in 1992, in fulfilling and implementing the Agenda 21 that was agreed upon at the UN Conference on Environment and Development. They also participate, directly and indirectly, in negotiating environmental agreements on such issues as climate change, biodiversity, and technology transfer. Explicit activist organizations still exist but in many countries they are merely a small part of what has become an expansive "non-governmental" realm, or environmental movement sector (Rootes 1999). And quite often new activists are as much in opposition to old activists as they are to the established powers-that-be.

The large variety of non-governmental organizations that are part of what I term professional environmentalism makes it difficult to generalize, but there are nonetheless some characteristic features that many of these organizations seem to share, particularly in terms of their cognitive praxis. On the one hand they employ members of staff who do most of the work. They are, to be sure, open to volunteer and amateur involvement, but these organizations are formalized in the sense of having some people who are employed to make, or produce, environmental knowledge. On the other hand there is another defining characteristic: the priority that is given to expertise. All these organizations are based on a particular kind of expert competence be it legal, scientific, administrative, commercial, educational, or disruptive. They derive their organizational identity from a particular kind of cognitive input to environmental politics. They are the experts of activism. Like all producers of expert knowledge they are thus dependent on patrons to provide resources for collecting, analyzing, sifting, and presenting this expert knowledge.

Finally, these organizations are permanent, or at least established and with ambitions to be permanent, which means that organizational growth and survival are important factors in their choice of topics to work on and methods to apply. They need, in other words, to find a "niche" in the social ecology of knowledge production, neither duplicating what is done in other places nor competing with those who are able to do a particular task more effectively. This organizational dynamic, or niche-seeking, is perhaps the main factor behind the specialization and division of labor that exists among professional environmentalists. The problem, however, is that there is no organized coordination of activity, no collective setting of agenda, and, more seriously, no accountability to any particular user of the knowledge that is produced. These organizations are accountable only to their formal directors, either elected governing boards (as is the case with the large membership-based organizations) or self appointed leaders, who operate much like the directors of business firms.

The identity of these organizations is derived primarily from their representative character; they have defined themselves as giving voice to a particular section of the public. This means that their own mode of operation is based not only on a view of representation, but is also grounded in one or another ideological perspective.

While many if not most of the non-governmental organizations are primarily concerned with achieving political results, that is, in affecting or influencing policies, laws, and agreements, there are other organizations whose primary activity consists of knowledge-making and dissemination. Throughout the world there has been developed independent think-tanks of various kinds as well as units associated with universities, intergovernmental agencies, research and consulting firms that all provide information and education in environmental policy and the sub-sets of substantive issues that comprise environmental politics.[1]

Some of these "green experts" are directly associated with local activists and civic groups and provide advice or training of one kind or another. Members of the Wuppertal Institute in Germany, the Centre for Science and Environment in India, and the Worldwatch Institute in the United States are all examples of professional environmentalists who mediate between the more "traditional" scientists and engineers at universities and the general public and its environmentalist representatives.

The "knowledge" products of these green experts are highly varied but in general terms we can divide them into three major types. On the one hand there are the factual reports about particular environmental issues – transportation, industrial pollution, climate change, energy technology – that are primarily collections of scientific information: popularizations at best, vulgarizations at worst. These reports, such as those produced by the Worldwatch Institute, are typically written by journalists with some scientific training, or by scientists with some journalistic training, and they tend to be sector-specific, policy-oriented and directed to non-expert readers.

The recent volumes produced by Hilary French of Worldwatch Institute and Anil Agarwal and his colleagues at the CSE on global environmental negotiations provide good examples of both the strengths and limitations of this kind of cognitive praxis (French 2000; Agarwal *et al.* 1999). They are both based primarily on solid investigative journalism that includes participant observation of key negotiating meetings, and they are filled with up-to-date references to media coverage and a vast range of official and organizational documentation. What is striking, however, is how little reference there is to the extensive academic literature that has been produced on green matters over the past ten years. Especially valuable, for instance, is the work of people like Sheila Jasanoff and Bran Wynne on the ways in which scientific knowledge enters into environmental political negotiations (e.g. Jasanoff 1990; Wynne 1994; Jasanoff and Wynne 1998). It sometimes seems as if academics and activists were living on, and trying to save, two different planets.

In the case of automotive transportation the World Resources Institute has produced a number of reports about the "costs" in human lives and in natural resources of automobiles, and has also produced a book on the need for a totally different approach to transportation, with a large number of specific policy suggestions for reforms at different levels of policy-making (Nadis and MacKenzie 1993). However in this report as in so many other factual, scientific-technical, reports, the input from those social scientists and historians who have tried to put much of this scientific–technical environmental knowledge-production into some kind of broader context is conspicuous by its absence.

A second type of knowledge produced by green experts is what might be termed material for popular education: training books, textbooks, pamphlets, CD-roms, websites, instruction manuals, and the like that are for use in courses, seminars, or study groups of various kinds. There is often a specific audience or readership, for whom these materials are designed, sometimes on a contractual basis. Many of these products are collections of useful practical experiences, or "best practices" (how to save energy, consume environmentally friendly products, institute environmental management procedures) that can be applied by the reader. Others are more specific "brands" of advice, such as the particular program of environmental improvements that the Natural Step proposes to companies.

Finally, and perhaps most significantly, there are the products that are visionary or innovative in their combinations of different approaches, the proposal of new concepts, or the formulation of new strategies, or new orientations for particular actor-groups or social constituencies. Wolfgang Sachs, for example, from the Wuppertal Institute in Germany, has for many years produced a kind of literature that falls somewhere between environmental social science and journalism. Like the works by Lester Brown and Hilary French from the Worldwatch Institute, Vandana Shiva from India, Helena Norberg-Hodge from the International Society for Ecology and Culture, and, for that matter, Murray Bookchin of the Social Ecology Institute, these are polemical writings that are meant to contribute to environmental consciousness-raising but are not associated with any one particular political group or organization. We can see these political green experts as a new variety of "movement intellectual" who, on an individual level, often think of themselves as part of a movement and yet express their opinions and offer their political suggestions more or less as professional experts, since they are either employed by a green think-tank or earn their living, to a large extent, by their speaking and writing (Eyerman and Jamison 1991; Eyerman 1994).

Relations among these various professional environmentalists are extremely complicated and roles shift as staff members of large organizations sometimes spend time at a think-tank and the experts at think-tanks sometimes set themselves up as consultants. The movement intellectuals often play a mediating role among organizations, and even help to form new organizations or alliances on particular occasions, such as the media-oriented protest events that are arranged at major international gatherings. Professional environmentalists occasionally combine forces on projects or on the preparation of particular meetings or reports that are supported by international foundations and, sometimes, by national governments. And there are a large number of working relationships that have been established over the years among many of these professional environmentalists and other kinds of professional – those in business, the media, in universities, on international bodies, as well as in other NGO sectors (there is, for example, a great deal of overlap between environmentalist and developmental intellectuals).

All of these contingencies or contextual factors make it extremely difficult to assess the quality of the expertise they produce, since much of the material is not subjected to the traditional academic procedures of "peer reviewing" but, rather, is selected on the basis of organizational profiles or identities, personal career trajectories, or the commercial strategies of publishers and companies. In competition with one another – for funding, for readers, for publishing contracts – green experts have little incentive to cooperate, and they also have little reason to develop a more comprehensive program for knowledge production among themselves. The ad hoc, or temporary nature of their contacts with academic researchers, usually on a project-by-project basis, is another factor that affects the coherence of the material that is produced. Some topics are "over-studied" and over-discussed, while others are neglected entirely. As with the scientific world, a tendency exists to follow fashion, or "go for the money." And there is the separation – in "lifestyle," in visibility, and in access to political influence – between the primarily locally based environmentalists and the increasingly cosmopolitan or internationally oriented professional environmentalists.

While the works that are produced by professional environmentalists continue to find audiences – and indeed finding audiences, selling products, "public relations" have become an important element of the cognitive praxis of many environmental organizations – the knowledge that is produced is rarely subjected to serious academic scrutiny. The academic worlds and the activist worlds seldom meet, and I have gotten a clear impression after reading much of the recent literature that the gap is growing. Academic writers seem not to be following particularly closely what activists are discussing in their popular writings, while professional activists seem to be uninterested and uninfluenced by the concepts and new theories and approaches that are being developed in the academic world.

Perhaps the main challenge for professional environmentalists – in both the academic and the non-governmental domains – is to help to re-establish a sense of coherence in relation to all the increasingly disparate movements, networks, campaigns, and alliances. For the large organizations this would involve the development of an explicit process of organizational reflection by which the aims and strategies that first inspired the organization are continually examined and brought up to date. In Europe this means, in particular, a much more open-ended discussion about the impact of Europeanization on environmental policy, that is, the emergence of the European Union as a major actor. Many professional organizations are well connected to their own national policy bodies and environmental authorities, but increasingly the challenge is to extend their international range, or global reach. For the transnational organizations such as Greenpeace and WWF the challenge is to develop new forms of communication with other national groups and organizations and with the new "players" in environmental politics – in business and academic life, civil society and government. Much like companies, the transnational NGOs have pursued their own organizational aims, largely without any broader political or social strategy; but as corporations and corporate interest organizations increasingly seek to set the overall agenda for environmental politics the NGOs need to articulate a clearer and more coherent political program.

Militant environmentalism

For all their differences the community-based and professional environmentalists are mainly interested in changing policies and affecting political decisions; however, there are a large number of environmentalists whose main concerns are moral or spiritual. But, as with political environmentalists, the moralists also are highly varied and contradictory in their aims. My distinction between the militant and the personal is intended to convey the fact that there is a fundamental difference between those who practice their environmental morality in public and those who practice it more privately. In the first category, which I call "militant environmentalism," we have the groups that have broken away, usually for ideological reasons, from the mainstream organizations – the so-called splinter groups – as well as the ever more militant groups that have sprung up in recent years in many parts of the world to liberate animals, reclaim the streets, and generally to disrupt the normal operations of social and economic activity (Taylor 1995).

Friends of the Earth can be considered to be the first splinter organization. David Brower, director of the Sierra Club for many years, in the late 1960s found himself in conflict with his board of directors over the strategy and orientation of the organization. By 1970 he felt that his view of environmental politics had become more environmental, more radical, than many of the other members of his organization. In many ways, this was a typical pattern of development in the environmental movement as it emerged in the 1960s and 1970s, as "new-fangled" environmentalists found themselves uncomfortable and unsatisfied with the priorities and political directions of the established organizations to which many of them belonged. Some of those new-fangled environmentalists have since joined the "mainstream" and become leaders of newly established professional organizations in their own right. In many countries, for example, Friends of the Earth and Greenpeace practice many of the same things as the older organizations – lobbying, consulting, etc. – and have become largely indistinguishable from the mainstream. Nonetheless there remains a difference in relation to both direct action and militance. Organizations like Greenpeace and Friends of the Earth provide latent support for militant environmentalists that older organizations seldom do.

In the 1980s and 1990s splinter organizations emerged, such as Earth First! and the Sea Shepherds. These organizations have brought new issues on to the agenda, as well as developing new methods of protest. Many of these more recent organizations have been inspired by the so-called deep ecology, and have also been influenced by anarchist, syndicalist, and even terrorist political and ideological traditions. On a cosmological level militant environmentalists share a belief in what might be termed "species equality," a form of biocentrism or ecocentrism that places human beings on an equal footing with other life forms (for critical discussion, see e.g. Ferry 1995; Taylor 1995; Harvey 1996).

Carolyn Merchant has given this framework the name "partnership ethics" in order to accentuate the dimension of sharing – of resources, space, nature – that is central to many militant environmentalists (Merchant 1999). The idea of partnership, for Merchant and many other radical ecologists, is related to the "gender equality" that has been propounded by feminists, and there is, in much militant environmentalism, a strong influence from "ecofeminist" thinkers such as Merchant and Vandana Shiva (see Eckersley 1992; Dowie 1996). As Merchant puts it, "A new cultural politics and a new environmental ethic arising out of women's experiences and needs can provide an ethic of sustainability. Many of the goals and gains of feminists are central to that new discourse and ethic. Women's interests and nature's interests intertwine. The goal is a sustainable partnership with the natural world" (Merchant 1999: 205).

We should recognize, however, that there are widely divergent meanings of both deep ecology and partnership ethics, most especially perhaps in terms of the role they play in the identity of the activists. A useful rule of thumb is whether the ideas of deep ecology or animal liberation or partnership ethics serve as an ideology or as a utopia, in the sense that Karl Mannheim once defined those terms (Mannheim 1936). An ideology relates to a pre-conceived framework of belief, while a utopia describes not-yet-existing relations and orients behavior to exemplifying the utopian vision. The ideological "use" of deep ecology is thus a translation of the idea of species equality to a principle of action, while the utopian use is a translation of much the same idea to a criterion of living experimentation. Where the one tends to "reduce" the ideas to a code of conduct, the other opens the ideas to innovative application.

"Deep ecology" as a label for the more spiritually minded, and often violently driven, environmental activists who occupy building sites and prevent forests from being cut, is, in any case, something quite different from deep ecology as it was first discussed by Arne Næss, the Norwegian philosopher, who coined the term. For Næss, deep ecology was to be distinguished from the shallow, from the mundane, political struggle, and it was not so much proposed as an alternative to traditional environmental politics as a necessary complement. But for Næss, it was also a philosophy, a kind of belief system, inspired by respect and humility for non-human nature, that was strongly influenced by Indian philosophy and, particularly, by the teachings of Gandhi (Rothenberg 1995). So it may be seen as unfortunate that deep ecology has been associated with violent environmental protests since, for Næss, the essence of environmentalism is non-violence and a kind of dialogic compassion for the other, for the "enemy." According to David Rothenberg, the environmental philosopher who has translated Næss into English:

Before turning to ecological matters, Næss worked for many years to demonstrate that Gandhi's collection of aphorisms, life experiences, protests and mediations constituted a coherent philosophy, not a bag of contradictory assertions and behaviors. Self-realization according to Gandhi is the root of Næss's entire philosophy of deep ecology... The power of nonviolence is built upon belief in the essential oneness of all life. (Rothenberg 1995: 208)

As an ideology for militant environmentalism, deep ecology has taken on a life of its own. It developed in the United States in the 1980s primarily as a way to react to the increasing rapaciousness of the forestry companies in the American western states (Taylor 1995). Like many other ideologies before and since, deep ecology "has become an attractive phrase for many people, who tend to bend the term to their needs without bothering to learn what it was originally meant to imply" (ibid.: 203). The founders of Earth First! and other spiritually-minded American environmentalists adapted deep ecology to their own purposes, and, by so doing, gave it an extremist connotation. Later, activists in Britain, in launching their own brand of militance to oppose the proliferation of highways across the countryside, transferred deep ecology back to Europe, apparently after discovering it in publications of the American organization, Earth First! (Wall 1999).

If the mainstream organizations stand for a kind of "incorporation" of activism into the dominant culture, splinter groups can be characterized as a sort of a "residual" cultural formation in relation to the emergent ecological culture. On the one hand, they are often infused with political ideologies, such as anarchism and even terrorism, that are part of a tradition of protest in many countries. On the other hand, they are characterized by their defense of "traditional" practices and ways of life and for the protection of animal species that seem to be in danger of elimination. Their resistance is based on an active identification with tradition: small-scale farming or shopkeeping, for example. Finally, these groups oppose any and all sorts of incorporation, and see the dominant culture of commercialization and globalization as their main enemy.

When Raymond Williams referred to residual cultural formations he was thinking of such things as a "rural way of life" or a sense of rural community, which, although weakened, and all but incorporated into the dominant culture, could nonetheless provide sources of opposition and alternative values that were still vibrant and alive. As he put it:

> The residual, by definition, has been effectively formed in the past, but it is still active in the cultural process, not only and often not at all as an element of the past, but as an effective element of the present. Thus certain experiences, meanings, and values which cannot be expressed or substantially verified in terms of the dominant culture are nevertheless lived and practised on the basis of the residue – cultural as well as social – of some previous social and cultural institution. (Williams 1977: 122)

Militant environmentalists, in their active resistance, are an important part of the emergent culture but, like community-based activists, they have a tendency to "reduce" the struggle to the defense of one particular value and to disregard the need for compromise and innovation. Their protest can thus become what Williams termed "archaic," defending a remnant of the past that cannot realistically or meaningfully be revived in anything but a symbolic manner. This is even more apparent in the case of the animal liberation groups that sprang up in the 1990s, particularly among the youth sub-cultures that were often of a vegan orientation. In Sweden and Finland, where these groups are perhaps especially prominent and visible, it is not deep ecology as much as a traditional Nordic primitivism from the Viking age that seems to be an active ingredient in the "cosmology" of the animal liberation struggles.

While Earth First! activists appropriated deep ecology into the strongly religious, or spiritual, American environmental discourse, Nordic animal rights activists have primarily appropriated the ideas of the philosopher Peter Singer, who was one of the first to call for the liberation of animals in the 1970s. But while Singer, then as now, has developed his arguments for animal liberation from a primarily utilitarian perspective, the young activists in Sweden and Finland have frequently translated Singer's ideas into a very different kind of discursive framework (Singer 1975; Lundmark 2000). For many of the militants there is an interest in paganism and in anti-modernism as well as in animal liberation. More significantly, perhaps, an animistic set of beliefs that includes an active attempt to identify with the feelings of animals is being mobilized. When questioned, animal liberationists give voice to a kind of natural religion in which animals are imputed to have the same moral rights as well as the same kind of emotional capacity as humans. It is the suffering of animals – in scientific experiments, in captivity, in food industries – that most infuriates them. As one of them has put it: "People can be superior to other animals in many ways, but when it comes to suffering all have the same capacity to feel pain" (quoted in Lundmark 2000: 118).

Personal environmentalism

The final category of ecological resistance is the most amorphous and variegated. It includes all of the myriad attempts to make the political personal, from the mystical teachings of new age philosophy to the individual efforts to shop in an environmentally conscious manner. What is striking about personal environmentalism is its increasing diversification over time, the fact that ecological, or green, life-styles and attitudes have spread into so many different kinds of life-worlds since they first began to be articulated in the 1960s and 1970s. Very few global citizens have remained unaffected by ecological ideas in their personal behavior, although the sheer variety of what is called "ecological" makes it hard to define what it means in regard to broader patterns of cultural transformation.

A popular book written in 1968 saw in the hippies the main contributors to the *Greening of America*, and, since the 1960s, it has been many an aging hippie who has found new ways to "keep on keepin' on," as we used to say. The hippies provided a spiritual, or, at least, a spirited contribution to the fledgling environmental movement, stimulated by psychedelic drugs, Asian and native American religious traditions, and ideas about personal liberation that were promulgated by a number of well-known psychologists such as David Cooper, R. D. Laing, Eric Fromm, Gregory Bateson, and Norman O. Brown (Cooper 1968). Members of the counterculture expressed themselves not just by wearing colorful clothes but also in their voluntary simplicity and a youthful openness to non-Western cultures that led many to move to the countryside and take journeys to the East, as well as to take ecological ideas and environmental problems seriously. In Sweden the migration of young people to the rural areas was called a "green wave," and throughout the industrialized world there was a growth of communes and production collectives in the 1970s, many of which have continued to provide training courses and living experiments in what might be termed the spiritual sides of ecology ever since.

As the environmental movement developed the spiritual dimension has tended to take on a life of its own, and, particularly as political campaigns have lost much of their mass attraction, the personal and the political have tended to separate out. In the late 1970s, an American journalist, Mark Satin, tried to fashion a new kind of political movement out of spiritual or personal approaches to environmentalism, but, then as now, new age politics proved to be a contradiction in terms (Satin 1979). The "new age" grew into a substantial and innovative genre of music and art, and, further, inspired a number of schools of therapy. Further, it became an important and influential cultural realm, or spiritual network, with activities spread throughout the world. What has changed through the years is the diversity of the new age culture, which has increased enormously, as has the commercial tone of much of what is on offer. Even the new age has been colonized by the dominant culture.

However, new-age culture continues to be rejected by many of the wings of the environmental movement, even by those – such as the new proponents of the "abstract wild" like Jack Turner – who could be thought to be sympathetic (Turner 1996). And it has brought on many a backlash from defenders of traditional age-old values. In its mysticism and its spiritual eclecticism, its mingling, or mangling, of the reasonable and the unreasonable, those who believe in science and modern rationality continue to find new age culture an easy target for scorn and moral outrage (e.g. Gross and Levitt 1994). And yet the new age continues to grow.

In the 1990s there emerged a somewhat different kind of spiritual, or ethical, discourse, or range of discourses, that were developed in the name of ecology. Inspired in large measure by the diffusion of genetically modified organisms, the very ideas of life and human existence have been seen to be challenged. Ethics has become a popular subject on university courses, as well as in popular literature, and new alliances, or networks, of activity have taken shape, often bringing the religious-minded and the environmentally minded together.

The less spiritual aspects of personal environmentalism took on a new importance in the 1990s, particularly in relation to the marketing of bio-technologies (see Durant 1998). There is a widely felt anxiety about these genetically-modified organisms (GMOs) that seems to indicate that the human exploitation of non-human reality has reached a new kind of threshold. Whatever value genetic technologies may have – and there is no denying that, in both food production and in medicine, there is much that they can contribute – large sections of the public remain unconvinced.[2]

But although opposition to GMOs has provided a focus of contention for many consumers and consumer organizations, green consumerism is filled with ambiguities. For those who are already involved in environmental politics in an organized way, then it is meaningful to connect lifestyle and politics. In relation to food consumption, in particular, "eating green" can become an important part of one's identity, and, at least, on the individual level, a way to internalize ecology (Halkier 1999). Similarly, gardening and various forms of ecological craftsmanship may provide satisfaction in a contemporary, fragmented life-style. Describing the so-called "ecological footprint" that we leave behind as we travel through life has become an important task for many personal environmentalists and, in recent years, the organization Friends of the Earth has even provided some quantitative methodological guidelines (Wackernagel and Rees 1996).

One difficulty in aggregating from individual experiences, and individual footprints, is in knowing what is ecological. There are so many different forms of eco-labelling and so many different criteria, or schools, of ecological, or organic, or biodynamic, or health food, that the meaning of "ecological consumption" tends to dissolve. Consumption choices are not made in a vacuum, but are rather part of broader strategies of everyday life that are difficult to conduct in a rational fashion. In one Danish study of ecological consumption among young parents, three main strategies were identified: the "bothered," who found ecological considerations in relation to food consumption a nuisance rather than a concern; the "believers," who bought ecological food as a matter of principle, and the "pragmatists," the vast majority who allowed the various contingencies of everyday life to determine their patterns of food purchase.[3]

The difficulty of generalizing from the particular is obvious, yet an understanding of the cultural dynamics of personal environmentalism requires an in-depth investigation among relatively small groups of people. The motivations that stimulate new age cultural expression and green consumerism are obviously varied, and it has proved difficult to turn a personal commitment into a more all-encompassing process of social and cultural change. But there can be little doubt that personal environmentalism will continue to flourish and grow, and, in particular, will provide serious problems for the biotechnology industries in their attempts to market their products with success.

Building bridges, making spaces

In this review of some of the main forms of critical ecology I have identified a number of dilemmas that affect the kinds of knowledge that are being made, and, in particular, the kinds of barrier or constraint that the emerging ecological culture is up against. One of the most significant problems is that however much we do, and however creative we try to be, there are simply fewer places in which we are allowed to operate. There is a diminishing public space that is open for the flowering of the ecological culture. It gets harder and harder to share the earth.

A major part of the problem is the aggressive nature of the dominant culture. Through its enormous array of products, its seemingly endless capacity to commercialize any possible human need or vice, and, not least, its colonization of other life worlds, the dominant culture draws us into its grasping arms. Even in the various projects of "public participation" that have been carried out around the world in the quest for sustainable development it is the private sector, the business culture, that all too often takes the lead. It is not that business involvement is not desirable, it is that all business involvement carries a price-tag with it. No company, no money-making operation is interested in doing something for nothing.

So it is crucially important that in our societies we have other, non-corporate, spaces for social learning and cognitive praxis. We need a public sphere that means something; we need to have opportunities for coming together, for sharing what we know, for discussing freely and critically the challenges that confront us collectively as communities and societies. Effective public engagement in environmental politics needs people who are willing to be involved, who, in one of its various forms, have an "ecological consciousness"; but there are also a number of supportive conditions, or social innovations, that are even more important if that consciousness is to be cultivated and able to contribute to cultural transformation.

From research into Local Agenda 21 projects, as well as into a wide range of other examples of public participation in the quest for sustainable development around the world, we are able to identify some factors that make it possible to combine, or recombine, the different critical ecologies into meaningful activity. One feature of many of the projects that I studied is that they have both the support of some centrally placed public authorities – we may term these "enlightened civil servants" – as well as a receptive local base of support. People must feel that their participation is meaningful. Enlightened civil servants are important as promoters of social innovations and they are the ones who must translate a new approach or method or concept into the relevant public (or private) space. In the making of the so-called Infralab, or Infrastructural laboratory in the Netherlands, for example, where local citizens are brought into decision-making processes on a regular and organized basis, it was an official at the Ministry of Transportation who simply realized that things had to be done differently concerning new transportation projects. In the "green guides" program in Denmark, as well as in countless other projects of urban ecology or local energy planning, civil servants in the Ministry of the Environment were given the task of making participation happen. It was necessary for public officials to break out of their normal routines, to socially innovate. Enlightened civil servants, often together with people who work for a non-governmental organization, have served to bring both professionalism and valuable "official" connections to a wide range of projects (see Jamison, ed. 1998).

At the same time, bridge-builders are needed; those who can facilitate interaction across and among various social divisions and boundaries. These functions are increasingly undertaken by *ad hoc* networks that are either established for particular campaigns or events or operate within particular sectors or areas of interest. There are now climate action networks, renewable energy networks, organic agriculture networks, ecological design networks and environmental justice networks that bring together people who work in professional organizations or environmental think-tanks with local activists and personal environmentalists.

In 1999 I was invited to a meeting of the Sustainable and Peaceful Energy Network for Asia (SPENA). In many ways, SPENA is a good example of both the strengths and weaknesses of the kind of networks that are so crucial for effective environmental politics. SPENA is composed of energy activists from different Asian countries and at the meeting I attended, the network's second annual gathering, the group comprised a retired engineering professor from India, university professors from Taiwan, Thailand and the Philippines, a long-time activist of all trades from Malaysia, several people from anti-nuclear groups in Japan (whence came both the initiative and the funding), and a number of young people involved in grass-roots projects. There were also a few friends from Europe who came to share our experiences as well as representatives from Greenpeace and a couple of international environmental think-tanks based in Asia.

On a beautiful tropical island, for four days we discussed strategy together, and it was remarkable to see how much useful work could be done, how many experiences could be exchanged, and how much inspiration such a gathering could give. The opportunity to meet and most especially to learn from others in a varied field is extremely important. Most of those who are active need to do too many things to support their activism (and/or academic work). We need to raise funds, report to funders, fill out forms, follow rules, as well as carry out all the routine tasks of our lives, which leaves less time for meeting on a regular basis.

There is an important role for us all to play in keeping open space for communication and recombination. Indeed, this is an increasingly crucial, but often neglected, task in the evolving politics of the environment. In the 1960s and 1970s, as we have seen, environmental and other new social movements carved out public spaces for creative experimentation that provided opportunities for interaction among concerned scientists and concerned citizens. There were science shops, alliances of workers and academics, radical science journals, citizen review boards, renewable energy workshops and a rather wide-ranging search for new forms of cognitive praxis and public involvement in knowledge-making.

In the intervening years, the conditions for such interaction have changed dramatically, as environmental movements have become differentiated and subdivided, and as activism has become more and more a business like any other. In addition, universities throughout the world have grown ever more commercialized, and the academic way of life has come to be strongly colored by the acquisitive and highly competitive values of the marketplace. Academics are more or less required to become entrepreneurs if they are to be successful in their careers; they must seek funds and opportunities for research as well as making direct and indirect connections with business firms. There is nothing intrinsically wrong with opening universities to the commercial marketplace so long as opportunities remain for other kinds of activity. But in many countries the space for critical reflection is getting smaller and, if it exists at all, it is seldom found at universities.

This means that there need to be stronger efforts to provide a counter-weight to the commercializing tendencies that dominate our contemporary world. In relation to environmentalism, somewhere in the interface between universities, public agencies and non-government organizations, we require a more explicit place for "strategic reflection": for questioning and developing alternatives to the dominant culture's ongoing incorporation of the quest for sustainable development. In some countries this kind of strategic activity has been institutionalized in organs for technology or risk assessment, often closely associated with regional and national parliaments. But as the closing of the Office of Technology Assessment, the advisory body for the US Congress that was established in the early 1970s and closed in the late 1990s, clearly testifies, these officially mandated "public spaces" for reflection and debate are highly politicized and dependent on the support and patronage of ruling elites. As it has developed in Europe technology assessment has primarily been a way to tame and domesticate debate, and, even in countries like Denmark and the Netherlands, where technology assessment has been perhaps most highly developed, it has been difficult for the institutionalized bodies to play more than a marginal role in policy-making. Innovative practices, such as the Danish consensus conferences, have emerged, but the kind of broad, public debates that characterized the "social movement" period of environmentalism in the 1970s has not been able to be replicated in these official organs and formal institutions (see Miettinen 1999). Efforts to mobilize resistance to globalization in organizations such as the French-initiated Attac campaign point to the importance of popular, voluntary forms of organization that are often missing in professional institutions (Clinell 2000).

Universities have traditionally prided themselves on their autonomy and their pursuit of academic freedom, and those remain important values to uphold. But they should not become vague abstractions, defending "neutrality" and inaction at the expense of critical reflection. As many universities now align themselves ever more closely to corporate and business interests at least some of them, or some who work within the universities, need to contribute more of our resources, our time, and intellectual energy to working with other "actors" in the society. The risks are fairly obvious: while the brokers of green business are busily recruiting the most enterprising and entrepreneurial, it is often the most militant and extreme of the "critical ecologists" who remain willing to take them on.

NOTES

This chapter draws on research conducted in the PESTO project, as well as in the project, The Transformation of Environmental Activism (TEA), supported by the European Union and coordinated by Christopher Rootes. On both projects, research assistance has been provided by Magnus Ring.

1 The largely non-reflective attitudes to science in environmental movement organizations have been discussed in a number of writings by Steven Yearley (e.g. Yearley 1991, 1994, 1995). Wolfgang Rudig has recently examined the work of a number of environmental think-tanks as part of a British research program in the public understanding of science (Rudig 2000), but otherwise these forms of cognitive praxis, curiously, have remained unexamined by both environmental social scientists, and students of science and technology.

2 Skepticism about the new products has been particularly intense in Europe. For a recent overview see *Scientific American*, April 2001.

3 The study was conducted by Bente Halkier as part of the Danish Strategic Environmental Research Program and involved a number of focus group interviews with parents of small children. What the study revealed was how varied are the meanings of political, or ecological, consumption when examined in detail. Even among those parents who were sympathetic to environmental concerns and arguments there was an easily reached threshold of "guilt" and even annoyance when too many decisions and choices are relegated to the individual level.

7   Concluding reflections

A time to plant, a time to reap . . .

Pete Seeger, "Turn, Turn, Turn" (1954)

Environmental action and environmental discourse, when carried on in the name of "sustainable development," implicitly or explicitly position themselves with respect to the crisis of justice and the crisis of nature. Different actors produce different types of knowledge; they highlight certain issues and underplay others. How attention is focused, what implicit assumptions are cultivated, what hopes are entertained, and what agents are privileged depends on the way the debate on sustainability is framed.

Wolfgang Sachs, Planet Dialectics (1999: 77–78)

A summing-up

Around 1987 the environmental movement began to take on a new character. Metaphorically we might say the seeds that had been planted in the cultural soil had started to take root. The utopian practices which had characterized much of the activity of environmental movements up until then have gradually given way to the somewhat more complicated and diffuse work of instituting and implementing: cultivating and nurturing the seeds that have been planted. As a result the underlying meanings of environmental politics have come to be fundamentally altered. Other interests have had to be taken into account in the launching of campaigns, the development of programs and the taking of initiatives. The terms of discussion have shifted from making particular improvements or pointing to particular environmental problems to integrating environmental concerns into all other kinds of social, economic, and political activities.

In this volume, I have put into a broader historical perspective some of the original visions and practices of the environmental movement, and have traced what has happened to them over the past thirty years. The theoretical contribution incorporates recent experiences of institutionalization and professionalization that have affected environmentalism to highlight fundamental processes of cultural and cognitive change. In so doing some of the underlying conflicts in the cultural transformations that are currently taking place in our societies in the name of ecology have been brought to light.

My account has been based on the assumption that in the quest for more sustainable paths to socio-economic development there have emerged a number of tensions within and between countries, and especially between the rich, advanced, nations of the North and the less developed, all-too-impoverished nations of the South. Using the concepts I developed with Ron Eyerman in writing on social movements, I focus on the cognitive dimensions of these tensions to provide a better understanding of the various programs and activities that different actors are pursuing. This focus on the intellectual content of "greening" is needed for practitioners and analysts alike, many of whom tend to disregard the views expressed by other participants in the quest for sustainable development.

While representatives of the bureaucratic culture, the domain of the state, have emphasized the formal aspects of knowledge production, agents of the economic culture have increasingly directed their attention to institutional and instrumental innovations, and to fostering new forms of management and accounting. The representatives of civic culture have sought primarily to mobilize latent forms of knowledge in the quest for sustainable development and have emphasized the significance of lay, or local, knowledge in political processes and policy-making. In his recent attempt to disentangle the different meanings of sustainable development Wolfgang Sachs has focused his attention on the definitions of "finiteness" that are contained within the several perspectives (Sachs 1999: 78ff). Where one perspective has the quest for sustainability as a "contest," a matter of competition and economic growth (the "economic" culture), another frames the quest in systemic, holistic, terms, from an "astronaut's" perspective, as Sachs calls it (the "bureaucratic" culture). A third approach sees the quest for sustainability from the vantage-point of the individual, or what Sachs terms the "home" perspective: an approach to sustainable development articulated by representatives of the "civic" culture.

As readers will gather, the research presented here has not been written with what Robert Merton once termed "disinterestedness." My observations and empirical investigations have been conducted in direct relation to the theoretical approach that I outlined in chapter 1.

In terms of methodology I have attempted to combine what anthropologists term "participatory observation" with intellectual engagement, seeking to confront the "discourses" or theories of environmental politics and the broader politics of knowledge with some of the emerging practices that are taking place.

I have tried to raise some doubts about how well the available interpretations help us understand what is actually going on in the world of environmental politics. "Ecological modernization," for instance, is a misleading term with which to describe green commercial activities. These activities of green business are filled with both modernizing and anti-modernizing tendencies, and, even more, they are shaped by changing conditions, opportunities, and contingencies.

"Deep ecology" may be a misleading term as all too often it takes on the function of ideology. The deep ecologist originally was meant simply to go further with his or her involvement in environmentalism than the "shallow" pragmatic, ecologist was wont to do in order to explore the deeper philosophical aspects of the environmental problematic, that is, to conduct what Arne Næss called "ecophilosophy" (Næss 1973). But as deep ecology became an ideological term it tended to become a concept to distinguish the radical, or the extremist, from the more pragmatic or practical-minded. So it became counter-productive in that it helped to strengthen a kind of backlash or rejection of environmental arguments. The deep ecologist, for better or worse, has also tended to spawn the not-so-deep anti-ecologist.

So it seems we need to modify our use of terminology. More fluid terms are needed: dialectical, open-ended terms to characterize the ebbs and flows, nuances and subtleties and the ambiguities of environmental politics.

From tensions to regimes

In ideal-typical terms three cognitive regimes have manifested themselves in the most recent phase of environmental politics as the emerging ecological culture wages its two-pronged battle against incorporation and reaction. These regimes are grounded in different types of human agency, each with its own characteristic form of social action and particular constituencies and actor-networks. In cognitive terms, we may distinguish not only the various kinds of knowledge-production that are favored by each of the regimes but also the different "tacit," or embodied, forms of knowledge that are mobilized. The division into regimes follows the cultural theory that I have used throughout this volume, in which environmental politics are characterized in relation to conflicting "cultural formations" (see Table 3).

Each regime has its own distinctive approach to both sustainable development, and to scientific and technological development, and, further, to

Table 3 *Cognitive regimes of sustainable development*

	Residual	Dominant	Emerging
Type of agency	local/national	transnational	synthetic
Forms of social action	traditionalist resistance	commercial brokerage	exemplary mobilization
Type of knowledge	factual/lay	scientific/managerial	contextual/situated
Tacit forms	place/roots	discipline/skills	experiences

knowledge-making in general. Each has its own preferred types of institutional, or organizational, "learning," and each has different reasons for
pursuing its agenda. In relation to public engagement each regime implies
quite different conceptions of agency and social action. At work in each
of the three main strategies there is a different processual logic, based on
what might be termed different normative or motivational systems. Each
may be seen to be mobilizing, or utilizing, different types of formalized,
or explicit, as well as informal or "tacit," forms of knowledge. Each tends
to be based on a separate sphere of society, and, indeed, one of the main
problems is that different strategies tend to compete for resources and
influence.

On the one hand, there are the locally based initiatives, where forms
of action are often a kind of protest, either directly against a new project
"from above" or indirectly, as a defense of a traditional form of existence,
way of life, or national prerogative. The pursuit of environmental sustainability provides a catalyst in many of these cases for mobilization and revitalization of traditional knowledge and national identities. As with many
earlier forms of populism, however, these local initiatives have a difficult
time achieving legitimacy and credibility, due both to their popular modes
of knowledge-making and their often too-personal forms of decision-
making.

On the other hand, with many of the various projects of so-called "ecological modernization," participation is primarily conceived as top-down,
with members of the public presented with the role of environmentally
conscious consumer, or offered opportunities for ecological employment.
Here, legitimacy is achieved at the cost of incorporation and subservience
to commercial agendas and strategies. Knowledge-making is dominated
by a managerial mindset, and the tacit dimension that is mobilized is
the skills and organizational routines that are embedded in established
institutions.

In these ways the emerging ecological culture represents a kind of synthesis, or transcendence, of the dominant and the residual, or what we can think of as established and populist regimes. The form of action is flexible and often presents experiments or examples of "what can be done." Knowledge is mobilized which is both transdisciplinary in a formal sense that draws on many disciplines and traditions, as well as contingent, in a tacit sense that depends on context and the recombining of knowledge. The form of agency is both direct and representative, or, rather, we may see it as an evolving "hybrid" combination of the local and the global, what has been termed local cosmopolitanism or global ecological citizenship (Beck 1999).

Back to the garden

Are the ecological transformations that we have examined here ultimately meaningful? Do they indicate the emergence of a new kind of human consciousness, a new kind of relationship between human and non-human nature? Can we see the making of a new cultural formation in the quest for sustainable development? Of course it is not possible to provide definitive answers to these questions, only to indicate some partial responses. There have been major barriers to institutional reform and to radical technological innovation that have slowed progress considerably. I have indicated how dissension and conflict and competition have distracted many agents for change from achieving their goals. It is clear that established power-holders, be they in the business world, local communities, or in environmental organizations have tried to limit the range and meaning of environmental politics and thus its impact and effect. But I have also shown how people have persevered with the struggle, amending it, moving it around, coming up with new ideas. For, as the old civil rights song would have it, "the movement's movin' on."

Perhaps the most important effect that environmentalism has had over the past thirty years is to help people worldwide to rediscover their relationship with the earth. Environmental movements, or the emerging ecological culture, have contributed to a project of global public cultivation, or enlightenment, by which millions of people have learned each in their own way why the survival of our natural surroundings is important for the human species. The "land ethic" was what Aldo Leopold called it back in the 1940s, and it has, of course, taken many forms in the years since, some of which are community-based (e.g. collective gardens), some of which are professional (e.g. organic agriculture), some of which are militant (e.g. occupying virgin forests) and some of which, or most of which, are personal. Perhaps it is in this personal dimension that a common denominator can be found among all the different forms of "critical" or social or cultural ecology that have been discussed in these pages, as an emerging culture struggles to stay free from the greedy commercial tentacles of global capitalism.

We might recall the Diggers, as they marched up St. George's Hill near Walton in Surrey in 1649 to share the earth, to dig together, and to practice a new creed – The Law of Freedom in a Platform – that was an early, perhaps the very first, environmentalist manifesto. "There should be no buying and selling of the Earth, nor of the fruits thereof," Gerrard Winstanley wrote (1652/1973: 127); and he continued:

The Earth is to be planted, and the fruits reaped, and carried into Barns and Store-houses by the assistance of every family: And if any man or family want Corn, or other provision, they may go to the Storehouses, and fetch without money: If they want a Horse to ride, go into the fields in Summer, or to the Common Stables in Winter, and receive one from the Keepers, and when your journey is performed, bring him where you had him, without money. If any want food or victuals, they may either go to the Butchers shops, and receive what they want without money; or else go to the flocks of sheep, or herds of cattel, and take and kill what meat is needful for their families, without buying and selling. (ibid.: 128)

Winstanley's vision was radical in the seventeenth century, and it has remained radical to this day. With its sense of solidarity and understanding of the collective nature of human sustenance it has served as a core, or underlying meaning for the varied and myriad attempts throughout subsequent centuries to develop an ecological society. But after some thirty years of an emerging environmental culture that has spread the vision far and wide the old idea might just have come a bit closer to realization.

References

Aall, Carlo (1999) Norway: From Environmental Protection to Sustainability 'Light'?, in Lafferty, ed.

Abram, David (1996) *The Spell of the Sensuous*. New York: Vintage

Adams, William (1990) *Green Development*. London: Routledge

Adorno, Teodor and Max Horkheimer (1972/1944) *The Dialectic of Enlightenment*. London: Herder and Herder

Agarwal, Anil and Sunita Narain (1991) *Global Warming in an Unequal World. A Case of Environmental Colonialism*. New Delhi: Centre for Science and Environment

Agarwal, Anil, Sunita Narain and Anju Sharma, eds. (1999) *Green Politics. Global Environmental Negotiations 1*. New Delhi: Centre for Science and Environment

Akula, Vikram (1995) Grassroots Environmental Resistance in India, in Taylor, ed.

Alberoni, Francesco (1984) *Movement and Institution*. New York: Columbia University Press

Andersen, Mikael Skou (1994) *Governance by Green Taxes: Making Pollution Prevention Pay*. Manchester University Press

(1997) Conflict and Compromise in Environmental Policy: Capacity Building in Denmark, in Jänicke and Weidner, eds.

Andersen, Michael Skou and Duncan Liefferink, eds. (1997) *European Environmental Policy. The Pioneers*. Manchester University Press

Andringa, Jose and Johan Schot (1997) Public Participation in Environmental Science and Technology: The Dutch National Experience 1960s–1990s, in Jamison and Østby, eds.

Andringa, Jose, Marco Giuliani, Patrick van Zwanenberg and Magnus Ring (1998) Participation by Mandate: Reflections on Local Agenda 21, in Jamison, ed.

Archibugi, Daniele and Bengt-Åke Lundvall, eds. (2001) *The Globalizing Learning Economy*. Oxford University Press

Aronowitz, Stanley (1993) *Roll Over Beethoven. The Return of Cultural Strife*. Hanover, N.H.: Wesleyan University Press

Ashford, Nicholas and Ralph Meima (1993) *Designing the Sustainable Enterprise*. Summary Report, Second International Research Conference, The Greening of Industry Network.

Athanasiou, Tom (1996) *Divided Planet. The Ecology of Rich and Poor*. Boston: Little Brown

Baark, Erik (1997) Environmental Technology Policy in a Consensus Mode: The Case of Denmark, in Jamison and Østby, eds.

Baark, Erik and Andrew Jamison (1986) The Technology and Culture Problematique, in Baark and Jamison, eds.

(1990) Biotechnology and Culture: Public Debates and Their Impact on Government Regulation in the United States and Denmark, in *Technology in Society*, no. 1

Baark, Erik and Andrew Jamison, eds. (1986) *Technological Development in China, India and Japan: Cross-cultural Perspectives*. London: Macmillan

Bach Tan Sinh (1998) Sustainable Development in Vietnam: Institutional Challenges for Integration of Environment and Development. Hanoi: National Institute for Science, Technology Policy and Strategy Studies (Ph.D. dissertation)

Bacon, Francis (1620/1947) *Novum Organum* (Book 1), as translated and excerpted in Saxe Commins and Robert Linscott, eds., *Man and the Universe: The Philosophers of Science*. New York: Random House

Baker, Susan, *et al.*, eds. (1997) *The Politics of Sustainable Development: Theory, Policy and Practice Within the European Union*. London: Routledge

Barber, Benjamin (1984) *Strong Democracy: Participatory Politics for a New Age*. Berkeley: University of California Press

Bauman, Zygmunt (1987) *Legislators and Interpreters*. Cambridge: Polity Press

Becher, Tony (1989) *Academic Tribes and Territories: Intellectual Enquiry and the Cultures of Disciplines*. London: Taylor and Francis.

Beck, Ulrich (1992/1986) *Risk Society. Towards a New Modernity*. London: Sage

(1988/1995) *Ecological Politics in an Age of Risk*. Cambridge: Polity Press

(1998) *Vad innebär globaliseringen? (Was ist Globalisierung?)*. Göteborg: Daidalos

(1999) *World Risk Society*. Cambridge: Polity Press

Beck, Ulrich, Anthony Giddens and Scott Lash (1994) *Reflexive Modernisation*. Cambridge: Polity Press

Beder, Sharon (1997) *Global Spin. The Corporate Assault on Environmentalism*. Totnes, Devon: Green Books

Bell, Michael (1998) *An Invitation to Environmental Sociology*. Thousand Oaks, CA: Pine Forge Press

Ben-David, Joseph (1971) *The Scientist's Role in Society*. Englewood Cliffs: Prentice-Hall

Benthall, Jeremy, ed. (1972) *Ecology, the Shaping Inquiry*. London: Longman

Berg, Maxine (1980) *The Machinery Question and the Making of Political Economy*. Cambridge University Press

Berger, Peter and Thomas Luckmann (1967) *The Social Construction of Reality: A Treatise in the Sociology of Knowledge*. New York: Doubleday

Berggren, Niclas (1997) *Teskedsjobben – en kritisk granskning av idéerna om "gröna jobb."* Stockholm: Timbro

Berry, Wendell (1990) *What Are People For?* San Francisco: North Point Press

Bichsel, Anne (1996) NGOs as agents of public accountability and democratization in intergovernmental forums, in Lafferty and Meadowcroft, eds.

Birnbaum, Norman (1988) *The Radical Renewal: The Politics of Ideas in Modern America*. New York: Pantheon

Blowers, Andrew and Stephen Young (2000) Britain: Unsustainable Cities, in Low *et al.*, eds.

Böhme, Gernot, *et al.* (1978) The "Scientification" of Technology, in Wolfgang Krohn, *et al.*, eds., *The Dynamics of Science and Technology*. Dordrecht: Reidel

Bookchin, Murray (1963) *Our Synthetic Environment* (pseudonym: Lewis Herber). New York: Knopf

(1971) *Post-Scarcity Anarchism*. Montreal: Black Rose Books

(1982) *The Ecology of Freedom*. Palo Alto, CA: Cheshire Books

(1994) *Which Way for the Ecology Movement?* Edinburgh and San Francisco: AK Press

Borish, Steven M. (1991) *The Land to the Living: The Danish Folk High Schools and Denmark's Non-violent Path to Modernization*. Nevada City, CA: Blue Dolphin Publishing

Bovin, Kristina dn Sindre Magnusson (1997) *49 Local Initiatives for Sustainable Development*. Stockholm: The Swedish Society for Nature Conservation

Boyle, Godfrey and Peter Harper, eds. (1976) *Radical Technology*. London: Wildwood House

Bramwell, Anne (1989) *Ecology in the 20th Century. A History*. New Haven: Yale University Press

Brand, Ellis and Theo de Bruijn (1998) *Evaluation Report of the Greening of Industry Network*. University of Twente, Center for Clean Technology and Environmental Policy

Brand, Karl-Werner (1990) Cyclical Aspects of New Social Movements: Waves of Cultural Criticism and Mobilization Cycles of New Middle-Class Radicalism, in R. Dalton and M. Kuechler, eds., *Challenging the Political Order: New Social and Political Movements in Western Democracies*. Cambridge: Polity Press

(1999) Dialectics of Institutionalisation: The Transformation of the Environmental Movement in Germany, in Rootes, ed.

Buell, Lawrence (1996) *The Environmental Imagination. Thoreau, Nature Writing and the Formation of American Culture*. Cambridge, MA: Harvard University Press

Buriks, Carla (1989) Waste-reduction Technologies. Unpublished MA thesis in Science and Technology Policy. Lund University

Carson, Rachel (1962) *Silent Spring*. Boston, MA: Houghton Mifflin

Castells, Manuel (1996) *The Rise of the Network Society*. Oxford: Blackwell

Chambers, Robert (1997) *Whose Reality Counts? Putting the First Last*. London: Intermediate Technology Publications

Clarke, Sarah and Susse Georg (1995) *From Greening to Sustaining: Transformational Challenges for the Firm* (Summary Report. Third International Research Conference, Greening of Industry Network). Technical University of Denmark: Unit for Technology Assessment

Climell, Bim (2000) *Attac – gräsrötternas revolt mot marknaden*. Stockholm: Agora

Cohen, Maurie (1999) Science and Society in Historical Perspective: Implications for Social Theories of Risk, in *Environmental Values*, no. 2

Cohen, Maurie (2000) Ecological Modernisation, Environmental Knowledge and National Character: A Preliminary Analysis of the Netherlands, in Mol and Sonnenfeld, eds.

(1999) *Risk in the Modern Age. Social Theory, Science and Environmental Decision-Making*. Basingstoke: Macmillan

Commoner, Barry (1971) *The Closing Circle*. New York: Knopf

(1972) The Social Use and Misuse of Technology, in Benthall, ed.

(1976) *The Poverty of Power. Energy and the Economic Crisis*. New York: Knopf

(1991) *Making Peace With the Planet*. New York: Pantheon

Connelly, James and Graham Smith (1999) *Politics and the Environment: From Theory to Practice*. London: Routledge

Cooper, David, ed. (1968) *The Dialectics of Liberation*. Harmondsworth: Penguin

Costanza, Robert, *et al.* (1997) *An Introduction to Ecological Economics*. Boca Raton, FL: St. Lucie Press

Cotgrove, Stephen (1982) *Catastrophe or Cornucopia: The Environment, Politics and the Future*. Chichester: John Wiley

Couch, Stephen and Steve Kroll-Smith (1997) Environmental Movements and Expert Knowledge: Evidence for a New Populism (manuscript)

Cramer, Jacqueline, Ron Eyerman and Andrew Jamison (1987) The Knowledge Interests of the Environmental Movement and Its Potential for Influencing the Development of Science, in Stuart Blume, *et al.*, eds., *The Social Direction of the Public Sciences*. Dordrecht: Reidel

Cramer, Jacqueline, Kurt Fischer and Johan Schot (1991) *The Greening of Industry: Research Needs and Policy Implications* (Summary Report. First International Research Conference). The Greening of Industry Network

Daly, Herman (1999) *Ecological Economics and the Ecology of Economics*. Cheltenham: Edward Elgar

Darier, Eric, ed. (1999) *Discourses of the Environment*. Oxford: Blackwell

de Solla Price, Derek (1963) *Little Science, Big Science*. New York: Columbia University Press

DeSimone, Livio and Frank Popoff (2000) *Eco-efficiency. The Business Link to Sustainable Development*. Cambridge, MA: MIT Press

Dekker, Kees, Mario Diani, Andrew Jamison and Lise Kvande (1998) Representing the Public: New Roles for Environmental Organizations, in Jamison, ed.

Della Porta, Donatella and Mario Diani (1999) *Social Movements. An Introduction*. Oxford: Blackwell

Diani, Mario and Paolo Donati (1999) Organisational Change in Western European Environmental Groups: A Framework for Analysis, in Rootes, ed.

Dickson, David (1974) *Alternative Technology and the Politics of Technical Change*. Glasgow: Fontana

Dobson, Andrew (2000) *Green Political Thought*. London: Routledge

Douglas, Mary (1966) *Purity and Danger: An Analysis of Concepts of Pollution and Taboo*. London: Routledge & Kegan Paul

(1970) *Natural Symbols: Explorations in Cosmology*. London: Cresset

(1972) Environments at Risk, in Benthall, ed.

(1978) *Implicit Meanings: Essays in Anthropology.* London: Routledge and Kegan Paul

Douglas, Mary and Aaron Wildavsky (1982) *Risk and Culture: An Essay on the Selection of Technical and Environmental Dangers.* Berkeley: University of California Press

Dowie, Mark (1996) *Losing Ground: American Environmentalism at the Close of the Twentieth Century.* Cambridge, MA: MIT Press

Dryzek, John (1997) *The Politics of the Earth. Environmental Discourses.* Oxford University Press

Durant, John, Martin Bauer and George Gaskell, eds. (1998) *Biotechnology in the Public Sphere. A European Sourcebook.* London: Science Museum

Eckersley, Robin (1992) *Environmentalism and Political Theory. Toward an Ecocentric Approach.* Albany: SUNY Press

The Ecologist (1972) *A Blueprint for Survival.* Harmondsworth: Penguin

Edelstein, Michael (1988) *Contaminated Communities. The Social and Psychological Impacts of Residential Toxic Exposure.* Boulder, CA: Westview Press

Eder, Klaus (1996) The Institutionalisation of Environmentalism: Ecological Discourse and the Second Transformation of the Public Sphere, in Lash *et al.,* eds.

Edquist, Charles, ed. (1997) *Systems of Innovation.* London: Pinter

Edquist, Charles and Bengt-Åke Lundvall (1993) Comparing the Danish and Swedish Systems of Innovation, in Nelson, ed.

Edquist, Charles and Edquist, Olle (1980) *Social Carriers of Techniques for Development.* Stockholm: SAREC

Edwards, Bob (1995) With Liberty and Environmental Justice for All: The Emergence and Challenge of Grassroots Environmentalism in the United States, in Taylor, ed.

Elander, Ingemar and Rolf Lidskog (2000) The Rio Declaration and Subsequent Global Initiatives, in Low *et al.,* eds.

Elzinga, Aant (1985) Research, Bureaucracy and the Drift of Epistemic Criteria, in Björn Wittrock and Aant Elzinga, eds., *The University Research System.* Stockholm: Almqvist and Wiksell

Elzinga, Aant and Andrew Jamison (1981) *Cultural Components in the Scientific Attitude to Nature. Eastern and Western Modes?* Lund: Research Policy Institute

(1984) Making Dreams Come True: On the Role of Practical Utopias in Science, in Everett Mendelsohn and Helga Nowotny, eds., *Nineteen Eighty-Four: Science Between Utopia and Dystopia.* Dordrecht: Reidel

(1986) The Other Side of the Coin: The Cultural Critique of Technology in India and Japan, in Baark and Jamison, eds.

(1995) Changing Policy Agendas in Science and Technology, in Sheila Jasanoff *et al.,* eds., *Handbook in Science and Technology Studies.* London: Sage

Elzinga, Aant, Andrew Jamison and Conny Mithander (1998) Swedish Grandeur: Contending Reformulations of the Great Power Doctrine, in Hård and Jamison, eds.

Engberg, Lars (2000) Reflexivity and Political Participation – a Study of Re-embedding Strategies. Roskilde University Center. (Ph.D. dissertation)

Eyerman, Ron (1994) *Between Culture and Politics.* Cambridge: Polity Press

Eyerman, Ron and Andrew Jamison (1989) Environmental Knowledge as an Organizational Weapon: The Case of Greenpeace, in *Social Science Information*, no. 2

(1991) *Social Movements. A Cognitive Approach.* Cambridge: Polity Press

(1998) *Music and Social Movements.* Cambridge University Press

Ezrahi, Yaron, *et al.*, eds. (1994) *Technology, Pessimism and Postmodernism.* Dordrecht: Kluwer

Ferry, Luc (1995) *The New Ecological Order.* University of Chicago Press

Fischer, Frank (2000) *Citizens, Experts and the Environment. The Politics of Local Knowledge.* Durham: Duke University Press

Fischer, Frank and Maarten Hajer, eds. (1999) *Living With Nature. Environmental Politics as Cultural Discourse.* Oxford University Press

Fischer, Kurt and Johan Schot, eds. (1993) *Environmental Strategies for Industry. International Perspectives on Research Needs and Policy Implications.* Washington: Island Press

Flam, Helena, ed. (1994) *States and Anti-Nuclear Movements.* Edinburgh University Press

Foucault, Michel (1973) *The Order of Things.* New York: Vintage Books

Fox, Stephen (1985) *The American Conservation Movement: John Muir and His Legacy.* Madison: University of Wisconsin Press

Frank, Andre Gunder (1978) *World Accumulation 1492–1789.* London: Macmillan

Frankel, Carl (1998) *In Earth's Company. Business, Environment and the Challenge of Sustainability.* Gabriola Island, BC: NewSociety Publishers

Freeman, Christopher (1987) *Technology Policy and Economic Performance: Lessons from Japan.* London: Pinter

French, Hilary (2000) *Vanishing Borders. Protecting the Planet in the Age of Globalization.* New York: W. W. Norton

Frängsmyr, Tore, ed. (1989) *Science in Sweden. The Royal Academy of Sciences 1739–1989.* Canton, MA: Science History Publications

Fuller, Steve (1988) *Social Epistemology.* Bloomington: Indiana University Press

Gadgil, Madhav and Ramachandra Guha (1992) *This Fissured Land. An Ecological History of India.* Berkeley: University of California Press

Galbraith, John (1967) *The New Industrial State.* New York: New American Library

Gan Lin (1995) The Shaping of Institutions in Global Environmental Policy. Roskilde University Center (Ph.D. Dissertation)

(1999) Implementation of Agenda 21 in China: Institutions and Obstacles, in *Environmental Politics*, no. 1

Gandhi, M.K. (1908/1938) *Hind Swaraj, or Indian Home Rule.* Ahmedabad: Navajivan Publishing House

Gellen, Martin (1970) The Making of a Pollution-Industrial Complex, *Ramparts*, May

Georgescu-Roegen, Nicholas (1971) *The Entropy Law and the Economic Process.* Cambridge, MA: Harvard University Press

Gibbons, Michael *et al.* (1994) *The New Production of Knowledge.* London: Sage

Giddens, Anthony (1990) *The Consequences of Modernity.* Cambridge: Polity Press

(1994) *Beyond Left and Right. The Future of Radical Politics.* Cambridge: Polity Press

(1998) *The Third Way.* Cambridge: Polity Press

Giddens, Anthony and Will Hutton, eds. (2000) *On The Edge. Living with Global Capitalism.* London: Jonathan Cape

Gieryn, Thomas (1999) *Cultural Boundaries of Science. Credibility on the Line.* University of Chicago Press

Gillberg, Minna (1999) From Green Image to Green Practice. Normative Action and Self-Regulation. Lund: Department of Sociology (Ph.D. dissertation)

Goldsmith, Maurice and Alan Mackay, eds. (1966) *The Science of Science.* Harmondsworth: Penguin

Golinski, Jan (1998) *Making Natural Knowledge. Constructivism and the History of Science.* Cambridge University Press

Gooch, Pernille (1998) At the Tail of the Buffalo. Van Gujjar Pastoralists between the Forest and the World Arena. Lund: Department of Sociology (Ph.D. dissertation)

Gorelick, Steven (1998) *Small is Beautiful, Big is Subsidised. How our Taxes Contribute to Social and Environmental Breakdown.* Dartington: International Society for Ecology and Culture

Gottlieb, Robert (1993) *Forcing the Spring: The Transformation of the American Environmental Movement.* Washington: Island Press

Gould, Kenneth, Allan Schnaiberg and Adam Weinberg (1996) *Local Environmental Struggles. Citizen Activism in the Treadmill of Production.* Cambridge University Press

Gouldner, Alvin (1979) *The Future of Intellectuals and the Rise of the New Class.* New York: Seabury

(1980) *The Two Marxisms.* New York: Oxford University Press

(1985) *Against Fragmentation.* New York: Oxford University Press

Groenewegen, Peter, (1996) *The Greening of Industry Resource Guide and Bibliography.* Washington: Island Press

Gross, Paul and Norman Levitt (1994) *Higher Superstition. The Academic Left and Its Quarrels with Science.* Baltimore: Johns Hopkins University Press

Guha, Ramachandra (1991) Lewis Mumford, The Forgotten American Environmentalist: An Essay in Rehabilitation, in *Capitalism, Nature, Socialism* (October)

(1992) Prehistory of Indian Environmentalism. Intellectual Traditions, in *Economic and Political Weekly*, January 4–11

(2000) *Environmentalism. A Global History.* New York: Longman

Haas, Peter, *et al.*, eds. (1993) *Institutions for the Earth: Sources of Effective International Environmental Protection.* Cambridge, MA: MIT Press

Habermas, Jürgen (1971/1964) *Knowledge and Human Interests.* Boston: Beacon

Haila, Yrjö (1997) "Wilderness" and the Multiple Layers of Environmental Thought, in *Environment and History*, no. 3, 1997

(1998) Environmental Problems, Ecological Scales and Social Deliberation, in Peter Glasbergen, ed., *Co-operative Environmental Governance.* Dordrecht: Kluwer

(1999) The North As/And the Other: Ecology, Domination, Solidarity, in Fischer and Hajer, eds.

Hajer, Maarten (1995) *The Politics of Environmental Discourse*. Oxford University Press
(1996) Ecological Modernisation as Cultural Politics, in Lash, *et al.*, eds.
Hajer, Maarten and Sven Kesselring (1999) Democracy in the Risk Society? Learning from the New Politics of Mobility in Munich, in *Environmental Politics*, no. 3
Halkier, Bente (1999) Consequences of the Politicization of Consumption: The Example of Environmentally Friendly Consumption Practices, in *Journal of Environmental Policy and Planning*, no. 1
Hannerz, Ulf (1992) *Cultural Complexity. Studies in the Social Organization of Meaning*. New York: Columbia University Press
Hannigan, John (1995) *Environmental Sociology. A Social Constructionist Perspective*. London: Routledge
Haraway, Donna (1991) *Simians, Cyborgs, and Women: The Reinvention of Nature*. New York: Chapman and Hall
Hård, Mikael (1994a) Technology as Practice. Local and Global Closure Processes in Diesel-engine Design, *Social Studies of Science* 24: 549–585
(1994b) *Machines Are Frozen Spirit: The Scientification of Refrigeration and Brewing in the Nineteenth Century – A Weberian Interpretation*. Frankfurt: Campus
Hård, Mikael and Andrew Jamison (1997) Alternative Cars: The Contrasting Stories of Steam and Diesel Automotive Engines, in *Technology in Society*, no. 3
Hård, Mikael and Andrew Jamison, eds. (1998) *The Intellectual Appropriation of Technology: Discourses on Modernity, 1900–1939*. Cambridge, MA: MIT Press
Harding, Sandra (1998) *Is Science Multicultural? Postcolonialisms, Feminisms and Epistemologies*. Bloomington: Indiana University Press
Harvey, David (1996) *Justice, Nature and the Geography of Difference*. Oxford: Blackwell
Hawken, Paul, Amory Lovins and Hunter Lovins (1999) *Natural Capitalism: Creating the next Industrial Revolution*. Boston: Little, Brown, and Co.
Hays, Samuel (1959) *Conservation and the Gospel of Efficiency*. Cambridge, MA: Harvard University Press
(1987) *Beauty, Health and Permanence: Environmental Politics in the United States, 1955–1985*. Cambridge University Press
Herf, Jeffrey (1984) *Reactionary Modernism: Technology, Culture and Politics in Weimar and the Third Reich*. Cambridge University Press
Hermele, Kenneth (2000) Framtidsfabriken, in *Ordfront*, no. 1–2
Hill, Christopher (1965) *Intellectual Origins of the English Revolution*. Oxford University Press
(1975) *The World Turned Upside Down. Radical Ideas During the English Revolution*. Harmondsworth: Penguin
Hillary, Ruth, ed. (1997) *Environmental Management Systems and Cleaner Production*. Chichester: John Wiley
Hobsbawm, E. J. (1962) *The Age of Revolution*. London: Weidenfeld and Nicolson
(1979) *The Age of Capital 1848–1875*. New York: New American Library
Holm, Jesper (1999) LA21 and Political Modernisation: Toward a New Environmental Rationality in Denmark?, in Lafferty, ed.

Huff, Toby (1993) *Rise of Early Modern Science: India, China and the West.* Cambridge University Press

Hughes, Thomas and Agatha Hughes, eds. (1990) *Lewis Mumford: Public Intellectual.* New York: Oxford University Press

Hukkinen, Janne (1999) *Institutions in Environmental Management: Constructing Mental Models and Sustainability.* London: Routledge

Illich, Ivan (1973) *Tools for Conviviality.* London: Calder and Boyars

Irwin, Alan (1995) *Citizen Science. A Study of People, Expertise and Sustainable Development.* London: Routledge

Irwin, Alan and Brian Wynne, eds. (1995) *Misunderstanding Science.* Cambridge University Press

Jacob, James (1998) *The Scientific Revolution. Aspirations and Achievements, 1500–1700.* Atlantic Highlands: Humanities Press

Jacob, Margaret (1988) *The Cultural Meaning of the Scientific Revolution.* New York: Knopf

(1997) *Scientific Culture and the Making of the Industrial West.* New York: Oxford University Press

Jacob, Merle (1996) Sustainable Development: a Reconstructive Critique of the United Nations Debate. Gothenburg: Department of Theory of Science (Ph.D. dissertation)

Jacobs, Michael, ed. (1997) *Greening the Millennium: The New Politics of the Environment.* Oxford: Blackwell

Jacoby, Russell (1987) *The Last Intellectuals. American Culture in the Age of Academe.* New York: Basic Books

Jagtenberg, Tom and David McKie (1997) *Eco-impacts and the Greening of Postmodernity.* London: Sage

Jameson, Frederic and Masao Miyoshi, eds. (1999) *The Cultures of Globalization.* Durham: Duke University Press

Jamison, Andrew (1970) *The Steam-Powered Automobile: An Answer to Air Pollution.* Bloomington: Indiana University Press

(1971a) How Sweden Tackles Pollution, in *New Scientist*, 4 February

(1971b) Swedish Scientists: Saying What Should Be Done, in *Technology Review*, April

(1971c) The Lesson of the Askö Lab, in *New Scientist*, 9 December

(1972) Taking Science to the Streets, in *New Scientist*, 24 February

(1973) Science as Control. Environmental Research in Sweden, in *Nordisk Forum*, no. 2

(1977) On the Politicization of Energy in Denmark and Sweden, in *Nordisk Forum*, no. 3

(1982) National Components of Scientific Knowledge. A Contribution to the Social Theory of Science. Lund: Research Policy Institute (Ph.D. dissertation)

(1987) National Styles of Science and Technology: A Comparative Model, in *Sociological Inquiry*, no. 2

(1988) Social Movements and the Politicization of Science, in Andrew Jamison, ed., *Keeping Science Straight.* Gothenburg: Dept of Theory of Science

(1989) Technology's Theorists: Conceptions of Innovation in Relation to Scence and Technology Policy, in *Technology and Culture*, July

(1991) National Styles in Technology Policy: Comparing the Danish and Swedish State Programmes in Microelectronics/Information Technology, in Ulrich Hilpert, ed., *State Policies and Techno-Industrial Innovation*. London: Routledge

(1993) National Political Cultures and the Exchange of Knowledge: The Case of Systems Ecology, in Elisabeth Crawford, *et al.* eds., *Denationalizing Science*. Dordrecht: Kluwer

(1994) Western Science in Perspective and the Search for Alternatives, in Jean-Jacques Salomon, *et al.* eds. *The Uncertain Quest. Science, Technology and Development*. Tokyo: UN University Press

(1995) Debating the Car in the 1960s and 1990s: Similarities and Differences, in *Technology in Society*, no. 4

(1996) The Shaping of the Global Environmental Agenda: The Role of Non-governmental Organisations, in Lash *et al.* eds.

(1997) Sweden: The Dilemmas of Polarization, in Jamison and Østby, eds.

(1998) American Anxieties: Technology and the Reshaping of Republican Values, in Hård and Jamison, eds.

Jamison, Andrew, ed. (1998) *Technology Policy Meets the Public. PESTO Papers 2.* Aalborg University Press

(1999) *Public Engagement and Science and Technology Policy Options (PESTO)*, final report of European Union research project contract number SOE1-CT96-1016. Aalborg University: Department of Development and Planning report series 237

Jamison, Andrew and Erik Baark (1990) Modes of Biotechnology Assessment in the USA, Japan and Denmark, in *Technology Analysis and Strategic Management*, no. 2: 111–127

(1995) From Market Reforms to Sustainable Development. The Cultural Dimension of Science and Technology Policy in Vietnam and China, in Irene Nørlund *et al.* eds., *Vietnam in a Changing World*. London: Curzon Press

(1999) National Shades of Green: Comparing the Swedish and Danish Styles in Ecological Modernisation, in *Environmental Values*, no. 2: 199–218

Jamison, Andrew and Ron Eyerman (1994) *Seeds of the Sixties*. Berkeley: University of California Press

Jamison, Andrew, Ron Eyerman, Jacqueline Cramer with Jeppe Læssøe (1990). *The Making of the New Environmental Consciousness: A Comparative Study of the Environmental Movements in Sweden, Denmark and the Netherlands* Edinburgh University Press

Jamison, Andrew, Ron Eyerman and Jacqueline Cramer (1990) Where Do Intellectuals Come From? On the Formation of Intellectuals in the Environmental Movement, in A. Elzinga *et al.*, eds. *In Science We Trust? Moral and Political Issues of Science in Society*. Lund University Press

Jamison, Andrew and Per Østby, eds. (1997) *Public Participation and Sustainable Development. Comparing European Experiences. PESTO Papers 1.* Aalborg University Press

Jänicke, Martin and Helmut Weidner, eds. (1997) *National Environmental Policies – A Comparative Study of Capacity Building*. Berlin: Springer Verlag

Jardine, Lisa (1999) *Ingenious Pursuits. Building the Scientific Revolution*. London: Little, Brown and Company

Jasanoff, Sheila (1990) American Exceptionalism and the Political Acknowledgment of Risk, in *Daedalus*, Autumn

    (1999) The Songlines of Risk, in *Environmental Values*, no. 2: 135–52

Jasanoff, Sheila and Brian Wynne (1998) Science and Decision Making, in Steve Rayner and Elizabeth Malone, eds., *Human Choice and Climate Change*. Columbus, OH: Batelle Press

Jasanoff, Sheila *et al.* eds. (1995) *Handbook in Science and Technology Studies*. London: Sage

Jasper, James (1990) *Nuclear Politics: Energy and the State in the United States, Sweden and France*. Princeton University Press

    (1997) *The Art of Moral Protest. Culture, Biography, and Creativity in Social Movements*. Chicago: University of Chicago Press

Jørgensen, Ulrik and Peter Karnøe (1995) The Danish Wind-Turbine Story: Technical Solutions to Political Visions? in Rip *et al.* eds.

Kamieniecki, Sheldon, ed. (1993) *Environmental Politics in the International Arena. Movements, Parties, Organizations, and Policy*. Albany: SUNY Press

Kazin, Michael (1995) *The Populist Persuasion*. New York: Basic Books

Kellow, Aynsley (2000) Norms, Interests and Environmental NGOs: The Limits of Cosmopolitanism, in *Environmental Politics*, no. 3

King, Alexander, ed. (1991) *Culture, Globalization and the World-System*. London: Macmillan

Kingston, Jos (1976) It's Been Said Before and Where Did that Get Us?, in Boyle and Harper, eds.

Kitschelt, Herbert (1986) Political Opportunity Structures and Political Protest: Anti-Nuclear Movements in Four Democracies. *The British Journal of Political Science* 16: 57–85

Kolakowski, Leszek (1981) *Main Currents of Marxism*. Oxford University Press

Konttinen, Esa, *et al.* (1999) All Shades of Green. The Environmentalization of Finnish Society. University of Jyväskylä: SoPhi

Kosik, Karel (1976) *The Dialectics of the Concrete*. Dordrecht: Reidel

Kousis, Maria (1997) Grassroots Environmental Movements in Rural Greece: Effectiveness, Success and the Quest for Sustainable Development, in Baker, *et al.* eds.

    (1998) Ecological Marginalization in Rural Areas: Actors, Impacts, Responses, in *Sociologia Ruralis*, no. 1

    (1999) Sustaining Local Environmental Mobilisations: Groups, Actions and Claims in Southern Europe, in Rootes, ed.

Kristensen, Peer and Charles Sabel (1991) The Trusts and the Yeoman Republic, in Charles Sabel and Jonathan Zeitlin, eds., *Worlds of Possibilities*. Cambridge University Press

Kuhn, Thomas (1978) *The Essential Tension*. University of Chicago Press

Kwa, Chunglin (1986) Representations of Nature in Cybernetic and Evolutionary Ecology, in P. Weingartner and G. Dorn, eds., *Foundations of Biology*. Vienna: Hoelder-Pichler-Tempsky

    (1989) Mimicking Nature. The Development of Systems Ecology in the United States, 1950–1975. University of Amsterdam. (Ph.D. dissertation)

Læssøe, Jeppe (1994) Citizen Participation in the Process of Change Towards Ecological Sustainability – A Social Ecological Approach Based on New

Danish Experiences, in I. Hanouskova, *et al.*, eds., *Ecology and Democracy – the Challenge of the 21ˢᵗ Century*. Proceedings of an international conference held in the Czech Republic

(1999) Folkelig deltagelse i bæredygtig udvikling (manuscript)

Lafferty, William, ed. (1999) *Implementing LA21 in Europe. New Initiatives for Sustainable Development*. Oslo: ProSus

Lafferty, William and James Meadowcroft, eds. (1996) *Democracy and the Environment. Problems and Prospects*. Cheltenham: Edward Elgar

Lake, Robert (2000) Contradictions at the local scale: local implementation of Agenda 21 in the USA, in Low, *et al.*, eds.

Landes, David (1969) *The Unbound Prometheus. Technological Change and Industrial Development in Western Europe from 1750 to the Present*. Cambridge University Press

Lasch, Christopher (1991) *The True and Only Heaven. Progress and Its Critics*. New York: W. W. Norton

Lash, Scott, Bronislaw Szerszynski, and Brian Wynne, eds. (1996) *Risk, Environment, Modernity. Towards a New Ecology*. London: Sage

Latour, Bruno (1987) *Science in Action*. Milton Keynes: Open University Press

(1993) *We Have Never Been Modern*. Cambridge, MA: Harvard University Press

Latour, Bruno and Steve Woolgar (1979) *Laboratory Life. The Social Construction of Scientific Facts*. Beverly Hills: Sage

Leopold. Aldo (1949) *A Sand Country Almanac and Sketches Here and There*. New York: Oxford University Press

Leroy, Pieter (1995) Environmental Science as a Vocation. Inaugural lecture as Professor of Social and Political Sciences of the Environment at Catholic University of Nijmegen.

Leroy, Pieter and Nico Nelissen (1999) *Social and Political Sciences of the Environment*. Utrecht: International Books

Levine, George, ed. (1987) *One Culture. Essays in Science and Literature*. Madison: University of Wisconsin Press

Lichterman, Paul (1996) *The Search for Political Community. American Activists Reinventing Commitment*. Cambridge University Press

Lidskog, Rolf (1996) In Science We Trust? On the Relation Between Scientific Knowledge, Risk Consciousness and Public Trust, in *Acta Sociologica*, 39: 31–56

Lidskog, Rolf and Ingemar Elander (2000) After Rio: Environmental Policies and Urban Planning in Sweden, in Low *et al*. eds.

Lilley, Samuel (1973) Technological Progress and the Industrial Revolution, in Carlo Cipolla, ed., *The Fontana Economic History of Europe. Volume 3, The Industrial Revolution*. Glasgow: Fontana

Lindroth, Sten (1952) *Swedish Men of Science*. Stockholm: Almqvist and Wiksell

Linton, Magnus (2000) *Veganerna – en bok om dom som stör*. Stockholm: Atlas

Löfstedt, Ragnar (1996) The Use of Biomass in a Regional Context: The Case of Växjö Energi, Sweden, in *Biomass and Bioenergy*, no. 1

Lomborg, Bjørn (1998) *Verdens sande tilstand*. Copenhagen: Centrum

Lovins, Amory (1977) *Soft Energy Paths*. Harmondsworth: Penguin

Low, Nicholas, *et al.*, eds. (2000) *Consuming Cities. The Urban Environment in the Global Economy after the Rio Declaration*. London: Routledge

Luhmann, Niklas (1993) *Risk: A Sociological Theory.* Berlin: de Gruyter

Lukács, Georg (1971/1924) *History and Class Consciousness.* Cambridge, MA: MIT Press

Luke, Timothy (1999) *Capitalism, Democracy and Ecology.* Urbana: University of Illinois Press

(2000) A Rough Road out of Rio: the Right-Wing Reaction in the United States against Global Environmentalism, in Low, *et al.* eds.

Lundmark, Fredrik (2000) Människan i centrum. En studie av antropocentrisk värdegemenskap (Man in the Center. A Study of Anthropocentric Value Consensus) (Ph.D. dissertation). Stehag: Förlags AB Gondolin

Lundqvist, Lennart (1980) *The Hare and the Tortoise. Clean Air Politics in United States and Sweden.* Ann Arbor: University of Michigan Press

(1996) Sweden, in Peter Munk Christiansen, ed., *Governing the Environment: Politics, Policy, and Organisation in the Nordic Countries.* Oslo: Nordic Council of Ministers

Lundvall, Bengt-Åke, ed. (1992) *National Systems of Innovation – Towards a Theory of Innovation and Interactive Learning.* London. Pinter

Lundvall, Bengt-Åke and Susana Borras (1998) *The Globalising Learning Economy: Implications for Innovation Policy.* Brussels: European Commission

McCarthy, Fiona (1994) *William Morris.* London: Faber and Faber

McCormick, John (1991) *Reclaiming Paradise: The Global Environmental Movement.* Bloomington: Indiana University Press

MacKenzie, James and Michael Walsh (1990) *Driving Forces: Motor Vehicle Trends and their Implications for Global Warming, Energy Strategies and Transportation Planning.* Washington: World Resources Institute

McKibben, Bill (1989) *The End of Nature.* New York: Viking

Macnaghten, Phil and John Urry (1998) *Contested Natures.* London: Sage

MacRobie, George (1981) *Small is Possible.* New York: Harper and Row

McTaggart, David, with Robert Hunter (1978) *Greenpeace III. Journey into the Bomb.* London: Collins

Mandrou, Robert (1978) *From Humanism to Science 1480–1700.* Harmondsworth: Penguin

Mannheim, Karl (1936) *Ideology and Utopia.* London: Routledge

Marcuse, Herbert (1964) *One-Dimensional Man.* Boston: Beacon

Marx, Karl (1859/1963) *Preface to a Contribution to the Critique of Political Economy.* As translated in *Karl Marx: Selected Writings in Sociology and Social Philosophy,* edited by T. B. Bottomore and M. Rubel. Harmondsworth: Penguin

(1867/1976) *Capital. A Critique of Political Economy,* volume 1. Harmondsworth: Penguin

Marx, Karl and Friedrich Engels (1968) *Selected Works.* Moscow: Progress Publishers

Marx, Leo (1988) *The Pilot and the Passenger.* New York: Oxford University Press

Meadows, D., D. Meadows, J. Randers and W. Behrens (1972) *The Limits to Growth – A Report for the Club of Rome's Project on the Predicament of Mankind.* London: Pan

Melucci, Alberto (1989) *Nomads of the Present.* Philadelphia: Temple University Press

(1996) *Challenging Codes: Collective Action in the Information Age.* Cambridge University Press

Mendelsohn, Everett (1964) The Emergence of Science as a Profession in the Nineteenth Century, in Karl Hill, ed., *The Management of Scientists.* Boston, MA: Beacon

(1990) Prophet of Our Discontent: Lewis Mumford Confronts the Bomb, in Hughes and Hughes, eds.

(1994) The Politics of Pessimism: Science and Technology Circa 1968, in Ezrahi *et al.* eds.

Merchant, Carolyn (1980) *The Death of Nature.* San Francisco, CA: Harper and Row

(1999) Partnership Ethics and Cultural Discourse: Women and the Earth Summit, in Fischer and Hajer, eds.

Merton, Robert (1970/1938) *Science, Technology and Society in Seventeenth-Century England.* New York: Harper and Row

Miettinen, Reijo, ed. (1999) *Biotechnology and Public Understanding of Science.* Helsinki: Academy of Finland

Miljø-og Energiministeriet (1995) *Natur- og Miljøpolitisk Redegørelse 1995.* Copenhagen: Environment and Energy Ministry

Mills, C. Wright (1963) *The Sociological Imagination.* Harmondsworth: Penguin

Milton, Kay (1996) *Environmentalism and Cultural Theory.* London: Routledge

Mishan, E. J. (1969) *The Costs of Economic Growth.* Harmondsworth: Penguin

Mol, Arthur and David Sonnenfeld, eds. (2000*) Ecological Modernisation Around the World: Perspectives and Critical Debates.* London: Frank Cass

Morgan, Edward (1991) *The '60s Experience. Hard Lessons About Modern America.* Philadelphia: Temple University Press

Morris, William (1973) *Political Writings.* Edited by A. L. Morton. London: Lawrence and Wishart

Mumford, Lewis (1922) *The Story of Utopias.* New York: Boni and Liveright

(1926) *The Golden Day.* New York: Boni and Liveright

(1934) *Technics and Civilization.* New York: Harcourt, Brace and Company

(1938) *The Culture of Cities.* New York: Harcourt, Brace and Company

(1944) *The Condition of Man.* New York: Harcourt, Brace and Company

(1966) *Technics and Human Development. The Myth of the Machine Volume One.* New York: Harcourt, Brace and Jovanovich

(1970) *The Pentagon of Power. The Myth of the Machine Volume Two.* New York: Harcourt, Brace and Jovanovich

(1979) *Interpretations and Forecasts: 1922–1972.* New York: Harcourt, Brace and Jovanovich

Musson, A. E. and Eric Robinson (1969) *Science and Technology in the Industrial Revolution.* Manchester University Press

Nader, Ralph (1966) *Unsafe at Any Speed.* New York: Pocket Books

Nadis, Steve and James MacKenzie (1993) *Car Trouble.* Boston: Beacon Press

Næss, Arne (1973) *Ekologi, samfunn og livsstil.* Oslo: Universitetsforlaget (English translation published as *Ecology, Community and Lifestyle.* Cambridge University Press, 1989)

Nattrass, Brian and Mary Altomare (1999) *The Natural Step for Business. Wealth, Ecology and the Evolutionary Corporation.* Gabriola Island, BC: New Society Publishers

Needham, Joseph (1969) *The Grand Titration: Science and Society in East and West.* London: George Allen and Unwin

Nelson, Richard, ed. (1993) *National Innovation Systems: A Comparative Analysis* Oxford University Press

Noble, David (1977) *America By Design. Science, Technology and the Rise of Corporate Capitalism.* New York: Knopf

Norgaard, Richard (1994) *Development Betrayed. The End of Progress and a Coevolutionary Revisioning of the Future.* London: Routledge

O'Brien, Mary (2000) *Making Better Environmental Decisions. An Alternative to Risk Assessment.* Cambridge, MA: MIT Press

O'Riordan, Tim and Heather Voisey, eds. (1997) *Sustainable Development in Western Europe: Coming to Terms with Agenda 21.* London: Frank Cass

Pacey, Arnold (1990) *Technology in World Civilization.* Oxford: Basil Blackwell

Packard, Vance (1960) *The Waste Makers.* New York: Pocket Books

Passmore, John (1974) *Man's Responsibility for Nature: Ecological Problems and Western Traditions.* London: Duckworth

Peet, Richard and Michael Watts, eds. (1996) *Liberation Ecologies. Environment, Development, Social Movements.* London: Routledge

Pellow, David, Allan Schnaiberg and Adam Weinberg (2000) Putting the Ecological Modernisation Thesis to the Test: The Promises and Performances of Urban Recycling, in Mol and Sonnenfeld, eds.

Pells, Richard (1973) *Radical Visions and American Dreams. Culture and Social Thought in the Depression Years.* New York: Harper and Row

Pepper, David (1996) *Modern Environmentalism: An Introduction.* London: Routledge

Pezzoli, Keith (1997) Sustainable Development: A Transdisciplinary Overview of the Literature, in *Journal of Environmental Planning and Management*, no. 5

Picou, Steven (2000) The "Talking Circle" as Sociological Practice: Cultural Transformation of Chronic Disaster Impacts, in *Sociological Practice: A Journal of Clinical and Applied Sociology*, no. 2

Plumwood, Val (1993) *Feminism and the Mastery of Nature.* London: Routledge

Polanyi, Michael (1958) *Personal Knowledge.* London: Routledge and Kegan Paul

Porter, Roy (1986) The Scientific Revolution: a Spoke in the Wheel?, in Roy Porter and Mikulas Teich, eds., *Revolution in History.* Cambridge University Press

Pursell, Carroll (1993) The Rise and Fall of the Appropriate Technology Movement in the United States, 1965–1983, in *Technology and Culture*, no. 3

Putnam, Robert (1993) *Making Democracy Work: Civic Traditions in Northern Italy.* Princeton University Press

(2000) *Bowling Alone: The Collapse and Revival of American Community.* New York: Simon and Schuster

Ramphal, Shridath (1992) *Our Country, the Planet. Forging a Partnership for Survival.* Washington: Island Press

Rangan, Haripriya (1996) From Chipko to Uttaranchal, in Peet and Watts, eds.

Ravetz, Jerome (1973) *Scientific Knowledge and Its Social Problems*. Harmondsworth: Penguin

Redclift, Michael (1987) *Sustainable Development: Exploring the Contradictions*. London: Methuen

(1992) Sustainable Development and Global Environmental Change. Implications of a Changing Agenda, in *Global Environmental Change*, March

Redclift, Michael and Ted Benton, eds. (1994) *Social Theory and the Global Environment*. London: Routledge

Redclift, Michael and Graham Woodgate, eds. (1997) *The International Handbook of Environmental Sociology*. Cheltenham: Edward Elgar

Rees, William, *et al.* (1995) *Our Ecological Footprint: Reducing Human Impact on the Earth*. Gabriola Island, BC: New Society Publishers

Remmen, Arne (1995). Pollution Prevention, Cleaner Technologies and Industry, in Rip *et al.*, eds.

(1998) Innovation Concepts and Cleaner Technologies – Experiences from Three Danish Action Plans, in Jamison, ed.

Ridgeway, James (1970) *The Politics of Ecology*. New York: E. P. Dutton

Rifkin, Jeremy (1983) *Algeny*. Harmondsworth: Penguin

Rinkevicius, Leonardas (1997) Lithuania: Environmental Awareness and National Independence, in Jamison and Østby, eds.

(1998) Ecological Modernization and Its Perspectives in Lithuania: Attitudes, Expectations, Actions. Kaunas University of Technology (Ph.D. dissertation)

(2000) Ecological Modernisation as Cultural Politics: Transformation of Civic Environmental Activism in Lithuania, in Mol and Sonnenfeld, eds.

Rip, Arie, Tom Misa and Johan Schot, eds. (1995) *Managing Technology in Society. The Approach of Constructive Technology Assessment*. London: Pinter

Rivers, Patrick (1976) There's No Transport Like No Transport, in Boyle and Harper, eds.

Rootes, Christopher (1997) Environmental Movements and Green Parties in Western and Eastern Europe, in M. Redclift and G. Woodgate, eds., *International Handbook of Environmental Sociology*. Cheltenham: Edward Elgar

(1999) Acting Globally, Thinking Locally? Prospects for a Global Environmental Movement, in Rootes, ed.

Rootes, Christopher, ed. (1999) *Environmental Movements. Local, National and Global*. London: Frank Cass

Rose, Hilary (1994) *Love, Power and Knowledge. Toward a Feminist Transformation of the Sciences*. Cambridge: Polity Press

Rosenberg, Nathan (1982) *Inside the Black Box. Technology and Economics*. Cambridge University Press

Ross, Dorothy (1991) *The Origins of American Social Science*. Cambridge University Press

Rossi, Paolo (1970) *Philosophy, Technology and the Arts in the Early Modern Era*. New York: Harper Torchbooks

Roszak, Theodore (1973) *Where the Wasteland Ends: Politics and Transcendence in Post-Industrial Society*. New York: Anchor Books

198   References

Rothenberg, David (1993) *Hand's End: Technology and the Limits of Nature*.
    Berkeley: University of California Press
    (1995) Have a Friend for Lunch: Norwegian Radical Ecology Versus Tradition,
    in Taylor, ed.
Rowell, Andrew (1996) *Green Backlash. Global Subversion of the Environment
    Movement*. London: Routledge
Rucht, Dieter (1993) Think Globally, Act Locally?, in J. D. Liefferink, *et al.*, eds.
    (1995) Ecological Protest as Calculated Law-breaking: Greenpeace and Earth
    First! In Comparative Perspective, in W. Rüdig, ed., *Green Politics Three*.
    Edinburgh University Press
    (1999) The Impact of Environmental Movements in Western Societies, in
    M. Giugni, *et al.*, eds., *Do Movements Matter?* Minneapolis: University of
    Minnesota Press
Rucht, Dieter, ed. (1991) *Research on Social Movements. The State of the Art in
    Western Europe and the USA*. Frankfurt: Campus
Rüdig, Wolfgang (1990) *Anti-Nuclear Movements: A World Survey of Protest Against
    Nuclear Energy*. Harlow: Longman
    (2000) Mobilising Environmental Expertise: 'Alternative' Research Institutes
    in Germany (manuscript)
Runyan, Curtis (1999) The Third Force: NGOs, in *Worldwatch* (November/
    December)
Russell, Colin (1983) *Science and Social Change, 1700–1900*. Basingstoke:
    Macmillan
Sachs, Ignacy (1994) The Environmental Challenge, in Jean-Jacques Salomon,
    et al., eds., *The Uncertain Quest. Science, Technology and Development*. Tokyo:
    UN University
Sachs, Wolfgang (1992) *For Love of the Automobile: Looking Back at the History of
    Our Desires*. Berkeley: University of California Press
    (1999) *Planet Dialectics. Explorations in Environment and Development*. London:
    Zed Books
Said, Edward (1993) *Culture and Imperialism*. New York: Knopf
Sale, Kirkpatrick (1986) The Forest for the Trees. Can Today's Environmentalists
    Tell the Difference?, in *Mother Jones*, November
    (1993) *The Green Revolution: The American Environmental Movement
    1962–1992*. New York: Hill and Wang
    (1996) *Rebels Against the Future*. London: Quartet Books
Salomon, Jean-Jacques (1977) Science Policy Studies and the Development of
    Science Policy, in Derek de Solla Price and Ina Spiegel-Rösing, eds., *Science,
    Technology and Society: A Cross-Disciplinary Perspective*. London: Sage
Satin, Mark (1979) *New Age Politics. Healing Self and Society*. New York: Dell
Scheler, Max (1980/1924) *Problems of a Sociology of Knowledge*. London:
    Routledge
Schmidheiny, Stephan (1992) *Changing Course*. Cambridge, MA: MIT Press
Schnaiberg, Allan (1980) *The Environment: From Surplus to Scarcity*. New York:
    Oxford University Press
Schnaiberg, Allan and Kenneth Gould (1994) *Environment and Society:
    The Enduring Conflict*. New York: St. Martin's Press

Schot, Johan (1992) Constructive Technology Assessment and Technology Dynamics: The Case of Clean Technologies, in *Science, Technology and Human Values* 17: 36–56
(1998) Constructive Technology Assessment Comes of Age, in Jamison, ed.
Schot, Johan, Ellis Brand and Kurt Fischer (1997) *The Greening of Industry for a Sustainable Future: Building an International Research Agenda.* Rijswijk, NL: The Advisory Council for Research on Nature and Environment (RMNO)
Schumacher, E. F. (1973) *Small is Beautiful: Economics As If People Mattered.* London: Blond and Briggs
Sclove, Richard (1995) *Democracy and Technology.* New York: Guilford
Seeger, Pete (1993) *Where Have All the Flowers Gone. A Singer's Stories, Songs, Seeds, Robberies.* Bethlehem, PA: Sing Out Publications
Shapin, Steven (1996) *The Scientific Revolution.* University of Chicago Press
Shapin, Steven and Simon Schaffer (1985) *Leviathan and the Air-Pump: Hobbes, Boyle and the Experimental Life.* Princeton University Press
Shiva, Vandana (1988) *Staying Alive. Women, Ecology and Development.* London: Zed Books
(1997) *Biopiracy: The Plunder of Nature and Knowledge.* Boston: South End Press
(2000) *Stolen Harvest. The Hijacking of the Global Food Supply.* Cambridge, MA: South End Press
Shutkin, William (2000) *The Land That Could Be. Environmentalism and Democracy in the Twenty-first Century.* Cambridge MA: MIT Press
Singer, Peter (1975) *Animal Liberation: A New Ethics for Our Treatment of Animals.* New York Review of Books
Snow, C.P. (1959) *The Two Cultures.* Cambridge, MA: Harvard University Press
Söderqvist, Thomas (1986) *The Ecologists From Merry Naturalists to Saviours of the Nation.* Stockholm: Almqvist and Wiksell
Strømsnes, Kristin and Per Selle, eds. (1996) *Miljøvernpolitikk og miljøvernorganisering mot år 2000.* Otta: Tano Aschehoug
Swedberg, Richard (1991) *Joseph A. Schumpeter. His Life and Work.* Cambridge: Polity Press
Szasz, Andrew (1994) *Ecopopulism: Toxic Waste and the Movement for Environmental Justice.* Minneapolis: University of Minnesota Press
Szerszynski, Bronislaw (1996) On Knowing What to Do: Environmentalism and the Modern Problematic, in Lash *et al.*, eds.
Szerszynski, Bronislaw, *et al.* (1996) Introduction: Ecology, Realism and the Social Sciences, in Lash *et al.* eds.
(1997) The Varieties of Ecological Piety, in *Worldviews* 1: 37–5
(1999) Performing Politics: The Dramatics of Environmental Protest, in Larry Ray and Andrew Sayer, eds., *Culture and Economy: After the Cultural Turn.* London: Sage
Tambiah, Stanley (1990) *Magic, Science, Religion, and the Scope of Rationality.* Cambridge University Press
Tarrow, Sidney (1994) *Power in Movement. Social Movements and Contentious Politics.* Cambridge University Press

Taylor, Bron, ed. (1995) *Ecological Resistance Movements. The Global Emergence of Radical and Popular Environmentalism.* Albany: State University of New York Press

Taylor, Peter (1988) Technocratic Optimism, H. T. Odum and the Partial Transformation of Ecological Metaphor after World War II, in *Journal of the History of Biology* 21: 213–44

Teich, Mikulas and Robert Young, eds. (1973) *Changing Perspectives in the History of Science.* London: Heinemann

Thomas, John (1990) Lewis Mumford, Benton MacKaye, and the Regional Vision, in Hughes and Hughes, eds.

Thompson, E.P. (1963) *The Making of the English Working Class.* Harmondsworth: Penguin

(1977) *William Morris. From Romantic to Revolutionary* (revised edition) London: Merlin Press

Thoreau, Henry David (1854/1963) *Walden, or Life in the Woods.* New York: New American Library

Tichi, Cecelia (1987) *Shifting Gears. Technology, Literature, Culture in Modernist America.* Chapel Hill: University of North Carolina Press

Todd, Nancy Jack, ed. (1977) *The Book of the New Alchemists.* New York: E. P. Dutton

Torgerson, Douglas (1999) *The Promise of Green Politics. Environmentalism and the Public Sphere.* Durham, NC: Duke University Press

Touraine, Alain (1981) *The Voice and the Eye. An Analysis of Social Movements.* Cambridge University Press

(1985) An Introduction to Social Movements, in *Social Research*, no. 4: 749–787

(1988) *Return of the Actor. Social Theory in Postindustrial Society.* Minneapolis: University of Minnesota Press

(1991) Commentary on Dieter Rucht's Critique, in Rucht, ed.

Turner, Jack (1996) *The Abstract Wild.* Tucson: University of Arizona Press

Vaillancourt, Jean Guy (1995) Sustainable Development: A Sociologist's View of the Definition, Origins and Implications of the Concept, in Michael Mehta and Eric Ouellet, *Environmental Sociology – Theory and Practice.* York: Captus Press

van der Heiden, Hein-Anton (1997) Political Opportunity Structure and the Institutionalisation of the Environmental Movement, in *Environmental Politics*, no. 4

(1999) Environmental Movements, Ecological Modernisation and Political Opportunity Structures, in Rootes, ed.

van Zwanenberg, Patrick (1997) The British National Experience, in Jamison and Østby, eds.

Veblen, Thorstein (1915) *Imperial Germany and the Industrial Revolution.* New York: Macmillan

(1921) *The Engineers and the Price System.* New York: B. W. Huebsch.

(1923) *Absentee Ownership and Business Enterprise in Recent Times: The Case of America.* New York: B. W. Huebsch.

Vickers, Ian and Martin Cordey-Hayes (1999) Cleaner Production and Organizational Learning, in *Technology Analysis and Strategic Management*, no. 1

Vig, Norman and Michael Kraft, eds. (1999) *Environmental Policy in the 1990s: New Directions for the Twenty-First Century*. Washington: Congressional Quarterly Books

Vogel, David (1986) *National Styles of Regulation*. Ithaca, NY: Cornell University Press

von Wright, Georg Henrik (1993) *Myten om framsteget*. Stockholm: Bonniers

Wagner, Michael (1999) *Det polytekniske gennembrud. Romantikkens teknologiske konstruktion 1780–850*. Århus: Århus universitetsforlag

Wagner, Peter, Björn Wittrock and Richard Whitley, eds. (1991) *Discourses on Society. The Shaping of the Social Science Disciplines*. Dordrecht: Kluwer

Wainwright, Hilary and David Eliot (1982) *The Lucas Plan. A New Trade Unionism in the Making*. London: Allison and Busby

Wall, Derek (1999) Mobilising Earth First! in Britain, in Rootes, ed.

Ward, Barbara and Rene Dubos (1972) *Only One Earth. The Care and Maintenance of a Small Planet*. London: Andre Deutsch

Weale, Albert (1992) *The New Politics of Pollution*. Manchester University Press

Webster, Charles (1975) *The Great Instauration. Science, Medicine and Reform 1626–1660*. New York: Holmes and Meier

Whitehead, Alfred (1925) *Science and the Modern World*. New York: Macmillan

Wilkinson, Richard (1973) *Poverty and Progress: an Ecological Model of Economic Development*. London: Methuen

Williams, Raymond (1963) *Culture and Society 1780–1950*. Harmondsworth: Penguin

(1972) Ideas of Nature, in Benthall, ed.

(1977) *Marxism and Literature*. Oxford University Press

Winstanley, Gerrard (1973/1649) *The Law of Freedom in a Platform, or True Magistracy Restored*. Edited by Richard W. Kenny. New York: Schocken Books

Worster, Donald (1977) *Nature's Economy. The Roots of Ecology*. San Francisco: Sierra Club

(1993) *The Wealth of Nature. Environmental History and the Ecological Imagination*. Oxford University Press

Wynne, Bran (1992) Misunderstood Misunderstanding: Social Identities and the Public Uptake of Science, in *Public Understanding of Science*, no. 3

(1994) Scientific Knowledge and the Global Environment, in Redclift and Benton, eds.

(1995) Public Understanding of Science, in Jasanoff, *et al.*, eds.

(1996) May the Sheep Safely Graze? A Reflexive View of the Expert–Lay Knowledge Divide, in Lash, *et al.*, eds.

Yates, Frances (1964) *Giordano Bruno and the Hermetic Tradition*. New York: Vintage Books

Yearley, Steven (1991) *The Green Case: a Sociology of Environmental Issues, Arguments and Politics*. London: HarperCollins

(1992) Green Ambivalence about Science: Legal-Rational Authority and the Scientific Legitimation of a Social Movement, in *British Journal of Sociology*, no. 4

(1994) Social Movements and Environmental Change, in Redclift and Benton, eds.

(1995) The Environmental Challenge to Science Studies, in Jasanoff *et al.*, eds.

(1996) *Sociology, Environmentalism, Globalization*. London: Sage

Zilsel, Edgar (1941) The Sociological Roots of Science, in *American Journal of Sociology* 47: 245–279

Index of Names

Learning Resources
Centre